Mortgage-Backed Securities

THE FRANK J. FABOZZI SERIES

Mortgage-Backed Securities

Products, Structuring, and Analytical Techniques

FRANK J. FABOZZI

ANAND K. BHATTACHARYA

WILLIAM S. BERLINER

BICENTENNIAL
1807
WILEY
2007
BICENTENNIAL

John Wiley & Sons, Inc.

For general information on our other products and services or for technical support, please contact our Customer Care Department within the United States at (800) 762-2974, outside the United States at (317) 572-3993, or fax (317) 572-4002.

Wiley also publishes its books in a variety of electronic formats. Some content that appears in print may not be available in electronic books. For more information about Wiley products, visit our web site at www.wiley.com.

ISBN: 978-0-470-04773-6

Printed in the United States of America.

10 9 8 7 6 5 4 3 2

FJF
To my wife Donna and my children
Francesco, Patricia, and Karly

AKB
To my wife Marcia and my children
Christina and Alex

WSB
To Heidi, Morgan, and Zachary

Contents

PART THREE

Structuring   97

PART FOUR

Valuation and Analysis   **203**

Preface

Over the past quarter of a century, the residential mortgage market has grown into the largest market for consumer debt. The market for mortgage-backed securities or MBS, in which mortgage cash flows are packaged and distributed to investors, has grown concomitantly. According to the Securities Industry and Financial Markets Associations (formerly the Bond Market Association), the market for mortgage-related securities surpassed the U.S. Treasury market at the end of 1999 to become the largest cash financial market in the world. By the end of 2006, the total amount of MBS outstanding was $6.4 trillion, 49% larger than the market for Treasury debt.

In addition to their size, both the consumer mortgage and MBS markets have become increasingly flexible and dynamic. The MBS market has traditionally exhibited great creativity in constructing different products and structures to help a wide variety of investors meet their investment objectives, exemplifying the concept of financial market segmentation. Innovations first conceived in the 1980s, such as senior-subordinate structures and planned amortization class (PAC) bonds, have recently been joined by concepts such as super-stable or "sinker" bonds and corridor-cap floaters. In addition, complex analytical tools have been developed and refined in order to aid investors in valuing their holdings and assess relative value among competing investment alternatives.

The consumer mortgage market has also undergone a period of substantial innovation and change. A major change occurred in the late 1990s with the advent of "risk-based pricing," which allowed lenders to price the risks associated with each loan, instead of the earlier equivalent of "one-size-fits-all" loan pricing. This change, accompanied by increased marketing savvy on the part of lenders, has led to major changes in the primary mortgage market. These changes include:

■ *A proliferation in the types of different loan products.* This includes products that are pegged to different parts of the yield curve, such as adjustable rate mortgages (ARMs), as well as loans with more flexible amortization schemes.

■ *The growth of lending to borrowers with nontraditional financial pro-files*. This has led to the growth of market segments such as alt-A and subprime lending, as well as investment products designed to securitize these riskier products.

■ *The increased importance of mortgage borrowings to the overall finan-cial conditions of consumers*. This is reflected in the increased sensitiv-ity of borrowers to monthly payments, rather than rates, as well as the willingness of homeowners to finance their lifestyle by monetizing home equity through cash-out refinancings.

These changes in both the consumer and financial markets, as well as accompanying sharp increases in real estate prices throughout most of the United States, have created the need for a reassessment of the MBS uni-verse. This book attempts to fill that need.

This book is divided into four parts. Chapters 1 and 2 (Part One) provide an introduction to the mortgage and MBS markets. Part Two (Chapters 3 and 4) is a primer on prepayment and default metrics and behavior. Part Three of the book, Chapters 5 to 9, focuses on structur-ing. The emphasis in this part of the book is on the details of structur-ing, with an emphasis on defining both differences and commonalities across various mortgage products and techniques. In Part Four of the book (Chapters 10 to 12), the methodologies and techniques used to value MBS products and assess interest rate risk are described and illus-trated.

The Appendix, coauthored by Andrew Kalotay and Deane Yang of Andrew Kalotay Associates and Frank Fabozzi, describes a new *option theoretic approach* to MBS valuation. The commercial software for this methodology is referred to as the CLEAN (Coupled Lattice Efficiency Analysis) model. Unlike standard industry models that use the Monte Carlo approach described in Chapter 10, the model presented in the Appendix uses the same "recursive lattice" approach commonly used for valuing American equity and bond options. Introduced in December 2004, the model presented has been well received by market partici-pants, due to its speed and precision. It has been reported that it can value 10,000 MBS per minute, versus 100 securities using the Monte Carlo approach. As an indication of its growing acceptance by the mar-ket, the CLEAN model has been licensed by a risk management firm to value their clients' MBS portfolios, deployed by Beacon Capital Strate-gies (a fixed income trading platform) to provide indicative pricing of MBS, and used by Sector (a supplier of agency MBS data to market par-ticipants) to launch a new pricing service for MBS. Moreover, it is unique in that it models directly individual borrowers' refinancing deci-sions, in contrast to standard industry models, which use econometric models to extrapolate past aggregate behavior into the future. As such, it represents an important advance in modeling prepayments and valuing MBS, and the interest this novel approach is generating among market participants led us to include it in this text.

The authors would like to acknowledge the contributions of a number of individuals at Countrywide Securities Corporation to this project. William Shang, Joseph Janssen, and Kevin Doyle were extremely helpful in the writing of Chapter 9; their expertise was instrumental in discussing a series of dense and complex topics. Brian Stack contributed to the sections on private label structuring in Chapter 8, while Weiss Piloti edited virtually the entire book through multiple rewrites and revisions. Finally, thanks to Ron Kripalani, the President of CSC, for his support of this project.

Frank J. Fabozzi
Anand K. Bhattacharya
William S. Berliner

About the Authors

Frank J. Fabozzi is Professor in the Practice of Finance in the School of Management at Yale University. Prior to joining the Yale faculty, he was a Visiting Professor of Finance in the Sloan School at MIT. He is a Fellow of the International Center for Finance at Yale University and on the Advisory Council for the Department of Operations Research and Financial Engineering at Princeton University. Professor Fabozzi is the editor of the *Journal of Portfolio Management* and an associate editor of the *Journal of Fixed Income*. He earned a doctorate in economics from the City University of New York in 1972. In 2002 was inducted into the Fixed Income Analysts Society's Hall of Fame and is the 2007 recipient of the C. Stewart Sheppard Award given by the CFA Institute. He earned the designation of Chartered Financial Analyst and Certified Public Accountant. He has authored and edited numerous books in finance.

Anand K. Bhattacharya is a Managing Director at Countrywide Securities Corporation (CSC), a wholly owned affiliate of Countrywide Financial Corporation. He joined CSC in 1999, where he is responsible for the management of fixed income research and strategies. Immediately prior to joining Countrywide, he was Managing Director responsible for capital markets, risk management and portfolio management oversight at Imperial Credit Industries Inc (ICII) from March 1998 to January 1999. Prior to his employment at ICII, Dr. Bhattacharya held positions at Prudential Securities Inc. from 1990 to 1998 with the most recent position as Managing Director, Global Head of Fixed Income Research. His prior employment includes positions in fixed income research and product management at Merrill Lynch Capital Markets, Franklin Savings Association and its subsidiaries and Security Pacific Merchant Bank. Dr. Bhattacharya has written extensively in various facets of fixed income analysis and portfolio management. He has authored or coauthored over 65 publications in various academic and professional journals and industry handbooks. He holds a Ph.D. in Finance and Quantitative Methods from Arizona State University.

William S. Berliner is Executive Vice President in charge of the Mortgage Strategies group at Countrywide Securities Corporation. In this capacity, he oversees the generation of relative value analysis and strategies, and writes and edits many of the firm's reports and publications. He began his career in the Government Operations Department of Bear, Stearns and Co. in 1985. He moved to the Mortgage trading desk in 1987 as a clerk and joined the CMO desk in 1989. He worked on the CMO desk at Bear until 1993, when he left to join Nikko Securities, where he eventually ran CMO trading. He joined Countrywide as a trader in 1996 and moved to the Research Department in early 1998. Mr. Berliner has a BA in Interpersonal Communications from Rutgers College and an MBA in Finance from the Rutgers Graduate School of Business.

Introduction to Mortgage and MBS Markets

Overview of Mortgages and the Consumer Mortgage Market

The mortgage market in the United States has emerged as one of the world's largest asset classes. According to Federal Reserve statistics, the total face value of 1–4 family residential mortgage debt outstanding was approximately $9.5 trillion as of the third quarter of 2006. The growth of the mortgage market is attributable to a variety of factors. Most notably, strong sales and price growth in the domestic real estate markets and the increased acceptance of new loan products on the part of the consumer has dovetailed with increased comfort levels with respect to the credit quality of the sector and the acceptance of a variety of loan products as collateral for securitizations.

Due to a variety of reasons such as product innovation, technological advancement, and demographic and cultural changes, the composition of the primary mortgage market is evolving at a rapid rate—older concepts are being updated, while a host of new products is also being developed and marketed. Consequently, the mortgage-lending paradigm continues to be refined in ways that have allowed lenders to offer a large variety of products designed to appeal to consumer needs and tastes. This evolution has been facilitated by sophistication in pricing that has allowed for the quantification of the inherent risks in such loans. At the same time, structures and techniques that allow the burgeoning variety of products to be securitized have been created and marketed, helping to meet the investment needs of a variety of market segments and investor clienteles.

The purpose of this chapter is to explain mortgage products and lending practices. The chapter introduces the basic tenets of the primary mortgage market and mortgage lending, and summarizes the various product offerings in the sector. In conjunction with the following chapter on mortgage-backed securities (MBS) and the MBS market, this chapter also provides a framework for understanding the concepts and practices addressed in the remainder of this book.

OVERVIEW OF MORTGAGES

In general, a *mortgage* is a loan that is secured by underlying assets that can be repossessed in the event of default. For the purposes of this book, a mortgage is defined as a loan made to the owner of a 1–4 family residential dwelling and secured by the underlying property (both the land and the structure or "improvement"). After issuance, loans must be managed (or serviced) by units that, for a fee, collect payments from borrowers and pass them on to investors. *Servicers* are also responsible for interfacing with borrowers if they become delinquent on their payments, and also manage the disposition of the loan and the underlying property if the loan goes into foreclosure.

Key Attributes that Define Mortgages

There are a number of key attributes that define the instruments in question that can be characterized by the following dimensions:

- Lien status, original loan term
- Credit classification
- Interest rate type
- Amortization type
- Credit guarantees
- Loan balances
- Prepayments and prepayment penalties

We discuss each below.

Lien Status

The *lien status* dictates the loan's seniority in the event of the forced liquidation of the property due to default by the obligor. A *first lien* implies that a creditor would have first call on the proceeds of the liquidation of the property if it were to be repossessed. Borrowers often utilize *second lien* or *junior* loans as a means of liquefying the value of a home for the purpose of expenditures such as medical bills or college tuition or investments such as home improvements.

Original Loan Term

The great majority of mortgages are originated with a 30-year original term. Loans with shorter stated terms are also utilized by those borrowers seeking to amortize their loans faster and build equity in their homes more quickly. The 15-year mortgage is the most common short-amortization instrument, although issuance of loans with 20- and 10-year terms has grown in recent years.

Credit Classification

The majority of loans originated are of high-credit quality, where the borrowers have strong employment and credit histories, income sufficient to pay the loans without compromising their creditworthiness, and substantial equity in the underlying property. These loans are broadly classified as *prime loans*, and have historically experienced low incidences of delinquency and default.

Loans of lower initial credit quality which are more likely to experience significantly higher levels of default, are classified as *subprime loans*. Subprime loan underwriting often utilizes nontraditional measures to assess credit risk, as these borrowers often have lower income levels, fewer assets, and blemished credit histories. After issuance, these loans must also be serviced by special units designed to closely monitor the payments of subprime borrowers. In the event that subprime borrowers become delinquent, the servicers move immediately to either assist the borrowers in becoming current or mitigate the potential for losses resulting from loan defaults.

Between the prime and subprime sector is a somewhat nebulous category referenced as *alternative-A loans* or, more commonly, *alt-A loans*. These loans are considered to be prime loans (the "A" refers to the A grade assigned by underwriting systems), albeit with some attributes that either increase their perceived credit riskiness or cause them to be difficult to categorize and evaluate.

Mortgage credit analysis employs a number of different metrics, including the following.

Credit Scores   Several firms collect data on the payment histories of individuals from lending institutions and use sophisticated models to evaluate and quantify individual creditworthiness. The process results in a credit score, which is essentially a numerical grade of the credit history of the borrower. There are three different credit-reporting firms that calculate credit scores: Experian (which uses the Fair Isaacs or FICO model), Transunion (which supports the Emperica model), and Equifax (whose model is known as Beacon). While each firm's credit scores are based on different data sets and scoring algorithms, the scores are generically referred to as *FICO scores*.

Loan-to-Value Ratios   The *loan-to-value ratio* (LTV) is an indicator of borrower leverage at the point when the loan application is filed. The LTV calculation compares the face value of the desired loan to the market value of the property. By definition, the LTV of the loan in the purchase transaction is a function of both the down payment and the purchase price of the property. In a refinancing, the LTV is dependent upon the requested amount of the new loan and the market value of the property as determined by an appraisal. If the new loan is larger than the original loan, the transaction is referred to as a *cash-out refinancing*, while a refinancing where the loan balance remains unchanged is described as a *rate-and-term refinancing* or *no-cash refinancing*.

The LTV is important for a number of reasons. First, it is an indicator of the amount that can be recovered from a loan in the event of a default, especially if the value of the property declines. The level of the LTV also has an impact on the expected payment performance of the obligor, as high LTVs indicate a greater likelihood of default on the loan. Another useful measure is the *Combined LTV* (or CLTV), which accounts for the existence of second liens. A $100,000 property with an $80,000 first lien and a $10,000 second lien will have an LTV of 80% but a CLTV of 90%.

Income Ratios   In order to ensure that borrower obligations are consistent with their income, lenders calculate income ratios that compare the potential monthly payment on the loan to the applicant's monthly income. The most common measures are called front and back ratios. The *front ratio* is calculated by dividing the total monthly payments on the home (including principal, interest, property taxes, and homeowners insurance) by pretax monthly income. The *back ratio* is similar, but adds other debt payments (including auto loan and credit card payments) to the total payments. In order for a loan to be classified as prime, the front and back ratios should be no more than 28% and 36%, respectively. (Because consumer debt figures can be somewhat inconsistent and nebulous, the front ratio is generally considered the more reliable measure, and accorded greater weight by underwriters.)

Documentation   Lenders traditionally have required potential borrowers to provide data on their financial status, and support the data with documentation. Loan officers typically required applicants to report and document income, employment status, and financial resources (including the source of the down payment for the transaction). Part of the application process routinely involved compiling documents such as tax returns and bank statements for use in the underwriting process. However, a growing number of loan programs have more flexible documentation requirements, and lenders typically offer programs with a variety of documentation standards. Such programs include programs where pay stubs and tax returns are not required (especially in cases where existing customers refinance their loans), as well as "stated" programs (where income levels and asset values are provided, but not independently verified).

Characterizing Prime versus Subprime Loans

The primary attribute used to characterize loans as either prime or subprime is the *credit score*. Prime (or A-grade) loans generally have FICO scores of 660 or higher, income ratios with the previously noted maximum of 28% and 36%, and LTVs less than 95%. Alt-A loans may vary in a number of important ways. Alt-A loans typically have lower degrees of documentation, be backed by a second home or investor property, or have a combination of attributes (such as large loan size and high LTV) that make the loan riskier. While subprime loans typically have FICO scores below 660, the loan programs and grades are highly lender-specific. One lender might consider a loan with a 620 FICO to be a B-rated loan, while another lender would grade the same loan higher or lower, especially if the other attributes of the loan (such as the LTV) are higher or lower than average levels.

Interest Rate Type

Fixed rate mortgages have an interest rate (or *note rate*) that is set at the closing of the loan (or, more accurately, when the rate is "locked"), and is constant for the loan's term. Based on the loan's balance, interest rate, and term, a payment schedule effective over the life of the loan is calculated to amortize the principal balance.

Adjustable rate mortgages (ARMs), as the name implies, have note rates that change over the life of the loan. The note rate is based on both the movement of an underlying rate (the *index*) and a spread over the index (the *margin*) required for the particular loan program. A number of different indexes can be used as a reference rate in determining the loan's note rate the loan "resets," including the London Interbank Offering Rate (LIBOR), one-year Constant Maturity Treasury (CMT), or the 12-month Moving Treasury Average (MTA), a rate calculated from monthly averages of the one-year CMT. The loan's note rate resets at the end of the initial period and subsequently resets periodically, subject to caps and floors that limit how much the loan's note rate can change. ARMs most frequently are structured to reset annually, although some products reset on a monthly or semiannual basis. Since the loan's rate and payment can (and often does) reset higher, the borrower can experience "payment shock" if the monthly payment increases significantly.

Traditionally, ARMs had a one-year initial period where the start rate was effective, often referred to as the "teaser" rate (since the rate was set at a relatively low rate in order to entice borrowers.) The loans reset at the end of the teaser period, and continued to reset annually for the life of the loan. One-year ARMs, however, are no longer popular products, and have been replaced by loans that have features more appealing to borrowers.

At this writing, the ARM market is dominated by two different types of loans. One is the *fixed-period ARM* or *hybrid ARM*, which have fixed initial rates that are effective for longer periods of time (3-, 5-7-, and 10-years) after funding. At the end of the initial fixed rate period, the loans reset in a fashion very similar to that of more traditional ARM loans. Hybrid ARMs typically have three rate caps: initial cap, periodic cap, and life cap. The *initial cap* and *periodic cap* limit how much the note rate of the loans can change at the end of the fixed period and at each subsequent reset, respectively, while the *life cap* dictates the maximum level of the note rate.

At the opposite end of the spectrum is the *payment-option ARM* or *negative amortization ARM*. Such products begin with a very low teaser rate. While the rate adjusts monthly, the minimum payment is only adjusted on an annual basis and is subject to a payment cap that limits how much the loan's payment can change at the reset. In instances where the payment made is not sufficient to cover the interest due on the loan, the loan's balance increases in a phenomenon called "negative amortization." (The mechanics of negative amortization loans are addressed in more depth later in this chapter.)

Amortization Type

Traditionally, both fixed and adjustable rate mortgages were *fully amortizing loans*, indicating that the obligor's principal and interest payments are calculated in equal increments to pay off the loan over the stated term. Fully amortizing, fixed rate loans have a payment that is constant over the life of the loan. Since the payments on ARMs adjust periodically, their payments are recalculated at each reset for the loan's remaining balance at the new effective rate in a process called *recasting the loan*.

A recent trend in the market, however, has been the growing popularity of nontraditional amortization schemes. The most straightforward of these innovations is the *interest-only* or *IO product*. These loans require only interest to be paid for a predetermined period of time. After the expiration of the interest-only or *lockout period*, the loan is recast to amortize over the remaining term of the loan. The inclusion of principal to the payments at that point amortized over the remaining (and shorter) term of the loan causes the loan's payment to rise significantly after the recast, creating payment shock analogous to that experienced when an ARM resets.

The interest-only product was introduced in the hybrid ARM market, where the terms of the interest-only and fixed rate periods were contiguous. A byproduct of the interest-only ARM can be large changes in the borrower's monthly payment, the result of the combination of post-reset rate increases and the introduction of principal amortization. However, fixed rate, interest-only products have recently grown in popularity. These are loans with a 30-year maturity that have a fixed rate throughout the life of the loan, but have a fairly long interest-only period (normally 10 years, although 15-year interest-only products are also being produced.) The loans subsequently amortize over their remaining terms. These products were designed to appeal to borrowers seeking the lower payments of interest-only products without the rate risk associated with adjustable rate products.

Another recent innovation is the *noncontiguous interest-only hybrid ARM*, where the interest-only period is different from the duration of the fixed rate period. As an example, a 5/1 hybrid ARM might have an interest-only period of 10 years. When the fixed period of a hybrid ARM is concluded, the loan's rate resets in the same fashion as other ARMs. However, only interest is paid on the loan until the recast date. These products were developed to spread out the payment shock that occurs when ARM loans reset and recast simultaneously.

Credit Guarantees

The ability of mortgage banks to continually originate mortgages is heavily dependent upon the ability to create fungible assets from a disparate group of loans made to a multitude of individual obligors. These assets are then sold (in the form of loans or, more commonly, MBS) into the capital markets, with the proceeds being recycled into new lending. Therefore, mortgage loans can be further classified based upon whether a credit guaranty associated with the loan is provided by the federal government or quasi-governmental entities, or obtained through other private entities or structural means.

Loans that are backed by agencies of the Federal government are referred to under the generic term of *government loans*. As part of housing policy considerations, the Department of Housing and Urban Development (HUD) oversees two agencies, the Federal Housing Administration

(FHA) and the Veterans Administration (VA), that support housing credit for qualifying borrowers. The FHA provides loan guarantees for those borrowers who can afford only a low down payment and generally also have relatively low levels of income. The VA guarantees loans made to veterans, allowing them to receive favorable loan terms. These guarantees are backed by the U.S. Department of the Treasury, thus providing these loans with the "full faith and credit" backing of the U.S. government. Government loans are securitized largely through the aegis of the Government National Mortgage Association (GNMA or Ginnie Mae), an agency also overseen by HUD.

So-called *conventional loans* have no explicit guaranty from the federal government. Conventional loans can be securitized either as "private label" structures or as pools guaranteed by the two government-sponsored enterprises (GSEs), namely Freddie Mac (FHLMC) and Fannie Mae (FNMA). The GSEs are shareholder-owned corporations that were created by Congress in order to support housing activity. While neither enterprise has an overt government guaranty, market convention has always reflected the presumption that the government would provide assistance to the GSEs in the event of financial setbacks that threaten their viability. As we will see later in this chapter, the GSEs insure the payment of principal and interest to investors in exchange for a *guaranty fee*, paid either out of the loan's interest proceeds or as a lump sum at issuance.

Conventional loans that are not guaranteed by the GSEs can be securitized as private label transactions. Traditionally, loans were securitized in private label form because they were not eligible for GSE guarantees, either because of their balance or their credit attributes. A recent development is the growth of private label deals backed either entirely or in part by loans where the balance conforms to the GSEs' limits. In such deals, the originator finds it more economical to enhance the loans' credit using the mechanisms of the private market (most commonly through subordination) than through the auspices of a GSE.

Loan Balances

The agencies have limits on the loan balance that can be included in agency-guaranteed pools. The maximum loan sizes for 1–4 family homes effective for a calendar year are adjusted late in the prior year. The year-over-year percentage change in the limits is based on the October-to-October change in the average home price (for both new and existing homes) published by the Federal Housing Finance Board. Since their inception, Freddie Mac and Fannie Mae pools have had identical loan limits, because the limits are dictated by the same statute. For 2006, the single-family limit is $417,000; the loan limits are 50% higher for loans made in Alaska, Hawaii, Guam, and the U.S. Virgin Islands.

Loans larger than the conforming limit (and thus ineligible for inclusion in agency pools) are classified as "jumbo" loans and can only be securitized in private label transactions (along with loans that do not meet the GSEs' required credit or documentation standards, irrespective of balance). While the size of the private label sector is significant (as of the second quarter of 2006, approximately $1.7 trillion in balance was outstanding), it is much smaller than the market for agency pools. Moreover, as the conforming balance limits have risen due to robust real estate appreciation, the market share of agency pools relative to private label deals has grown.

Prepayments and Prepayment Penalties

Mortgage loans can prepay for a variety of reasons. All mortgage loans have a "due on sale" clause, which means that the remaining balance of the loan must be paid when the house is sold. Existing mortgages can also be refinanced by the obligor if the prevailing level of mortgage rates declines, or if a more attractive financing vehicle is proposed to them. In addition, the homeowner can make partial prepayments on their loan, which serve to reduce the remaining balance and shorten the loan's remaining term. As we will discuss later in this chapter, prepayments strongly impact the returns and performance of MBS, and investors devote significant resources to studying and modeling them.

To mitigate the effects of prepayments, some loan programs are structured with prepayment penalties. The penalties are designed to discourage refinancing activity, and require a fee to be paid to the servicer if the loan is prepaid within a certain amount of time after funding. Penalties are typically structured to allow borrowers to partially prepay up to 20% of their loan each year the penalty is in effect, and charge the borrower six months of interest for prepayments on the remaining 80% of their balance. Some penalties are waived if the home is sold, and are described as "soft" penalties; hard penalties require the penalty to be paid even if the prepayment occurs as the sale of the underlying property.

MORTGAGE LOAN MECHANICS

As described above, mortgage loans traditionally are structured as fully amortizing debt instruments, with the principal balance being paid off over the term of the loan. For a fixed rate product, the loan's payment is constant over the term of the loan, although the payment's breakdown into principal and interest changes each month. An amortizing fixed rate loan's monthly payment can be calculated by first computing the *mortgage payment factor* using the following formula:

$$\text{Mortgage payment factor} = \frac{\text{Interest rate}(1 + \text{Interest rate})^{\text{Loan term}}}{(1 + \text{Interest rate})^{\text{Loan term}} - 1}$$

Note that the interest rate in question is the monthly rate, that is, the annual percentage rate divided by 12. The monthly payment is then computed by multiplying the mortgage payment factor by the loan's balance (either original or, if the loan is being recast, the current balance).

As an example, consider the following loan:

Loan balance: $100,000
Annual rate: 6.0%
Monthly rate: 0.50% = 0.005
Loan term: 30 Years (360 Months)

The monthly payment factor is calculated as

$$\frac{0.05(1.005)^{360}}{(1.005)^{360} - 1} = 0.0059955$$

Therefore, the monthly payment on the subject loan is $100,000 × 0.0059955, or $599.55.

An examination of the allocation of principal and interest over time provides insights with respect to the buildup of owner equity. As an example, Exhibit 1.1 shows the total payment and the amount of principal and interest for the $100,000 loan with a 6.0% interest rate (or *note rate*, as it is often called) for the life of the loan.

The exhibit shows that the payment is comprised mostly of interest in the early period of the loan. Since interest is calculated from a progressively declining balance, the amount of interest paid declines over time. In this calculation, since the aggregate payment is fixed, the principal component consequently increases over time. In fact, the exhibit shows that the unpaid principal balance in month 60 is $93,054, which means that only $6,946 of the $35,973 in payments made by the borrower up to that point in time consisted of principal. However, as the loan seasons, the payment is increasingly allocated to principal. The crossover point in the example (i.e., where the principal and interest components of the payment are equal) for this loan occurs in month 222.

EXHIBIT 1.1   Monthly Payment Breakdown for a $100,000 Fixed Rate Loan at 6.0% Rate with a 30-Year Term (fixed payment of $599.55 per month)

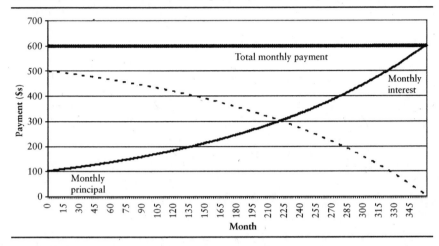

EXHIBIT 1.2   Balances for $100,000 6.0% Fixed Rate Loan over Different Original Terms

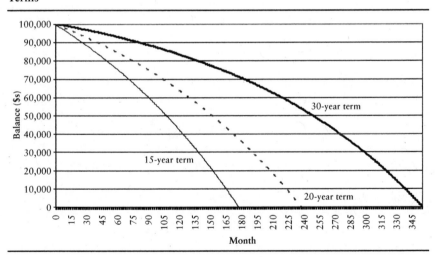

Loans with shorter amortization schedules (e.g., 15-year loans) allow for buildup of equity at a much faster rate. Exhibit 1.2 shows the outstanding balance of a $100,000 loan with a 6.0% note rate using 30-, 20-, and 15-year amortization terms. In contrast to the $93,054 remaining balance on the 30-year loan, the remaining balances on 20- and 15-year loan in month 60 are $84,899 and $76,008, respectively. In LTV terms, if the purchase price of the home is $125,000 (creating an initial LTV of

EXHIBIT 1.3   Remaining Principal Balance Outstanding for $100,000 6% Loan, Fully Amortizing versus 5-Year Interest-Only Loans

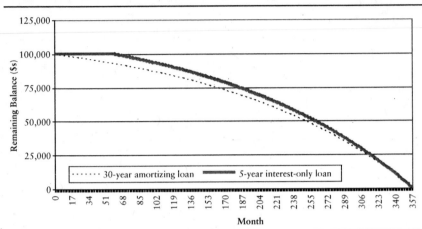

80%), the LTV in month 60 on the 15-year loan is 61% (versus 74% for the 30-year loan). Finally, while 50% of the 30-year loan balance is paid off in month 252, the halfway mark is reached in month 154 with a 20-year term, and month 110 for a 15-year loan.

Patterns of borrower equity accumulation due to amortization are important in understanding the attributes of interest-only loans. Exhibit 1.3 compares the remaining balances over time for the previously described fully amortizing $100,000 loan with a 6% rate, versus an interest-only loan with the same rate and term. A fully amortizing loan would have a monthly payment of $599.95, and would have reduced its principal balance by $6,946 at the end of five years. The interest-only loan, by definition, would amortize none of the principal over the same period. It would have an initial monthly payment at the 6% rate of $500, which would increase to $644 when the loan recasts in month 60. The 29% increase in the payment results from the loan's balance being amortized over the remaining term of 300 months. As Exhibit 1.3 indicates, the remaining balance of the interest-only loan amortizes faster than the fully amortizing loan because of the higher payment, although the interest-only loan's remaining balance is greater than that of the amortizing loan. The LTV of the amortizing loan (assuming a purchase price of $125,000 and an original LTV of 80%) declines to roughly 74% by month 60 and 72% in month 80. The interest-only loan has an 80% LTV through the first 60 months after issuance, but by month 80 the LTV declines to 77.5%.

For amortizing ARM loans, the initial payment is calculated at the initial note rate for the full 360-month term. At the first reset, and at every subsequent adjustment, the loan is recast, and the monthly payment schedule is recalculated using the new note rate and the remaining term of the loan. For example, payments on a five-year hybrid ARM with a 5.5% note rate would initially be calculated as a 5.5% loan with a 360-month term. If the loan resets to a 6.5% rate after five years (based on both the underlying index and the loan's margin), the payment is calculated using a 6.5% note rate, the remaining balance in month 60, and a 300-month term. In the following year, the payment would be recalculated again using the remaining balance and prevailing rate (depending on the performance of the index referenced by the loan) and a 288-month term. In this case, the loan's initial monthly payment would be $568; in month 60, the loan's payment would change to $624, or the payment at a 6.5% rate for 300 months on a $92,460 remaining balance.

The payments on an interest-only hybrid ARM are similar to those of a fixed rate, interest-only loan. Using the rate structure described above, an interest-only 5/1 hybrid ARM would have an initial payment of $458. After the 60-month fixed rate, interest-only period, the monthly payments would reset at $675, an increase of roughly 47%. This increase represents the payment shock discussed previously. Depending on the loan's margin and the level of the reference index, borrowers seeking to avoid a sharp increase in monthly payments often refinance their loans into cheaper available products. The desire to mitigate payment shock is also largely responsible for the growth in hybrid ARMs with noncontiguous resets. Since these loans essentially separate the rate reset and payment recast, the payment increases are spread over two periods, reducing the impact of a large one-time increase in payment.

The payment structure for negative-amortization ARM loans is different and complex. The most commonly issued form of products that allow negative amortization are so-called payment-option loans, which are variations on traditional annual-reset ARMs. The loans have an introductory rate that is effective for a short period of time (either one or three months). After the initial period, the loan's rate changes monthly, based on changes in the reference index. The borrower's minimum or "required" payment, however, does not change until month 13. The initial or teaser payment is initially calculated to fully amortize the loan over 30 years at the introductory rate. After a year, and in one-year intervals thereafter, the loan is recast. The minimum payment is recalculated based on the loan's margin, the index level effective at that time, and the remaining balance and term on the loan. However, the increase in the loan's minimum monthly payment is subject to a 7.5% cap.[1]

---

[1] Note that this cap functions differently than those in the hybrid market, which are based on changes in the loan's rate rather than payment.

The minimum payment may not be sufficient to fully pay the loan's interest, based on its effective rate. This may occur if the loan's index and margin are such that the minimum payment is lower than the interest payment, or if the minimum payment is constrained by the 7.5% payment cap. In that event, the loan undergoes negative amortization, where the unpaid amount of interest is added to the principal balance. Negative amortization is typically limited to 115% of the original loan balance (or 110% in a few states). If this threshold is reached, the loan is immediately recast to amortize the current principal amount over the remaining term of the loan. Under all circumstances, the loan is automatically recast periodically, with payments calculated based on the current loan balance and the remaining term of the loan. At this point, the payment change is *not* subject to the 7.5% payment cap—a condition that also holds true if the loan recasts because the negative amortization cap is reached. (The first mandatory recast is generally at the beginning of either year 5 or 10; in either case, the loan will subsequently recast every five years thereafter.)

RISKS ASSOCIATED WITH MORTGAGES AND MORTGAGE PRODUCTS

Holders of fixed income investments ordinarily deal with interest rate risk, or the risk that changes in the level of market interest rates will cause fluctuations in the market value of such investments. However, mortgages and associated mortgage products have additional risks associated with them that are unique to the products and require additional analysis. We conclude this chapter with a discussion of these risks.

Prepayment Risk

In a previous section, we noted that obligors have the ability to prepay their loans before they mature. For the holder of the mortgage asset, the borrower's prepayment option creates a unique form of risk. In cases where the obligor refinances the loan in order to capitalize on a drop in market rates, the investor has a high-yielding asset pay off, and it can be replaced only with an asset carrying a lower yield. Prepayment risk is analogous to "call risk" for corporate and municipal bonds in terms of its impact on returns, and also creates uncertainty with respect to the timing of investors' cash flows. In addition, changing prepayment "speeds" due to interest rate moves cause variations in the cash flows of mortgages and securities collateralized by mortgage products, strongly influencing their relative performance and making them difficult and expensive to hedge.

While we address both the factors driving prepayment behavior and the metrics used to measure prepayment speeds later in this text, a brief introduction at this juncture will be helpful. Prepayments are phenomena resulting from decisions made by the borrower and/or the lender, and occur for the following reasons:

- The sale of the property (due to normal mobility, as well as death and divorce).
- The destruction of the property by fire or other disaster.
- A default on the part of the borrower (net of losses).
- Curtailments (i.e., partial prepayments).
- Refinancing.

Prepayments attributable to reasons other than refinancings are referred to under the broad rubric of "turnover." Turnover rates tend to be fairly stable over time, but are strongly influenced by the health of the housing market, specifically the levels of real estate appreciation and the volume of existing home sales. Refinancing activity, however, generally depends on being able to obtain a new loan with either a lower rate or a smaller payment, making this activity highly dependent on the level of interest rates, the shape of the yield curve (since short rates strongly influence ARM pricing), and the availability of alternative loan products. In addition, the amount of refinancing activity can change greatly as the result of seemingly small changes in rates.

The paradigm in mortgages is thus fairly straightforward. Mortgages with low note rates (that are "out-of-the-money," to borrow a term from the option market) normally prepay fairly slowly and steadily, while loans carrying higher rates (and are "in-the-money") are prone to experience spikes in prepayments when rates decline. Clearly, this paradigm is dependent on the level of mortgage rates. Many loans that are out-of-the-money at this writing were fully in-the-money in mid-2003, when rates were at all-time loans and prepayment speeds skyrocketed.

It is important to understand how changes in prepayment rates impact the performance of mortgages and MBS. Since prepayments increase as bond prices rise and market yields are declining, mortgages shorten in average life and duration when the bond markets rally, constraining their price appreciation. Conversely, rising yields cause prepayments to slow and bond durations to extend, resulting in a greater drop in price than experienced by more traditional (i.e., option-free) fixed income products. As a result, the price performance of mortgages and MBS tends to lag that of comparable fixed maturity instruments (such as Treasury notes) when the prevailing level of yields increases.

This phenomenon is generically described as "negative convexity." The effect of changing prepayment speeds on mortgage durations, based on movements in interest rates, is precisely the opposite of what a bondholder would desire. (Fixed income portfolio managers, for example, extend durations as rates decline, and shorten them when rates rise.) The price performance of mortgages and MBS is, therefore, decidedly nonlinear in nature, and the product will underperform assets that do not exhibit negatively convex behavior as rates decline.

Exhibit 1.4 shows a graphic representation of this behavior. Investors are generally compensated for the lagging price performance of MBS through higher base-case yields. However, the necessity of managing negative convexity and prepayment risk on the part of investors involves fairly active management of MBS portfolios, and creates both higher hedging costs and the possibility of losses due to estimation and modeling error. In turn, this creates the desire on the part of some investors to limit their exposure to prepayments by investing in bonds where prepayment risk is transferred within the structure. This type of risk mitigation is central to the structured MBS market, and will be discussed in depth later in this text.

EXHIBIT 1.4   Performance Profile of Hypothetical Fixed Maturity Bond versus MBS

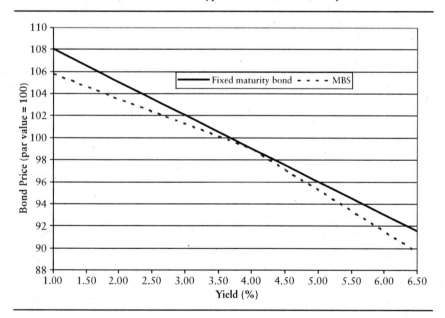

Credit and Default Risk

Analysis of the credit exposure in the mortgage sector is different from the assessment of credit risk in most other fixed income instruments because it requires:

- Quantifying and stratifying the characteristics of the thousands of loans that underlie the mortgage investment.
- Estimating how these attributes will translate into performance based on standard metrics, and the evaluation of reasonable best-, worst-, and likely-case performance.
- Calculating returns based on these scenarios.

In a prior section, some of the factors (credit scores, LTVs, etc.) that are used to gauge the creditworthiness of borrowers and the likelihood of a loan to result in a loss of principal were discussed. Many of the same measures are also used in evaluating the credit worthiness of a mortgage pool. For example, weighted average credit scores and LTVs are routinely calculated, and stratifications of these characteristics (along with documentation styles and other attributes) are used in the credit evaluation of the pool. In addition to these characteristics of the loans, the following metrics are also utilized in the a posteriori evaluation of a mortgage pool or security.

Delinquencies

These measures are designed to gauge whether borrowers are current on their loan payments or, if they are late, stratifying them according to the seriousness of the delinquency. The most common convention for classifying delinquencies is one promulgated by the Office of Thrift Supervision; this "OTS" method classifies loans as follows:

- Payment due date to 30 days late: *Current*
- 30–60 days late: *30 days delinquent*
- 60–90 days late: *60 days delinquent*
- More than 90 days late: *90+ days delinquent*

Defaults

At some point in their existence, many loans that are associated with delinquencies become current, as the condition leading to the delinquency (e.g., job loss, illness, etc.) resolves itself. However, some portion of the delinquent loan universe ends up in default. By definition, default is the point where the borrower loses title to the property in question. Default generally occurs for loans that are 90+ days delinquent, although loans where the borrower goes into bankruptcy may be classified as defaulted at an earlier point in time.

Loss Severity

Since the lender has a lien on the borrower's property, much of the value of the loan can be recovered through the foreclosure process. Loss severity measures the face value of the loss on a loan after foreclosure is completed. Depending on the type of loan, loss severities can average in the area of 20% to 40%, and can be heavily influenced by the loan's LTV (since a high LTV loan leaves less room for a decline in the value of the property in the event of a loss). However, in the event of a default, loans with relatively low LTVs can also result in losses, generally for two reasons:

- The appraised value of the property may be high relative to the property's actual market value.
- There are costs and foregone income associated with the foreclosure process.

As with prepayments, the measurement of estimated and historical credit performance is discussed later in this text.

In light of these factors, the process of evaluating the credit-adjusted performance of either a group of loans involves first gauging the expected delinquencies, defaults, and loss severities of the pool or security based on its credit characteristics. Subsequently, loss-adjusted yields and returns can be generated. It should be noted that investors in some segments of the MBS market do not engage in detailed credit analysis; buyers of agency pools, for example, generally rely on the guaranty of the agency in question. In addition to buyers of mortgages in whole-loan form, credit analysis is primarily undertaken by investors in the subordinate tranches of private label deals. As we will subsequently discuss, the performance of subordinates is highly sensitive to the credit performance of the collateral pool. This is both because of their role in protecting the senior classes from losses, as well as the sequential nature of loss allocations within the subordinate classes.

CHAPTER 2

Overview of the Mortgage-Backed Securities Market

The growth of the real estate and primary mortgage markets have, quite naturally, led to the rapid expansion of the mortgage-backed securities—or MBS—market. According to the Bond Market Association, there were $6.4 trillion in MBS outstanding at the end of the third quarter of 2006, which would make it roughly 49% larger than the Treasury market at that time. The size of the MBS market, as well as the broad range of products offered, reflect the growth and diversity of the market for fixed income investment vehicles. It has also caused fixed income investment managers to be cognizant of developments in the MBS markets and sensitive to factors driving MBS issuance and performance.

In the most general sense, originators securitize loans to tap the capital markets for funding and liquidity. Mortgage lenders accept applications, fund loans, sell them into the capital markets in the form of MBS, and then recycle the resulting proceeds into new lending. Before the development of the MBS markets, lenders made mortgage loans from deposits and typically held the loans in their portfolio. This resulted in periodic shortages of mortgage money when local financial conditions were relatively illiquid; in addition, lenders' profitability was tied to the shape of the yield curve and the ability to earn a spread over funding costs. The development of an actively traded market for mortgage products over the last quarter-century has resulted in the growth of a national primary mortgage market. Mortgage lending has evolved from a fragmented industry, where rates and availability of financing were

21

based on local liquidity conditions, to a market where sources and users of funds interact on a massive scale.

This chapter introduces concepts involved in the creation and trading of MBS in the primary and secondary markets. It discusses the mechanics of issuing different forms of MBS, along with many of the market practices, conventions, and terms associated with the MBS markets. In conjunction with the previous chapter on mortgage products, it also discusses how secondary market pricing and levels drive the pricing of mortgage loans to consumers.

CREATING DIFFERENT TYPES OF MBS

The fundamental unit in the MBS market is the *pool*. At its lowest common denominator, mortgage-backed pools are aggregations of large numbers of mortgage loans with similar (but not identical) characteristics. Loans with a commonality of attributes such as note rate (i.e., the interest rate paid by the borrower on the loan), term to maturity, credit quality, loan balance, and product type are combined using a variety of legal mechanisms to create relatively fungible investment vehicles. With the creation of MBS, mortgage loans were transformed from a heterogeneous group of disparate assets into sizeable and homogenous securities that trade in a liquid market.

The transformation of groups of mortgage loans with common attributes into tradable and liquid MBS occurs using one of two mechanisms. Loans that meet the guidelines of the agencies (i.e., Fannie Mae, Freddie Mac, and Ginnie Mae, as discussed in the prior chapter) in terms of credit quality, underwriting standards, and balance are assigned an insurance premium, called a *guaranty fee*, by the agency in question and securitized as an agency pool. Loans that either do not qualify for agency treatment, or for which agency pooling execution is not efficient, are securitized in nonagency or "private label" transactions. These types of securities do not have an agency guaranty, and must therefore be issued under the registration entity or "shelf" of the issuer.[1] As noted later in this chapter, the insurance (or "credit enhancement") for the loans is in the form of either a private guaranty or, more commonly, structured in

---

[1] The Securities Exchange Act of 1934 requires nonexempt entities to register their offerings with the Securities and Exchange Commission (SEC) prior to issuance. Because of their quasi-government status, securities issued by the GSEs are exempt from the SEC's registration requirements. "Shelf registration" refers to SEC rule 415, which modified registration requirements by allowing issuers to register securities up to two years before they are actually issued.

the deal through so-called "subordinate" classes. The senior portions of these deals are very similar in profile to agency pools, and are often referred to as *private label* or *senior pass-throughs.*[2]

Once a pool (in either agency or private label form) is created, it can be sold to investors in the form of a pass-through, in which principal and interest is paid to investors based on their pro rata share of the pool. However, the cash flows of pools can also be carved up to meet the requirements of different types of investors. The creation of so-called "structured securities" involves dividing (or "tranching") the underlying pools' cash flows into securities that have varying average lives and durations,[3] different degrees of prepayment protection or exposure, and (in the case of private label deals) different degrees of credit risk. These types of securities are broadly referred to as *collateralized mortgage obligations* (CMOs). The flexibility inherent in tranching, along with the broad range of loan instruments, allows the MBS market to reflect a large degree of market segmentation. In turn, this allows a wide range of investor types with different investment objectives and risk tolerances to invest in the MBS market, supplying the funds that ultimately are recycled into new mortgage lending.

It will be helpful at this juncture to briefly discuss and contrast the processes of creating and structuring agency CMOs and private label transactions. To create an agency CMO deal, the underwriter buys agency MBS pools in the primary or secondary markets and places them in a trust-like entity. The different tranches are then created from the principal and interest cash flows generated by the MBS pools (or "collateral"). In contrast, private label transactions are created by placing large numbers of loans directly in a securitization vehicle, from which the structured transaction is subsequently created by the issuer. (This accounts for why these transactions are sometimes referred to as "whole loan CMOs.")[4] While the agency transaction is an arbitrage of sorts, the

---

[2] The term "pass-through" indicates that principal and interest is passed on to the investor pro rata with their holding. Using this definition, the senior portion of a private label deal is technically not a pass-through, because principal is redistributed within the structure; however, the term is nonetheless utilized to describe the senior cash flows before they are restructured.

[3] The concepts of average life and duration are discussed in Chapter 11. *Duration* is a measure of the sensitivity of the price of a fixed income instrument to changes in interest rates.

[4] CMOs are also referred to as Real Estate Mortgage Investment Conduits, or REMICs. The terminology refers to a provision in the Tax Reform Act of 1986 in order to remedy some double taxation inefficiencies inherent in earlier collateralized structures. While the term REMIC is essentially a tax election, often the terms CMO and REMIC are used interchangeably.

private label securitization serves as the process by which loans are directly distributed into the capital markets.

A different subset of the MBS sector is the market for *mortgage strips*, or more precisely the market for principal-only and interest-only securities. Since mortgages are comprised of both principal and interest, the two components can be separated and sold independently. The holder of the *principal-only security* (or PO) receives only principal (scheduled and unscheduled) paid on the underlying loans. The holder of the *interest-only security* (or IO) receives the interest generated by the underlying loans. Although IOs are quoted with a principal balance, this balance is notional in nature; it is used only as a point of reference for settling the transaction and calculating monthly interest cash flows generated by the security. The most common mortgage strips are created simply by putting agency pools into a trust and splitting principal and interest cash flows into IOs and POs. (Note that IOs in this context should not be confused with interest-only loans discussed in Chapter 1; the two concepts are totally different, even though they do share some of the same nomenclature.)

The market for mortgage developed to allow MBS investors a means of trading directly on prepayment speeds and expectations. POs typically have long positive durations and rise in value when rates decline, while IOs have negative durations, behaving in a fashion similar to bond puts when rates rise. However, the critical driver of performance strips is prepayment expectations. POs perform well if prepayment speeds are fast, in the same way that returns would be enhanced if a zero-coupon bond were called prior to maturity at par. By contrast, IOs perform well if prepayment speeds are slow; they can be viewed as an annuity where the value increases the longer it remains outstanding.

While IOs and POs are most commonly created in trust form, both types of bonds can also be created as part of a CMO deal. Structured IOs and POs have a similar appeal to investors as strips, and are evaluated in a similar fashion. They are created as part of the process of structuring certain bonds with a targeted coupon or dollar price. If an investor seeks a bond with a lower dollar price, for example, the coupon on the bond must be reduced; this can be accomplished by stripping some coupon off the tranche in question and selling it as a structured IO. We discuss this topic in more depth in Chapter 7.

Agency MBS Creation

While both agency adjustable rate pools and private label securities have existed for many years, the agency fixed rate market remains the most widely quoted and liquid benchmark in the MBS market. Therefore, a discussion of pooling practices and the securitization process logically begins with the formation of fixed rate agency pools. In this section, we will first address the basics of agency fixed rate pools, which dictate to a large extent how such pools are created. Subsequently, we will discuss the creation of ARM pools, which have many similarities to fixed rate products but are pooled quite differently.

Fixed Rate Agency Pooling

Agency fixed rate MBS are traded according to their coupons, which are normally securitized in 50 basis point increments. There are liquid markets in both even coupons and half-coupons (e.g., 6.0% and 6.5%), although quarter- and eighth-coupon pools are sometimes originated. Loans, by contrast, are normally originated in increments of 12.5 basis points (or 1/8th of a percent). As part of the transformation process, certain cash flows from the loan interest stream are allocated for servicing and credit support payments. These apportionments are as follows:

- Guaranty fees (or "g-fees") are, as described earlier, fees paid to the agencies to insure the loan. Since these fees essentially represent the price of credit risk insurance, g-fees vary across loan types. In the conventional universe, g-fees vary depending on the perceived riskiness of the individual loans (based on credit metrics such as credit score, LTV, and documentation described in Chapter 1). However, high-volume lenders may be able to negotiate generally lower guaranty fees. For Ginnie Mae pools, the guaranty fee is almost always six basis points, reflecting the loan-level guarantees provided by the Federal Housing Administration and Veterans Administration.
- *Required servicing* or *base servicing* refers to a portion of the loan's note rate that must be held by the servicer of the loan. This entity collects payments from mortgagors, makes tax and insurance payments for the borrowers, and remits payments to investors. The amount of base servicing required differs depending on the agency and program. At this writing, base servicing is 25 basis points in the fixed rate passthrough market.
- *Excess servicing* is the amount of the loan's note rate in excess of the desired coupon remaining after the g-fees and base servicing are subtracted.

Both base and excess servicing (sometimes described as *mortgage servicing rights* or MSRs) can be capitalized and held by the servicer after the loan is funded. However, secondary markets exist for trading servicing, either in the form of raw mortgage servicing rights or interest-only securities created from excess servicing.

A simple schematic showing how two loans with different fixed note rates can be securitized into a 5.5% agency pass-through pool is shown in Exhibit 2.1. For both loans, the amount of base servicing and guaranty fee is the same, with the difference being the amount of excess servicing created by the issuer. This diagram ignores some of the complexities of pooling, however, which will be addressed later in this section.

General pooling practices in the fixed rate market mandate that the note rate of the loans must be greater than the pool's coupon. However, loans with a wide range of note rates can be securitized in pools. For example, Freddie Mac and Fannie Mae allow the note rate to be as much as 250 basis points higher than the coupon rate.[5] Pooling economics normally dictate that the note rate of the loan is between 25 and 75 basis points higher than the coupon rate since retaining large amounts of excess servicing is generally uneconomical. In addition, guaranty fees can be capitalized, or "bought down," and paid as an up-front fee to the GSE at the loan's funding. This typically occurs when the lender wishes

EXHIBIT 2.1   Cash Flow Allocation for a 5.5% Agency Pass-Through Pool for Loans with Different Note Rates

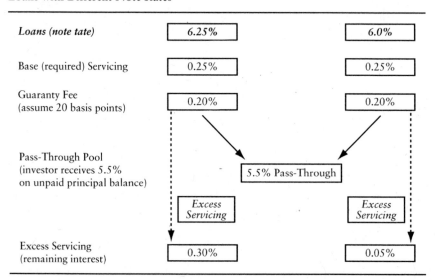

Loans (note tate)	6.25%	6.0%
Base (required) Servicing	0.25%	0.25%
Guaranty Fee (assume 20 basis points)	0.20%	0.20%
Pass-Through Pool (investor receives 5.5% on unpaid principal balance)	5.5% Pass-Through	
	Excess Servicing	*Excess Servicing*
Excess Servicing (remaining interest)	0.30%	0.05%

[5] Ginnie Mae pooling rules depend on the program used to securitize the loans. The Ginnie I program, where the majority of loans are pooled, requires that the note rate be 50 basis points over the coupon rate. The multi-issuer Ginnie II program allows the note rate to be up to 150 basis points higher than the coupon.

to create pools with relatively high coupon rates (e.g., pool a 6.25% loan into a 6.0% pool) based on market conditions, a practice known as "pooling up." (Naturally enough, pooling this loan into a 5.5% pool would be called "pooling down.") Because of the base servicing requirement, however, at this writing the spread between a loan's note rate and pooling coupon cannot be less than 25 basis points.

Once large numbers of loans are funded, lenders will group loans with the same coupon in order to form pools. To create a pool, the lender effectively transfers loans earmarked for a particular coupon to the agency and receives the same face value of MBS in exchange. The MBS received may consist of a pool collateralized by only its loans, or it may be part of a multi-issuer pool. After receiving the security, the lender can either sell the pool into the secondary market or (in the case of a depository) hold it in its investment portfolio.

The GSEs also buy loans for cash proceeds through what is called, appropriately enough, the *cash window*. This is often used for loan programs with unusual specifications such as certain documentation styles or loan-to-value ratios, as well as by smaller lenders that engage in piecemeal sales. Loans purchased through the cash window can either be securitized in multi-issuer pools or retained in the GSEs' portfolios.

Adjustable Rate Agency Pooling

As noted earlier in this section, pooling practices in the agency ARM market are currently somewhat different. As in the fixed rate market, a standard amount of base servicing is held on each loan, and guaranty fees are assigned and paid on the loans based on each loan's perceived riskiness. (Base servicing in the ARM market has historically been 37.5 basis points, but at this writing some lenders have begun to hold only 12.5 basis points of base servicing.) The lender's current production, with loans having a range of note rates, is then pooled, with the pool's coupon being an average of the net note rates in the pool weighted by the loans' balances. This is referred to as having a *weighted average coupon* or WAC coupon. Using this methodology means that:

- No excess servicing is held in order to decrease the net note rates of the loans to a targeted level.
- G-fees are generally not bought down, since buydown pricing is not efficient in the ARM sector.
- Pools will contain loans with note rates below the coupon rate.

There are important implications of this different pooling methodology. ARM pools typically are originated with uneven coupons taken to three decimal places (e.g., a pool might have an initial coupon of 5.092%). In addition, coupon rates on ARM pools (and, in fact, any security with a WAC coupon) change slightly over time, as individual loans in the pool are paid off. The result of these factors is that agency ARMs trade on a pool-specific basis, rather than by specific coupons as in the fixed rate universe. (There have been a number of initiatives designed to create ARM securities that can trade in forward markets more like those of the fixed rate universe, although none have yet been adopted in a broad fashion.)

Private Label Securitization

While the creation of private label deals is conceptually similar to agency pooling practices, the lack of involvement by the agencies necessitates significant differences. Since there is no guaranty fee, alternative forms of credit enhancement must be utilized as noted previously. Private credit enhancement is most commonly created in the form of subordination, which means that a portion of the deal is subordinate or "junior" in priority of cash flows, and is the first to absorb nonrecoverable losses in order to protect the remaining (or "senior") tranches. A common technique is to divide the subordinated part of the deal into different tranches, each with different ratings (which typically range from double-A to unrated first-loss pieces) and degrees of exposure to credit losses. (For example, the nonrated "first loss" tranche is the first to absorb losses; if this tranche is exhausted, the losses are then allocated to the tranche second-lowest in initial priority). Subordinate tranches trade at significantly higher yields than the seniors to compensate investors for the incremental riskiness and greater likelihood of credit-related losses.

Exhibit 2.2 shows an example of a senior/subordinate deal structured in this fashion. The amount of subordination required for a deal and the relative sizes of the different subordinate tranches (often referred to as the "splits") are dictated by the rating agencies, based upon their assessment of the likelihood of losses for the subject collateral. Prior to being structured, the senior portion of the deal in the example has cash flows that are very similar (but not identical) to agency pools, as noted previously. These private label pass-throughs are sometimes sold directly in unstructured form, although it is more common to see them restructured into tranches using the techniques we explore in Chapter 8.

Deals with *subordination* (also called *senior/sub deals*) typically have an additional feature designed to insure the adequacy of credit enhancement levels. All unscheduled principal payments (i.e., prepayments) are initially directed to the senior tranches, and the subordinates are locked out from prepayments (although they do receive scheduled principal payments, or amortizations). This feature causes the subordi-

EXHIBIT 2.2   Diagram of a Senior/Subordinate Structure

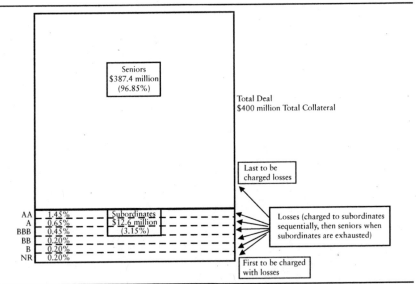

nation (as a percentage of the deal) to grow over time, and increases the degree of protection for the senior sector. The subordinates eventually begin to receive some unscheduled principal payments (although the actual schedule depends on the type of collateral), and ultimately receive prepayments pro rata with their size. The technique is referred to as "shifting interest," and deals with this type of subordination are commonly called *shifting interest structures.*

Other variations of the senior/subordinate structure are used in the MBS markets, especially for subprime and other loans that have a greater degree of default risk. Some deals are structured such that there is more loan collateral than bonds in a deal, lending additional credit support to the senior bonds (in addition to some subordinate classes). This structuring technique is referred to as *overcollateralization,* and deals structured in this fashion are referred to as OC *structures.* (We will more fully address techniques of credit enhancement and subordination in Chapters 8 and 9.)

As with agency ARM pools, private label deals typically securitize a wide range of note rates, due in part to the desire of issuers to capitalize on economies of scale by issuing large deals. However, the market for fixed rate securities is generally not receptive to WAC coupons. In order to create a fixed coupon rate, the loan collateral must be modified before the credit enhancement is structured. This technique is somewhat different from that utilized in creating agency pools. Both the range of note rates included in a deal, as well as the desire to include loans with note rates below the deal's coupon (once base servicing and fees are taken into account), necessitate the creation of WAC IOs and POs, securities unique to the private label market.

The decision with respect to which coupon is to be produced is a function of market conditions, including investor's interest rate and prepayment outlook. Once the coupon is designated, the loans are divided into "discount" and "premium" loan groups. This calculation subtracts the base servicing and fees from each loan's note rate to create the *net note rate*. The net note rate is then compared to the deal's designated coupon. Discount loans are those loans that have a net note rate lower than that of the deal's coupon; premium loans are those where the net note rate is above the deal coupon.

At this point, the two loan groups are each structured to give them the deal's coupon. The discount loans are "grossed up" to the deal's coupon rate by creating, for each note rate, a small amount of PO.[6] The amount of PO created for each rate stratum is computed based on the *PO Percentage*, which is calculated as follows:

$$\text{PO percentage} = [\text{Deal coupon} - \text{Note rate}] \div \text{Deal coupon}$$

The PO percentage for each note rate stratum is then multiplied by its face value, and the sum of the POs created for all discount note rates is the size of the WAC PO.

The loans in the premium loan group are stripped of some of the interest in order to reduce their net note rates to that of the deal coupon. The interest strip is assigned a notional value equal to the face value of the stratum. As an example, assume that $20 million face value of loans has a 6.5% note rate, and the designated deal coupon is 6.0%. Assuming 25 basis points of base servicing and no fees gives it a 6.25% net note rate. Therefore, 25 basis points of interest is stripped from these loans, creating $20 million notional value of a strip with a coupon of 0.25%. The notional value of the WAC IO is simply the combined notional value of all loans having premium net note rates, and its coupon is the average of the strip coupons weighted by their notional balances. (Note that in some cases the strip cash flows generated by the premium loans are held by the originator in the form of excess servicing, rather than securitized into a WAC IO.)

---

[6] By creating some PO for each strata, the available interest is allocated over a smaller amount of principal, effectively raising its net note rate to that of the deal coupon.

EXHIBIT 2.3 Example of Loan Stratification and Coupon Creation for a Hypothetical Private Label Deal (assuming 25 basis points base servicing, 0.9 basis points trustee fee, and a 5.75% security coupon)

	Note Rate	Net Note Rate[a]	Balance in Cohort	Difference— Net Note Rate and Coupon	Net Contri- bution to WAC[b]	PO %[c]	PO% × Balance	Face Value Added to WAC IO
Discount Loans	5.000%	4.741%	500,000	−0.0101	0.0000	17.5%	87,739	0
	5.125%	4.866%	2,600,000	−0.0088	0.0000	15.4%	399,722	0
	5.250%	4.991%	5,000,000	−0.0076	0.0000	13.2%	660,000	0
	5.375%	5.116%	8,000,000	−0.0063	0.0000	11.0%	882,087	0
	5.500%	5.241%	16,400,000	−0.0051	0.0000	8.9%	1,451,757	0
	5.625%	5.366%	21,000,000	−0.0038	0.0000	6.7%	1,402,435	0
	5.750%	5.491%	31,000,000	−0.0026	0.0000	4.5%	1,396,348	0
	5.875%	5.616%	37,000,000	−0.0013	0.0000	2.3%	862,261	0
	6.000%	5.741%	45,000,000	−0.0001	0.0000	0.2%	70,435	0
Premium Loans	6.125%	5.866%	55,000,000	0.0012	0.0012	0.0%	0	55,000,000
	6.250%	5.991%	70,000,000	0.0024	0.0024	0.0%	0	70,000,000
	6.375%	6.116%	41,000,000	0.0037	0.0037	0.0%	0	41,000,000
	6.500%	6.241%	42,000,000	0.0049	0.0049	0.0%	0	42,000,000
	6.625%	6.366%	37,000,000	0.0062	0.0062	0.0%	0	37,000,000
	6.750%	6.491%	30,500,000	0.0074	0.0074	0.0%	0	30,500,000
	6.875%	6.616%	22,000,000	0.0087	0.0087	0.0%	0	22,000,000
	7.000%	6.741%	21,000,000	0.0099	0.0099	0.0%	0	21,000,000
	7.125%	6.866%	8,000,000	0.0112	0.0112	0.0%	0	8,000,000
	7.250%	6.991%	4,000,000	0.0124	0.0124	0.0%	0	4,000,000
	7.375%	7.116%	3,000,000	0.0137	0.0137	0.0%	0	3,000,000
						Total	7,212,783	333,500,000

Total Deal Size	500,000,000
WAC IO Size[d]	333,500,000
WAC PO Size[e]	7,212,783

[a] Note rate less base servicing and trustee fee.
[b] For premium loans, the net contribution is defined as: Net note rate − Security coupon. It is 0 for discount loans.
[c] For discount loans, the PO percentage is defined as: (Security coupon − Net note rate)/Security coupon.
[d] The face value of the WAC IO is the sum of the face value of the premium loans.
[e] The face value of the WAC PO is the sum of the face value of the discount loans times the PO percentage.

The breakdown and grouping of loans backing a hypothetical private label deal, and the structuring of the loans into a pool with one fixed coupon rate, is shown in Exhibit 2.3. The exhibit shows the calculations for a package of loans with various note rate strata for a deal with a 5.75% coupon, assuming 25 basis points of base servicing and 0.9% trustee fee (which are both standard assumptions at this writing). All loans with note rates of 6.125% and higher are considered premium loans, since they will have a net note rate higher than the 5.75% cutoff; loans with note rates below 6.125% are classified as discount loans. Notice that changing the deal's coupon changes the sizes of the WAC IO and PO, as well as the WAC IO's coupon. In the example, lowering the deal coupon to 5.5% pushes $82 million face value of loans, with note rates of 5.75% and 5.875%, into the premium sector, increasing the WAC IOs notional face value from $333.5 million to $415.5 million. The face value of the WAC PO declines, however, from approximately $7.21 million to $2.72 million. Therefore, the "market conditions" influencing the choice of coupon include the preferences of investors for premium or discount coupons, as well as the relative demand for IOs and/or POs.

MBS TRADING

The structure of the MBS markets has long reflected the practices of both originators and borrowers in the primary mortgage market. This discussion is facilitated by a brief overview of the timeline of a mortgage loan, illustrated in Exhibit 2.4. A loan begins as an application, which may either be associated with a designated rate (making the loan "locked" or "committed") or carried as a floating rate obligation (to be locked at a point prior to funding). Borrowers that lock their loan at the time of application pay slightly more for their loans (in terms of either a rate differential or slightly higher fees) to account for the cost of hedging the loan for the period between application and funding. Most importantly, there is a lag between the points in time when borrowers apply for their loans and the loans are funded that lenders must take into account in managing their book of business, or *pipeline*. This lag reflects the time necessary for lenders to underwrite the loan and process the paperwork, which includes appraisals, title searches and insurance, geological and flood surveys, and credit analysis. In addition, purchase transactions often require additional time to process and register the underlying real estate transaction.

EXHIBIT 2.4   Timeline of Loan From Application to Agency Pooling

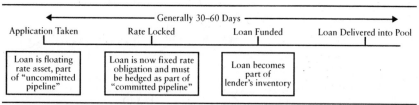

The lag between application and funding, which varies depending on the type of loans and market conditions, allows lenders to sell their expected production for settlement in the future. However, it also forces lenders to manage and hedge their production pipeline in order to control the variability of their proceeds and maximize their profitability. While hedging a loan pipeline is similar in concept to hedging other portfolios, it requires lenders to continuously be appraised of the rate of new applications (which adds to the position) as well as so-called "fall out," which occurs as some borrowers allow their loan applications to lapse. A fairly consistent amount of loans will fall out under all circumstances, reflecting transactions that fail to close for a variety of reasons. However, fallout of committed loans can change sharply if lending rates fluctuate. For example, a drop in rates typically causes an increase in the number of loans that fall out as applicants let their existing application lapse and apply for new loans. In the same fashion as negative convexity discussed in Chapter 1, changing fallout rates complicate the process of hedging by making changes in the pipeline's value nonlinear with respect to interest rates.

The need for lenders to sell their expected production for future settlement has resulted in the MBS market being structured as a so-called *forward market*. In a forward market, a trade is agreed upon between two parties at a price for settlement (i.e., the exchange of the item being traded for the agreed-upon proceeds) at some future date.

MBS Market Structure

The MBS market has evolved a number of conventions unique to the needs of both mortgage originators and investors. For example, settlements occur each month according to a predetermined calendar which specifies the delivery date for a variety of products over the course of each month. (The calendar is developed by the Bond Market Association (BMA) and published roughly six months in advance.) Prices are typically quoted for three settlements months (e.g., a quote sheet in March would post prices for April, May, and June settlement). However, trades can be executed farther in the future, subject to accounting and counterparty risk considerations.

Transactions in fixed rate pass-through securities can be effected in one of three ways:

■ *A preidentified pool or pools can be traded.* In this type of "specified pool" trade, the pool number and "original balance" of the pool (i.e., the amount of the pool as if it were a brand-new pool, before the effects of paydowns) are identified at the time the transaction is consummated.

- *A so-called to-be-announced (TBA) trade.* In this case, the security is identified (e.g., Fannie Mae 6.0s) and a price is set; but the actual pools identities are not provided by the seller until just before settlement. (This process is referred to as *pool allocation.*) The attributes of the pools that are eligible for delivery into TBA trades is specified by the BMA in order to effect a degree of standardization.
- *A "stipulated" trade.* This is a variation on a TBA trade, but the underlying characteristics of the pool are specified more precisely than in a standard TBA trade. In some cases, the pools in a stipulated trade are not deliverable, under the BMA rules, into TBA pools. In other instances, the pools can be delivered, but are viewed as having incremental value to investors and trade at a premium to TBAs.

The TBA market only exists, at this writing, in the fixed rate market for agency pools. As noted previously, there is currently no equivalent to the TBA in the ARM market for conventional ARMs because of the wide variety of product types and specifications in the ARM market. (There has been a TBA market in the Ginnie ARM product, but trading in that sector became fairly illiquid in the late 1990s.) ARM products trade almost entirely as either specified or stipulated (or "stipped," as it is sometimes called) pools, although they generally settle based on "good-day" delivery specified by the BMA calendar. Both agency and private label deals are settled at the end of the month; secondary trading typically occurs for settlement three business days after the trade is executed, for so-called "corporate settlement."

Financing and the Dollar Roll Market

An interesting attribute of forward markets that has appeal to MBS participants is the fact that they implicitly create a built-in financing vehicle. The forward market mechanism allows trading in the same securities for settlement in different months. As noted, originators generally sell their production for forward settlement in order to monetize and hedge their pipelines. However, there is also demand for MBS pools for settlement in the early or "front" months. For example, some types of investors (such as depository institutions) generally put securities on their books rather than forward obligations, which may not receive favorable accounting treatment. In addition, dealers acquiring agency pools as collateral for agency CMO deals must take delivery of the pools before their structured transaction settles. Therefore, MBS trading involves pricing the same securities for different settlement dates. In addition, dealers make active markets in TBAs for different settlements, simultaneously buying positions for one settlement month and selling the identical position for another. This type of transaction is known as a *dollar roll* or simply a "roll."

Simply put, valuing dollar rolls involves weighing the benefits and costs, over a holding period, of either:

1. Buying the security for the earlier (or "front") month, and owning (and financing) it for the period ending with the latter (or "back" month) settlement date.
2. Buying the security for the back month's settlement.

In the first case, where the security is bought for the front month, the investor receives coupon payments and reinvested interest for the holding period, along with principal payments (both amortizations and prepaid principal). The investor must also finance the position, typically through the repurchase market. In theory, the back month price is such that the investor is indifferent between the two alternatives. In practice, the price difference (or "drop") between the two settlement dates is often greater than that implied by the breakeven calculation, which means that the investor buying the position for back-month settlement is effectively financing the security at an implied repo rate lower than that available in the repurchase market. The trade-off is illustrated in Exhibit 2.5, which compares the total holding period proceeds garnered by buying in the front month and holding the security to the horizon vis-à-vis buying the bonds in the back months.

The factors that impact roll valuations are:

- The attributes of the security (including its coupon and, to a lesser extent, its age and WAC).
- The length of the holding period (i.e., the number of calendar days between the two settlement dates).
- The assumed prepayment speed.
- The cost of funding in the repo market.

When the drop expands beyond the implied cost of funds and the roll offers subrepo financing, it is referred to as trading "special." This condition can be caused by a number of factors, including:

- Heavy issuance by originators in the back month, pushing down the price for that settlement date.
- Strong demand in the front month for deal collateral, pushing up the front month price.
- A shortage of a particular security in the market. If a dealer fails to make delivery against a sale, they must pay accrued interest to the

EXHIBIT 2.5 Example of Calculation of Dollar Rolls

Security Assumptions

Coupon	6.0%
WAC	6.50%
WAM	358
Age	2
June price	100-24/32s
July price	100-19/32s
Drop (roll)	5/32s
Front-month settlement date (June)	6/13/2006
Back-month settlement date (July)	7/13/2006
Assumed prepayment speed (in CPR)	15%
(E) Assumed funding rate	5%
Delay days	24

Roll (Buy for July Settlement)

Proceeds at July price	$1,007,500
Number of days accrued	*13*
13 days of accrued interest at 6%	$2,000
Total invested	$1,009,500
Holding period (number of days between settlement dates)	*30*
(A) Reinvestment income[a]	$4,206
(B) Total future value—Rolling	$1,013,706

(D) Dollar Advantage (B–C)	$915
Roll special (in 32s)	3/32

Hold (Buy for June Settlement, Sell for July Settlement)

Future value of cash flows[b]	$19,323
July principal value	$991,497
July holding period	12
Accrued interest received for sale in July	$1,971
(C) Total future value	$1,012,791

Cash Flows

June principal payment	$14,355
June coupon interest payment (at 6.0%)	$5,000
Total June cash flow (received on July 25)	$19,355
Remaining balance on $1 million original balance in July (at 15% CPR)	$985,645

Calculating Breakeven Cost-of-Funds

Reinvestment income to breakeven to hold scenario (A–D)	$3,291
(F) Reinvestment rate to receive same proceeds as holding[c]	3.912%
Total future value at breakeven reinvestment rate	$1,012,791
Roll Special (in basis points) (E–F)	108.8

[a] The hold ing period is the period between 6/13/06 and 7/13/06 since the proceeds of a July purchase can be invested for that period of time.

[b] Because of delay days, cash flows for pools held on the June record date are paid on July 25; the future value calculation discounts these cash flows back to the July settlement date at the funding rate.

[c] This rate is the breakeven rate that changes the reinvestment proceeds such that the future values for both scenarios are the same.

seller on the face value of the sale, while not receiving any interest for the long position; "failing" on a trade is thus very expensive. This forces the dealer (or, in some cases, multiple dealers) to buy the security for delivery in the front month, which drives up the front month price and exacerbating the specialness of the roll. (A shortage can occur either because of unanticipated low issuance of a security, or the unwillingness of investors to roll them.)

Strictly speaking, MBS dollar rolls trade as an adjunct to the TBA market in the fixed rate sector. However, all sectors in the MBS market can be traded for a variety of settlements; an ARM pool, for example, can be priced for a number of different settlements, and originators can look to roll existing trades forward if they have difficulty funding enough loans to fill a trade. The calculation is similar to that done in the dollar roll market. Here, however, the price drop between regular and extended settlement is calculated based on the bond's coupon, expected prepayment speed, and expectations for repo rates over the horizon period.

However, the availability of the roll market and the potential for below-market funding often gives TBAs an intrinsic advantage over other products in the MBS sector. For example, an investor comparing a stipped pool to a TBA when rolls are special must account for the opportunity cost of eschewing the below-market financing available in the TBA market in valuing the alternative security. By implication, non-rolling MBS must trade more cheaply relative to TBAs during periods when dollar roll specials offer attractive financing rates.

THE ROLE OF THE MBS MARKETS IN GENERATING CONSUMER LENDING RATES

An ancillary benefit of the growth in the MBS sector and the integration of consumer mortgage markets is the increased rationality of loan pricing to the consumer. As the mortgage market has become increasingly national in scope over the years, the influence of local supply and demand conditions has become less important in determining market-clearing rates. At the same time, the importance of capital markets in the loan funding and risk transfer process has grown. Consequently, consumer borrowing rates have become directly linked with capital market rates and flows, as well as investor demand for the associated securities. In this section, we examine some of the links between the pricing of mortgage products to the consumer and developments in the capital markets. We initially use the fixed rate agency MBS markets as an example, and subsequently relate the rate setting processes to other markets and products.

In order to maximize their proceeds, the optimal coupon execution for different note rate strata is regularly calculated by the originator. Optimal execution is a function of the levels of pass-through prices for different coupons, as well as servicing valuations and guaranty fee buy-down pricing. Exhibit 2.6 shows two possible execution scenarios for a loan with a 6.25% note rate. In the example, securitizing the loan in the 6.0% pool is the best execution option, since it provides greater proceeds to the lender than by pooling into a 5.5% coupon.

Once the optimal execution is determined for each note rate strata, the associated points are then calculated. Points are up-front fees paid on the loan by the borrower, and are part of the all-in cost of any loan. (For loans with high note rates, negative points are "charged" or, in actuality, rebated to the borrower.) Points are the true expression of loan pricing by lenders, who typically quote current pricing in rate/point matrices with rates in 12.5 basis point increments. (Within reason, lenders will write loans with a wide range of note rates, but charge or rebate different points depending on the note rate.) As with the execution calculation, the calculation of points is based on market prices for pass-throughs and prevailing valuations for servicing and g-fee buydowns.

Exhibit 2.7 shows a hypothetical calculation of points for loans with 6.25% and 6.625% note rates, assuming that the best execution for both rate strata would be as 6.0% pools. The calculated points are shown at the bottom as the difference between the net value of the loan after pricing all components and its par value. Note that in order to securitize the 6.25% loan in a 6.0% pass-through, the guaranty fee must be bought down, as described previously. In practice, points would be simultaneously calculated for many rate levels, and would subsequently be posted in a rates/point matrix used to quote rates.

The calculation of the optimal MBS coupon for jumbo loans bears a strong resemblance to that of conforming loans, although some variables differ in practice (if not in concept). Valuing the cost of credit enhancement is one major difference between the sectors. Since the loans are not pooled into any of the agency programs, there is no guaranty fee calculation. As credit enhancement generally takes the form of subordination, the weighted average price of the various subordinate classes is taken into account in calculating valuation levels.

However, the calculation for evaluating the optimal coupon for jumbo securitizations is conceptually similar to that used for conforming loans bound for agency pools, in that the exercise involves evaluating various components of the loan. In this case, the components would include:

EXHIBIT 2.6   Pooling Options for a 6.25% Note Rate Loan Using Hypothetical Prices and Levels

	6.0% MBS	5.5% MBS	Comments
MBS pass-through price	101	99	TBA prices for forward settlement
Base servicing	1.0	1.0	*25 bps in both cases—assumes 4× multiple*[a]
Excess servicing:			
Amount in basis points	0	30	
Excess servicing value	0	1.2	*4× multiple for 30 bps for 5.5s*[a]
Guarantee fee buy-up/buydown:			
G-fee buy-up/(down) in basis points[b]	(20)	0	
G-fee buydown value	(0.60)	0.00	*Assumes 3× multiple for buydown*
Proceeds	101.4	101.2	
Total origination costs (includes allocation of G&A, hedging, and origination costs)	−1.65	−1.65	Assumed same in both cases
Net proceeds	99.8	99.6	

[a] For simplicity's sake, the multiples for base and excess servicing are assumed to be the same in this example. In addition, the value placed on servicing is a function of the different remittance styles utilized by Freddie Mac and Fannie Mae. As a result, the choice of remittance method may also affect the optimal pooling decision.

[b] The example assumes a 20 bps g-fee. Note that the g-fee buydown is paid to the GSE and is, therefore, treated as a negative value.

EXHIBIT 2.7   Sample Calculation of Points Given a Lending Rate (All Levels Hypothetical)

Note rate	6.25	6.625	Comments
Optimal pass-through coupon[a]	6.0	6.0	
MBS pass-through price	101	101	
Servicing values:			
Base servicing (2)	1.0	1.0	25 basis points, assuming a 4× multiple
Excess servicing (net of guaranty fee)[b]	0.0	0.7	Assuming 20 basis points of guaranty fee, there is no excess servicing for the 6.25% note rate, and 17.5 basis points for the 6.625% note rate—example assumes 4× multiple.
Guaranty fee buydown	−0.6	0	For 6.25% note rate, 20 basis points of g-fee must be bought down. No buydown is required for 6.625% note rate, since 20 basis point g-fee can be paid out of the note rate after base servicing.
Total value of servicing and buydowns	0.4	1.7	
Gross value	101.4000	102.7000	MBS price plus servicing value plus origination income
Total costs (including origination, administrative, and hedging costs, as well as an allocation for a targeted profit margin)	2.0	2.0	
Net value	99.4000	100.7000	Gross value less costs
Gross points	0.6000	−0.7000	100.00 less net value

[a] Determined by the methodology described in Exhibit 2.6.
[b] For this example, the assumed multiples are the same for both note rates. In practice, the multiples might be different, due to different valuations placed on the servicing of the two note rates.

- The price of the senior securities, generally quoted as a price spread behind similar coupon FNMAs (hence, the terminology of "x 32nds behind FNMAs").
- The weighted average price of the subordinate bonds.
- Proceeds realized from the sale of excess servicing, typically in the form of the WAC IO (for premium loans).
- The size and valuation of the WAC PO (for discount loans).

Once levels are established for each component, the optimal coupon can be selected for a deal. Unlike in the conforming agency market, where execution is calculated for each note rate strata, the optimal coupon for a jumbo deal is calculated for most expected production for the period under consideration. As described previously, this allows issuers to capitalize on economies of scale and spread the fixed costs of securitizations across as large a deal as possible.

Once the securitization coupon is established, points are calculated for each note rate strata. As with the optimal execution calculation, however, the variables are somewhat different, reflecting the different forms that credit enhancement takes in the jumbo market, different valuations techniques for the excess coupon generated by premium loans, and the ability to include discount loans in the pool through the creation of the WAC PO.

There have been some interesting historical shifts with respect to the securitization of loans with nontraditional attributes, such as reduced documentation, lower credit scores, and high LTV ratios. (These loans represent the alt-A product described in the previous chapter.) This market grew fairly rapidly in the late 1990s, and loans were typically securitized in private label structures irrespective of their balance. Around 2000, the GSEs began to offer guaranty fees on a wider variety of product attributes, and subsequently increased their market share of conforming-balance loans with alternative characteristics. By mid-2004, however, private label, conforming-balance deals became widely accepted in the capital markets. At that point, the choice of securitization vehicle for loans with alternative attributes began to be driven by best-execution considerations. A key trade-off is the relative pricing of the senior pass-through (which, like the jumbo senior pass-through, trades behind agency pass-throughs), along with the cost of paying the GSEs' guaranty fee versus creating private label credit enhancement through subordination.

CASH FLOW STRUCTURING

As noted previously, the cash flows generated by agency pools and senior private label pass-throughs are very similar in nature. Both securities can be structured to take advantage of demand for a variety of securities by different segments of the fixed income investment community. Various investor clienteles have different investment objectives and risk tolerances, and thus tend to invest in securities with different cash flow and performance attributes. Some different market segments include:

- Banks and other depository institutions, which generally seek short securities where they can earn a spread over their funding costs.
- Life insurance companies and pension funds, which typically invest in bonds with longer maturities and durations in order to immunize long-dated expected liabilities.
- Investment managers, who typically manage fixed income assets versus performance indexes.
- Hedge funds, which typically seek investment vehicles that offer the potential for very high-leveraged returns.

The nature of mortgage cash flows makes mortgage loans and mortgage-backed securities ideal vehicles for creating a variety of bonds. Their long-term principal and interest cash flows allow structurers to create securities of varying average lives and durations in order to meet the needs of different classes of investors. In addition, different structures allow different risks (both prepayment and, for private label deals, credit) to be transferred within the structure, and creates a rich environment for the wide variety of structures and structuring techniques discussed in Chapters 6 through 9.

However, mortgage structures are closed universes by nature, in that all balances and cash flows generated by the collateral within the structure must be taken into account. For example, a structure where the coupon of one bond is stripped below that of the collateral must allocate the incremental interest cash flows elsewhere in the structure. This shifting of interest cash flows can be done in a number of different forms, as we will discuss in Chapter 7. Another example might be a bond that pays principal to investors based on a schedule. This stabilizes the "scheduled" bond's average life and duration, but cash flow uncertainty is transferred to other bonds in the structure, giving their cash flows greater variability.

Therefore, the process of MBS structuring requires examining and valuing the trade-offs necessary to create a variety of bonds designed to meet the needs of multiple investor clienteles. To create a more desirable bond within a structure, for example, the underwriter must be able to sell the enhanced bond (or combination of bonds) at a better valuation than the original tranche, in order to offset the concession that must be given to attract investors to the bond with less-appealing attributes.

Understanding the trade-offs involved in structuring therefore requires an understanding of how the different structuring techniques work, and how they impact other bonds within the structure.

Prepayment and Default Metrics and Behavior

CHAPTER 3

Measurement of Prepayments and Defaults

It is essential for participants in the residential mortgage-backed securities market to understand the general prepayment and default nomenclature. The market is characterized by the usage of a variety of prepayment terms, some specific to certain asset classes, such as HEP, PPC, and MHP and default language such as CDR. In this chapter, the basic terms used to characterize residential mortgage-related prepayments and losses are discussed. Note that our focus is on describing the terminology and nomenclature and our discussion does not focus on the determinants or the modeling of prepayments and defaults.

Understanding the terms used in the market to define prepayments and defaults, as well as the methodologies used to generate these metrics, is important for the following reasons:

- Efficient risk-based pricing at the origination level.
- Evaluation of relative value within the MBS sector, as well as across the fixed income universe.
- Effective hedging and management of prepayment and credit risk exposure.
- Ex post performance attribution.

PREPAYMENT CONVENTION TERMINOLOGY

For fixed rate amortizing assets, such as fixed rate mortgages, home equity loans (HELs), and manufactured housing loans (MHs), the monthly scheduled payment, consisting of scheduled principal and interest payments, is constant throughout the amortization term. If the borrower pays more than the monthly scheduled payment, the extra payment will be used to pay down the outstanding balance faster than the original amortization schedule, resulting in a prepayment (or, as it is sometimes referenced, an "unscheduled principal payment"). If the outstanding balance is paid off in full, the prepayment is a "complete prepayment"; if only a portion of the outstanding balance is prepaid, the prepayment is called either a "partial prepayment" or "curtailment." Prepayments can be the result of natural turnover, refinancings, defaults, partial paydowns, and credit-related events. (Such an event might occur if a borrower improves or "cures" his/her credit, thus becoming eligible for a new loan with a lower interest rate.) The evaluation of prepayments is further complicated by the fact that there is an interplay between defaults, which are effectively "credit-related" prepayments, and prepayments attributable to declining interest rates.

Prepayments and defaults can be analyzed on both the loan and pool level. Loan-level prepayment analysis, which requires detailed loan level information, is more accurate than pool-level prepayment analysis, but is also more computationally intensive. Additionally, this type of analysis allows the inclusion of specific obligor and property characteristics as determinants of prepayments and defaults. Loan-level analysis involves amortizing each loan individually, tracking defaults and prepayments on an individual loan basis and combining these amount to calculate aggregated metrics. Due to the diversity of the characteristics of the underlying loans in most deals, loan level analysis is generally more accurate and has greater predictive capabilities.

Several conventions have been used as a benchmark for MBS prepayment rates: (1) Federal Housing Administration (FHA) experience; (2) the conditional prepayment rate; and (3) the Public Securities Association (PSA) prepayment convention. While the first convention is no longer used, we discuss it because of its historical significance.

In the earliest stages of the pass-through market's development, prepayments were not measured at all. Rather, cash flows were calculated assuming no prepayments for the first 12 years, at which time all the mortgages in the pool were assumed to prepay. This naive approach (referenced at the time as the "12 years and out" convention) was replaced by the "FHA prepayment experience" approach.

The prepayment experience for 30-year mortgages based on FHA tables on mortgage survival factors was once the most commonly used benchmark for prepayment rates. It called for the projection of the cash flow for a mortgage pool on the assumption that the prepayment rate would be the same as the FHA experience (referred to as "100% FHA"), or some multiple of FHA experience (faster or slower than the FHA's survival experience).

Despite the method's past popularity, prepayments based on FHA experience are not necessarily indicative of the prepayment rate for a particular pool, mainly because FHA prepayments are for mortgages originated over all sorts of interest rate periods. As prepayment rates are tied to interest rate cycles, an average prepayment rate for loans issued over various cycles is not very useful in estimating prepayments. Moreover, new FHA tables are published periodically, causing confusion about which FHA table prepayments should be based on. Finally, FHA mortgages are fundamentally different from non-FHA (or "conventional") loans. For example, FHA mortgages are assumable, while conventional loans typically have due-on-sale provisions. This difference causes FHA statistics to systematically underestimate prepayments speeds for non-FHA loans. Because estimated prepayments using FHA experience may be misleading, the resulting cash flow is not meaningful for valuing pass-throughs.

Conditional Prepayment Rate

A commonly used methodology for projecting prepayments and the cash flow of a pass-through assumes that some fraction of the remaining principal in the pool is prepaid each month for the remaining term of the mortgage. The prepayment rate assumed for a pool, called the *conditional prepayment rate* (CPR),[1] is based on the characteristics of the pool (including its historical prepayment experience) and the current and expected future economic environment. The advantage of this approach is its simplicity. Furthermore, changes in economic conditions that impact prepayment rates or changes in the historical prepayment pattern of a pool can be analyzed quickly.

Single Monthly Mortality Rate

The CPR is an annual rate. However, because mortgage cash flows are a monthly phenomenon, calculating the CPR requires the generation of a monthly prepayment rate, called the *single monthly mortality rate* (SMM). The SMM is the most fundamental measure of prepayment speeds; it is the unit upon which all other prepayment measures are based. SMM measures the monthly prepayment amount as a percentage of the previous month's outstanding balance minus the scheduled principal payment. Mathematically, the SMM is calculated as follows:

$$\text{SMM} = \frac{\begin{array}{c}\text{Total payment,}\\\text{including prepayments}\end{array} - \begin{array}{c}\text{Scheduled interest}\\\text{payment}\end{array} - \begin{array}{c}\text{Scheduled principal}\\\text{payment}\end{array}}{[\text{Unpaid principal balance} - \text{Scheduled principal payment}]} \quad (3.1)$$

---

[1] It is also called the *constant prepayment rate*.

For example, if the pool balance at month zero is \$10,000,000, assuming an interest rate of 12%, the scheduled principal and interest payments are \$2,920.45 and \$100,000 in month one, respectively. If the actual payment in month one is \$202,891.25, the SMM rate is 1%, calculated as

$$SMM = \frac{(202,891.25 - 100,000 - 2,920.45)}{(10,000,000 - 2,920.45)} = 1\%$$

Therefore, if a mortgage loan prepaid at 1% SMM in a particular month, this means that 1% of that month's scheduled balance (last month's outstanding balance minus the scheduled principal payment) has been prepaid.

Relationship between SMM and CPR

Given the SMM, a CPR can be computed using the following formula:

$$CPR = 1 - (1 - SMM)^{12}$$

For example, if the SMM is 1%, then the CPR is

$$CPR = 1 - (0.99)^{12} = 11.36\%$$

To convert an SMM into a CPR, the following formula is used:

$$SMM = 1 - (1 - CPR)^{1/12} \qquad\qquad (3.2)$$

For example, suppose that the CPR used to estimate prepayments is 6%. The corresponding SMM is

$$SMM = 1 - (1 - 0.06)^{1/12} = 1 - 0.94^{0.08333} = 0.005143$$

PSA Prepayment Benchmark

The Public Securities Association (PSA) prepayment benchmark is expressed as a monthly series of annual prepayment rates.[2] (While the PSA has changed its name to the Bond Market Association, the benchmark is still referred to as the PSA prepayment benchmark.) The basic PSA model assumes that prepayment rates are low for newly originated mortgages and then will speed up as the mortgages become seasoned.

---

[2] This benchmark is commonly referred to as a prepayment model, suggesting that it can be used to estimate prepayments. Characterization of this benchmark as a prepayment model is inappropriate. It is simply a market convention.

The PSA standard benchmark assumes the following prepayment rates for 30-year mortgages:

1. A CPR of 0.2% for the first month, increased by 0.2% per year per month for the next 29 months when it reaches 6% per year.
2. A 6% CPR for the remaining years.

This benchmark, referred to as "100% PSA" or simply "100 PSA," is graphically depicted in Exhibit 3.1. Mathematically, 100 PSA can be expressed as follows:

If $t \le 30$ then CPR = 6% $\times$ $(t/30)$
If $t > 30$ then CPR = 6%

where t is the number of months since the mortgage was originated. Since the CPR prior to month 30 rises at a constant rate, this period is sometimes referred to as the *ramp*, and loans are considered to be "on the ramp" when they are less than 30 months old.

Slower or faster speeds are then referred to as some percentage of PSA. For example, 50 PSA means one-half the CPR of the PSA benchmark prepayment rate; 150 PSA means 1.5 times the CPR of the PSA benchmark prepayment rate; 300 PSA means three times the CPR of the benchmark prepayment rate. This is illustrated graphically in Exhibit 3.2 for 50 PSA, 100 PSA, and 150 PSA. A prepayment rate of 0 PSA means that no prepayments are assumed.

It is important to note that mortgage pools will typically be comprised of loans having different origination months and, therefore, different ages. In practice, the *weighted average loan age* (or WALA) of a pool or security is used as a proxy for its age. However, a large dispersion of loan ages within a pool will distort the PSA calculation.

EXHIBIT 3.1   Graphical Depiction of 100 PSA

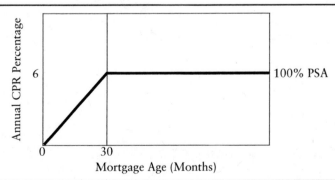

EXHIBIT 3.2 Graphical Depiction of 50 PSA, 100 PSA, and 300 PSA

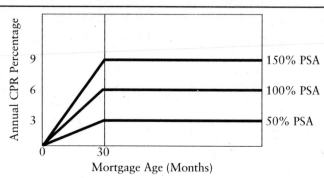

Calculating Monthly Prepayment Speeds

Assuming that the weighted average loan age of a pool is known, converting SMMs and CPRs into a PSA rate is straightforward. An SMM of x% means that approximately x% of the remaining mortgage balance at the beginning of the month, less the scheduled principal payment, will prepay that month. That is,

Prepayment for month t
= SMM × (Beginning mortgage balance for month t
– Scheduled principal payment for month t)

For example, suppose that an investor owns a pass-through in which the remaining mortgage balance at the beginning of some month is $290 million. Assuming that the SMM is 0.5143% and the scheduled principal payment is $3 million, then the estimated prepayment for the month is

$$0.005143 \times (\$290,000,000 - \$3,000,000) = \$1,476,041$$

The CPR is converted to an SMM using equation (3.2). For example, the SMMs for month 5, month 20, and months 31 through 360 assuming 100 PSA are calculated as follows:

For month 5:

CPR = 6% (5/30) = 1% = 0.01
SMM = $1 - (1 - 0.01)^{1/12} = 1 - (0.99)^{0.083333} = 0.000837$

For month 20:

CPR = 6% (20/30) = 4% = 0.04
SMM = $1 - (1 - 0.04)^{1/12} = 1 - (0.96)^{0.083333} = 0.003396$

For month 31-360:

$$CPR = 6\%$$
$$SMM = 1 - (1 - 0.06)^{1/12} = 1 - (0.94)^{0.083333} = 0.005143$$

The SMMs for month 5, month 20, and months 31 through 360 assuming 165 PSA are computed as follows:

For month 5:

$$CPR = 6\% \ (5/30) = 1\% = 0.01$$
$$165 \ PSA = 1.65 \ (0.01) = 0.0165$$
$$SMM = 1 - (1 - 0.0165)^{1/12} = 1 - (0.9835)^{0.08333} = 0.001386$$

For month 20:

$$CPR = 6\% \ (20/30) = 4\% = 0.04$$
$$165 \ PSA = 1.65 \ (0.04) = 0.066$$
$$SMM = 1 - (1 - 0.066)^{1/12} = 1 - (0.934)^{0.08333} = 0.005674$$

For month 31–360:

$$CPR = 6\%$$
$$165 \ PSA = 1.65 \ (0.06) = 0.099$$
$$SMM = 1 - (1 - 0.099)^{1/12} = 1 - (0.901)^{0.08333} = 0.007828$$

Notice that the SMM assuming 165 PSA is not just 1.65 times the SMM assuming 100 PSA. It is the CPR that is a multiple of the CPR assuming 100 PSA.

The SMMs for month 5, month 20, and months 31 through 360 assuming 50 PSA are as follows:

For month 5:

$$CPR = 6\% \ (5/30) = 1\% = 0.01$$
$$50 \ PSA = 0.5 \ (0.01) = 0.005$$
$$SMM = 1 - (1 - 0.005)^{1/12} = 1 - (0.995)^{0.08333} = 0.000418$$

For month 20:

$$CPR = 6\% \ (20/30) = 4\% = 0.04$$
$$50 \ PSA = 0.5 \ (0.04) = 0.02$$
$$SMM = 1 - (1 - 0.02)^{1/12} = 1 - (0.98)^{0.08333} = 0.001682$$

For month 31–360:

CPR = 6%
50 PSA = 0.5 (0.06) = 0.03
$$SMM = 1 - (1 - 0.03)^{1/12} = 1 - (0.97)^{0.08333} = 0.002535$$

Once again, notice that the SMM assuming 50 PSA is not just one-half the SMM assuming 100 PSA. It is the CPR that is a multiple of the CPR assuming 100 PSA.

Illustration of Monthly Cash Flow Construction

We now show how to construct a monthly cash flow for a hypothetical pass-through given a PSA assumption. For the purpose of this illustration, the underlying mortgages for this hypothetical pass-through are assumed to be fixed rate, level payment mortgages with a weighted average coupon (WAC) rate of 6.0%. It will be assumed that the pass-through rate is 5.5% with a weighted average maturity (WAM) of 358 months. In Chapters 6 and 7, we will use this pass-through to illustrate structuring techniques utilized in the CMO markets.

Exhibit 3.3 shows the cash flow for selected months assuming 100 PSA. The cash flow is broken down into three components: (1) interest (based on the pass-through rate), (2) the regularly scheduled principal payment, and (3) prepayments based on 100 PSA.

Let's walk through Exhibit 3.3 column by column.

Column 1. This is the month.

Column 2. This column gives the outstanding mortgage balance at the beginning of the month. It is equal to the outstanding balance at the beginning of the previous month reduced by the total principal payment in the previous month.

Column 3. This column shows the SMM for 100 PSA. Two things should be noted in this column. First, for month 1, the SMM is for a pass-through that has been seasoned three months because the WAM is 357 months. This results in a CPR of 0.8%. Second, from month 27 on, the SMM is 0.00514 which corresponds to a CPR of 6%.

Column 4. The aggregate monthly mortgage payments are shown in this column. Notice that the total monthly mortgage payment declines over time, as prepayments reduce the mortgage balance outstanding. (In the absence of prepayments, this figure would remain constant.) In

EXHIBIT 3.3 Monthly Cash Flow for a $400 Million Pass-Through with a 5.5% Pass-Through Rate, a WAC of 6.0%, and a WAM of 358 Months, Assuming 100% PSA

(1) Month	(2) Outstanding Balance	(3) SMM	(4) Mortgage Payment	(5) Net Interest	(6) Scheduled Prinicipal	(7) Prepayments	(8) Total Principal	(9) Cash Flow
1	400,000,000	0.00050	2,402,998	1,833,333	402,998	200,350	603,349	2,436,682
2	399,396,651	0.00067	2,401,794	1,830,568	404,810	266,975	671,785	2,502,353
3	398,724,866	0.00084	2,400,187	1,827,489	406,562	333,463	740,025	2,567,514
4	397,984,841	0.00101	2,398,177	1,824,097	408,253	399,780	808,033	2,632,130
5	397,176,808	0.00117	2,395,766	1,820,394	409,882	465,892	875,773	2,696,167
6	396,301,034	0.00134	2,392,953	1,816,380	411,447	531,764	943,211	2,759,591
7	395,357,823	0.00151	2,389,738	1,812,057	412,949	597,362	1,010,311	2,822,368
8	394,347,512	0.00168	2,386,124	1,807,426	414,386	662,652	1,077,038	2,884,464
9	393,270,474	0.00185	2,382,110	1,802,490	415,758	727,600	1,143,357	2,945,847
10	392,127,117	0.00202	2,377,698	1,797,249	417,063	792,172	1,209,235	3,006,484
11	390,917,882	0.00219	2,372,890	1,791,707	418,300	856,336	1,274,636	3,066,343
12	389,643,247	0.00236	2,367,686	1,785,865	419,470	920,057	1,339,527	3,125,391
13	388,303,720	0.00253	2,362,089	1,779,725	420,571	983,303	1,403,873	3,183,599
14	386,899,847	0.00271	2,356,101	1,773,291	421,602	1,046,041	1,467,643	3,240,934
15	385,432,204	0.00288	2,349,724	1,766,564	422,563	1,108,239	1,530,802	3,297,366
16	383,901,402	0.00305	2,342,961	1,759,548	423,454	1,169,864	1,593,318	3,352,866
17	382,308,084	0.00322	2,335,813	1,752,245	424,273	1,230,887	1,655,159	3,407,405
18	380,652,925	0.00340	2,328,284	1,744,659	425,020	1,291,274	1,716,294	3,460,953
19	378,936,632	0.00357	2,320,377	1,736,793	425,694	1,350,996	1,776,690	3,513,483
20	377,159,941	0.00374	2,312,095	1,728,650	426,296	1,410,023	1,836,319	3,564,968
21	375,323,622	0.00392	2,303,442	1,720,233	426,824	1,468,325	1,895,148	3,615,382
22	373,428,474	0.00409	2,294,420	1,711,547	427,278	1,525,872	1,953,150	3,664,697
23	371,475,324	0.00427	2,285,034	1,702,595	427,657	1,582,637	2,010,294	3,712,889
24	369,465,030	0.00444	2,275,288	1,693,381	427,962	1,638,590	2,066,553	3,759,934
25	367,398,478	0.00462	2,265,185	1,683,910	428,192	1,693,706	2,121,898	3,805,808
26	365,276,580	0.00479	2,254,730	1,674,184	428,347	1,747,956	2,176,303	3,850,488
27	363,100,276	0.00497	2,243,928	1,664,210	428,427	1,801,315	2,229,742	3,893,952
28	360,870,534	0.00514	2,232,783	1,653,990	428,430	1,853,758	2,282,189	3,936,178
29	358,588,346	0.00514	2,221,300	1,643,530	428,358	1,842,021	2,270,379	3,913,909
30	356,317,967	0.00514	2,209,875	1,633,124	428,286	1,830,345	2,258,631	3,891,755
100	223,414,587	0.00514	1,540,329	1,023,984	423,256	1,146,847	1,570,104	2,594,087
101	221,844,483	0.00514	1,532,407	1,016,787	423,185	1,138,773	1,561,958	2,578,745
102	220,282,525	0.00514	1,524,526	1,009,628	423,114	1,130,740	1,553,853	2,563,482
103	218,728,672	0.00514	1,516,686	1,002,506	423,042	1,122,749	1,545,791	2,548,297
104	217,182,881	0.00514	1,508,885	995,422	422,971	1,114,799	1,537,770	2,533,191
105	215,645,111	0.00514	1,501,125	988,373	422,900	1,106,891	1,529,790	2,518,164

EXHIBIT 3.3 (Continued)

(1)	(2)	(3)	(4)	(5)	(6)	(7)	(8)	(9)
Month	Outstanding Balance	SMM	Mortgage Payment	Net Interest	Scheduled Prinicipal	Prepayments	Total Principal	Cash Flow
200	100,719,066	0.00514	919,770	461,629	416,174	515,859	932,033	1,393,662
201	99,787,032	0.00514	915,039	457,357	416,104	511,066	927,170	1,384,527
202	98,859,862	0.00514	910,333	453,108	416,034	506,298	922,332	1,375,439
203	97,937,531	0.00514	905,651	448,880	415,964	501,555	917,518	1,366,399
204	97,020,012	0.00514	900,994	444,675	415,893	496,836	912,730	1,357,405
205	96,107,283	0.00514	896,360	440,492	415,823	492,142	907,966	1,348,457
300	28,001,417	0.00514	549,218	128,340	409,211	141,907	551,118	679,457
301	27,450,299	0.00514	546,393	125,814	409,142	139,073	548,215	674,028
302	26,902,085	0.00514	543,583	123,301	409,073	136,254	545,326	668,628
303	26,356,758	0.00514	540,787	120,802	409,003	133,450	542,453	663,255
304	25,814,305	0.00514	538,006	118,316	408,934	130,660	539,595	657,910
305	25,274,710	0.00514	535,239	115,842	408,865	127,885	536,751	652,593
350	3,725,850	0.00514	424,402	17,077	405,773	17,075	422,848	439,925
351	3,303,002	0.00514	422,219	15,139	405,704	14,901	420,605	435,744
352	2,882,397	0.00514	420,048	13,211	405,636	12,738	418,374	431,585
353	2,464,023	0.00514	417,887	11,293	405,567	10,587	416,154	427,447
354	2,047,869	0.00514	415,738	9,386	405,499	8,447	413,946	423,332
355	1,633,924	0.00514	413,600	7,489	405,430	6,318	411,749	419,237
356	1,222,175	0.00514	411,473	5,602	405,362	4,201	409,563	415,164
357	812,613	0.00514	409,357	3,724	405,294	2,095	407,388	411,113
358	405,224	0.00514	407,251	1,857	405,225	0	405,225	407,082

[a] Since the WAM is 358 months, the underlying mortgage pool is seasoned an average of two months. Therefore, the CPR for month 28 is 6%.

essence, the payment is calculated each month as a function of the WAC, the remaining balance at the end of the prior month, and the remaining term (i.e., the original WAM minus the number of months since issuance). For example, the payment in month 10 of $2,376,474 can be generated on a calculator by inputting $391,508,422 as the balance or present value, 0.5% (6.0% divided by 12) as the rate, and 348 months as the remaining term.[3]

Column 5. The monthly interest paid to the pass-through investor is found in this column. This value is determined by multiplying the outstanding mortgage balance at the beginning of the month by the pass-through rate of 5.5% and dividing by 12.

---

[3] The calculation can also be presented as a series of formulae, which are available in Chapter 21 of Frank J. Fabozzi, *Fixed Income Mathematics: Analytical and Statistical Techniques* (New York: McGraw-Hill, 2006).

Column 6. This column shows the regularly scheduled principal repayment, or amortization. This is the difference between the total monthly mortgage payment [the amount shown in column (4)] and the gross coupon interest for the month. The gross coupon interest is 6.0% multiplied by the outstanding mortgage balance at the beginning of the month, then divided by 12.

Column 7. The prepayment for the month is reported in this column. The prepayment is found by using equation (2):

$$SMM \times (\text{Beginning mortgage balance for month } t \\ - \text{Scheduled principal payment for month } t)$$

So, for example, in month 100, the beginning mortgage balance is $223,414,587, the scheduled principal payment is $423,356, and the SMM at 100 PSA is 0.00514301 (only 0.00514 is shown in the exhibit to save space), so the prepayment is:

$$0.00514301 \times (\$223,414,587 - \$423,356) = \$1,146,847$$

Column 8. The total principal payment, which is the sum of columns (6) and (7), is shown in this column.

Column 9. The projected monthly cash flow for this pass-through is shown in this last column. The monthly cash flow is the sum of the interest paid to the pass-through investor [column (5)] and the total principal payments for the month [column (8)].

Exhibits 3.4 and 3.5 show selected monthly cash flows for the same pass-through assuming 165 PSA and 250 PSA, respectively.

A more recent addition to MBS prepayment terminology is the *prospectus prepayment curve* (PPC). While the logic underlying the PSA convention (i.e., that loans prepay faster as they age, all other factors constant) remains in force, newer types of alternative and expanded-criteria loans (such as alt-A products) exhibit a faster prepayment ramp, due in part to the effects of credit curing on prepayments. This has created the needs for prepayment vectors that are specific to both different product classifications, as well as the loan- and borrower-level attributes of the pool in question.

This resulted in the development of PPC curves, which are actually prepayment vectors specified in a deal's prospectus supplement. Typically, 100% PPC is the base-case prepayment assumption used to create the deal. PPC curves (or ramps) are generally specified as a beginning and terminal CPR, along with the associated time period. A typical ramp might be speci-

EXHIBIT 3.4 Monthly Cash Flow for a $400 Million Pass-Through with a 5.5% Pass-Through Rate, a WAC of 6.0%, and a WAM of 358 Months, Assuming 165% PSA

(1)	(2)	(3)	(4)	(5)	(6)	(7)	(8)	(9)
Month	Outstanding Balance	SMM	Mortgage Payment	Net Interest	Scheduled Prinicipal	Prepayments	Total Principal	Cash Flow
1	400,000,000	0.00083	2,402,998	1,833,333	402,998	331,173	734,171	2,567,505
2	399,265,829	0.00111	2,401,007	1,829,968	404,678	441,424	846,102	2,676,070
3	398,419,727	0.00139	2,398,350	1,826,090	406,251	551,451	957,702	2,783,793
4	397,462,024	0.00167	2,395,027	1,821,701	407,717	661,161	1,068,878	2,890,579
5	396,393,146	0.00195	2,391,039	1,816,802	409,073	770,461	1,179,534	2,996,336
6	395,213,612	0.00223	2,386,386	1,811,396	410,318	879,258	1,289,576	3,100,972
7	393,924,036	0.00251	2,381,072	1,805,485	411,452	987,459	1,398,910	3,204,395
8	392,525,126	0.00279	2,375,097	1,799,073	412,471	1,094,972	1,507,443	3,306,516
9	391,017,683	0.00308	2,368,464	1,792,164	413,376	1,201,705	1,615,081	3,407,245
10	389,402,602	0.00336	2,361,178	1,784,762	414,165	1,307,567	1,721,732	3,506,494
11	387,680,870	0.00365	2,353,241	1,776,871	414,836	1,412,469	1,827,305	3,604,176
12	385,853,565	0.00393	2,344,658	1,768,496	415,390	1,516,319	1,931,709	3,700,205
13	383,921,856	0.00422	2,335,434	1,759,642	415,825	1,619,031	2,034,855	3,794,497
14	381,887,001	0.00451	2,325,575	1,750,315	416,140	1,720,516	2,136,656	3,886,971
15	379,750,345	0.00480	2,315,086	1,740,522	416,334	1,820,689	2,237,023	3,977,545
16	377,513,322	0.00509	2,303,974	1,730,269	416,407	1,919,465	2,335,872	4,066,142
17	375,177,450	0.00538	2,292,246	1,719,563	416,359	2,016,761	2,433,120	4,152,683
18	372,744,330	0.00567	2,279,911	1,708,412	416,189	2,112,495	2,528,685	4,237,096
19	370,215,645	0.00597	2,266,975	1,696,822	415,897	2,206,589	2,622,486	4,319,308
20	367,593,159	0.00626	2,253,448	1,684,802	415,482	2,298,964	2,714,446	4,399,248
21	364,878,713	0.00656	2,239,339	1,672,361	414,945	2,389,544	2,804,490	4,476,850
22	362,074,223	0.00685	2,224,657	1,659,507	414,286	2,478,256	2,892,542	4,552,049
23	359,181,681	0.00715	2,209,413	1,646,249	413,504	2,565,029	2,978,533	4,624,783
24	356,203,147	0.00745	2,193,616	1,632,598	412,601	2,649,793	3,062,394	4,694,992
25	353,140,753	0.00775	2,177,279	1,618,562	411,575	2,732,482	3,144,057	4,762,619
26	349,996,696	0.00805	2,160,413	1,604,152	410,429	2,813,031	3,223,460	4,827,612
27	346,773,236	0.00835	2,143,028	1,589,377	409,162	2,891,380	3,300,542	4,889,919
28	343,472,694	0.00865	2,125,139	1,574,250	407,775	2,967,468	3,375,244	4,949,494
29	340,097,450	0.00865	2,106,757	1,558,780	406,269	2,938,286	3,344,555	4,903,335
30	336,752,895	0.00865	2,088,533	1,543,451	404,769	2,909,369	3,314,138	4,857,589
100	164,905,045	0.00865	1,136,936	755,815	312,411	1,423,706	1,736,116	2,491,931
101	163,168,929	0.00865	1,127,102	747,858	311,257	1,408,698	1,719,955	2,467,813
102	161,448,973	0.00865	1,117,352	739,974	310,108	1,393,831	1,703,938	2,443,913
103	159,745,035	0.00865	1,107,687	732,165	308,962	1,379,102	1,688,064	2,420,229
104	158,056,971	0.00865	1,098,106	724,428	307,821	1,364,510	1,672,332	2,396,759
105	156,384,639	0.00865	1,088,608	716,763	306,684	1,350,055	1,656,739	2,373,502

EXHIBIT 3.4 (Continued)

(1)	(2)	(3)	(4)	(5)	(6)	(7)	(8)	(9)
Month	Outstanding Balance	SMM	Mortgage Payment	Net Interest	Scheduled Principal	Prepayment	Total Principal	Cash Flow
200	52,224,616	0.00865	476,917	239,363	215,794	449,870	665,664	905,026
201	51,558,952	0.00865	472,792	236,312	214,997	444,119	659,116	895,427
202	50,899,837	0.00865	468,702	233,291	214,203	438,424	652,627	885,918
203	50,247,209	0.00865	464,648	230,300	213,412	432,786	646,198	876,497
204	49,601,012	0.00865	460,629	227,338	212,624	427,203	639,827	867,165
205	48,961,185	0.00865	456,644	224,405	211,838	421,676	633,514	857,919
300	10,199,637	0.00865	200,055	46,748	149,057	86,936	235,993	282,741
301	9,963,644	0.00865	198,324	45,667	148,506	84,900	233,406	279,073
302	9,730,238	0.00865	196,609	44,597	147,958	82,886	230,843	275,440
303	9,499,394	0.00865	194,908	43,539	147,411	80,893	228,305	271,844
304	9,271,090	0.00865	193,222	42,492	146,867	78,923	225,790	268,283
305	9,045,299	0.00865	191,551	41,458	146,325	76,975	223,300	264,757
350	1,137,497	0.00865	129,569	5,214	123,882	8,768	132,650	137,863
351	1,004,848	0.00865	128,449	4,606	123,424	7,624	131,049	135,654
352	873,799	0.00865	127,338	4,005	122,969	6,495	129,463	133,468
353	744,336	0.00865	126,236	3,412	122,514	5,379	127,893	131,305
354	616,443	0.00865	125,144	2,825	122,062	4,276	126,338	129,164
355	490,104	0.00865	124,062	2,246	121,611	3,187	124,799	127,045
356	365,306	0.00865	122,989	1,674	121,162	2,112	123,274	124,948
357	242,032	0.00865	121,925	1,109	120,715	1,049	121,764	122,873
358	120,268	0.00865	120,870	551	120,269	0	120,269	120,820

[a] Since the WAM is 358 months, the underlying mortgage pool is seasoned an average of two months. Therefore, the CPR for month 28 is $1.65 \times 6\%$.

fied as "8–20% CPR over 12 months." This translates to an assumption of 8% CPR in the first month, increasing 1.09% per month for the next 11 months, and terminating at 20% CPR in month 12. However, there is no industry standardization for the usage of this terminology, as the specification is issue-dependent. As a result, investors must confirm how "100% PPC" is defined for each particular issue before performing further analysis.

The language utilized in a deal's prospectus supplement is illuminating. For example, the document for Countrywide's CWALT 2005-J9 deal has language as follows:

> Prepayments of mortgage loans commonly are measured relative to a prepayment standard or model. The model used in this prospectus supplement assumes a constant prepayment rate ("CPR") or an assumed rate of prepayment each month of the then—outstanding

EXHIBIT 3.5 Monthly Cash Flow for a $400 Million Pass-Through with a 5.5% Pass-Through Rate, a WAC of 6.0%, and a WAM of 358 Months, Assuming 250% PSA

(1)	(2)	(3)	(4)	(5)	(6)	(7)	(8)	(9)
Month	Outstanding Balance	SMM	Mortgage Payment	Net Interest	Scheduled Principal	Prepayment	Total Principal	Cash Flow
1	400,000,000	0.00126	2,402,998	1,833,333	402,998	502,964	905,962	2,739,295
2	399,094,038	0.00168	2,399,974	1,829,181	404,504	670,653	1,075,156	2,904,337
3	398,018,882	0.00211	2,395,937	1,824,253	405,842	838,007	1,243,849	3,068,102
4	396,775,033	0.00253	2,390,887	1,818,552	407,012	1,004,812	1,411,824	3,230,376
5	395,363,209	0.00296	2,384,826	1,812,081	408,010	1,170,856	1,578,866	3,390,947
6	393,784,343	0.00340	2,377,756	1,804,845	408,834	1,335,924	1,744,759	3,549,604
7	392,039,584	0.00383	2,369,681	1,796,848	409,483	1,499,803	1,909,287	3,706,135
8	390,130,297	0.00427	2,360,606	1,788,097	409,955	1,662,281	2,072,236	3,860,333
9	388,058,061	0.00470	2,350,537	1,778,599	410,247	1,823,147	2,233,394	4,011,994
10	385,824,667	0.00514	2,339,483	1,768,363	410,359	1,982,191	2,392,550	4,160,913
11	383,432,117	0.00558	2,327,451	1,757,397	410,290	2,139,205	2,549,495	4,306,893
12	380,882,621	0.00603	2,314,452	1,745,712	410,039	2,293,986	2,704,025	4,449,737
13	378,178,597	0.00648	2,300,497	1,733,319	409,604	2,446,332	2,855,937	4,589,255
14	375,322,660	0.00692	2,285,600	1,720,229	408,986	2,596,046	3,005,032	4,725,261
15	372,317,628	0.00737	2,269,773	1,706,456	408,185	2,742,932	3,151,118	4,857,573
16	369,166,510	0.00783	2,253,033	1,692,013	407,201	2,886,803	3,294,003	4,986,017
17	365,872,507	0.00828	2,235,395	1,676,916	406,033	3,027,473	3,433,506	5,110,421
18	362,439,001	0.00874	2,216,878	1,661,179	404,683	3,164,763	3,569,446	5,230,625
19	358,869,555	0.00920	2,197,499	1,644,819	403,151	3,298,500	3,701,651	5,346,470
20	355,167,904	0.00966	2,177,278	1,627,853	401,438	3,428,516	3,829,955	5,457,808
21	351,337,949	0.01013	2,156,236	1,610,299	399,547	3,554,651	3,954,198	5,564,497
22	347,383,751	0.01060	2,134,396	1,592,176	397,477	3,676,750	4,074,227	5,666,403
23	343,309,524	0.01107	2,111,779	1,573,502	395,232	3,794,667	4,189,898	5,763,400
24	339,119,626	0.01154	2,088,411	1,554,298	392,812	3,908,261	4,301,074	5,855,372
25	334,818,552	0.01201	2,064,314	1,534,585	390,221	4,017,402	4,407,624	5,942,209
26	330,410,929	0.01249	2,039,516	1,514,383	387,462	4,121,967	4,509,428	6,023,811
27	325,901,500	0.01297	2,014,043	1,493,715	384,535	4,221,839	4,606,374	6,100,090
28	321,295,126	0.01345	1,987,921	1,472,603	381,446	4,316,914	4,698,360	6,170,962
29	316,596,767	0.01345	1,961,180	1,451,069	378,196	4,253,755	4,631,952	6,083,020
30	311,964,815	0.01345	1,934,798	1,429,839	374,974	4,191,490	4,566,464	5,996,303
100	108,745,344	0.01345	749,744	498,416	206,017	1,460,065	1,666,082	2,164,498
101	107,079,262	0.01345	739,658	490,780	204,262	1,437,677	1,641,939	2,132,719
102	105,437,324	0.01345	729,708	483,254	202,522	1,415,613	1,618,135	2,101,389
103	103,819,189	0.01345	719,892	475,838	200,796	1,393,869	1,594,665	2,070,503
104	102,224,524	0.01345	710,208	468,529	199,086	1,372,441	1,571,526	2,040,056
105	100,652,997	0.01345	700,655	461,326	197,390	1,351,324	1,548,713	2,010,039

EXHIBIT 3.5 (Continued)

(1)	(2)	(3)	(4)	(5)	(6)	(7)	(8)	(9)
Month	Outstanding Balance	SMM	Mortgage Payment	Net Interest	Scheduled Principal	Prepayment	Total Principal	Cash Flow
200	21,191,894	0.01345	193,525	97,130	87,566	283,894	371,460	468,589
201	20,820,434	0.01345	190,922	95,427	86,820	278,907	365,727	461,154
202	20,454,707	0.01345	188,353	93,751	86,080	273,998	360,078	453,828
203	20,094,629	0.01345	185,820	92,100	85,347	269,164	354,510	446,611
204	19,740,119	0.01345	183,320	90,476	84,620	264,405	349,024	439,500
205	19,391,095	0.01345	180,854	88,876	83,899	259,719	343,618	432,494
300	2,546,812	0.01345	49,953	11,673	37,219	33,759	70,978	82,651
301	2,475,835	0.01345	49,281	11,348	36,902	32,808	69,710	81,058
302	2,406,124	0.01345	48,618	11,028	36,587	31,875	68,462	79,490
303	2,337,662	0.01345	47,964	10,714	36,276	30,958	67,234	77,948
304	2,270,428	0.01345	47,319	10,406	35,967	30,058	66,025	76,431
305	2,204,403	0.01345	46,682	10,104	35,660	29,174	64,834	74,938
350	222,803	0.01345	25,379	1,021	24,265	2,671	26,936	27,957
351	195,867	0.01345	25,038	898	24,058	2,311	26,369	27,267
352	169,498	0.01345	24,701	777	23,853	1,959	25,812	26,589
353	143,685	0.01345	24,369	659	23,650	1,615	25,265	25,923
354	118,420	0.01345	24,041	543	23,449	1,278	24,726	25,269
355	93,694	0.01345	23,717	429	23,249	948	24,196	24,626
356	69,498	0.01345	23,398	319	23,051	625	23,676	23,994
357	45,822	0.01345	23,084	210	22,854	309	23,163	23,373
358	22,659	0.01345	22,773	104	22,660	0	22,660	22,764

[a] Since the WAM is 358 months, the underlying mortgage pool is seasoned an average of two months. Therefore, the CPR for month 28 is $2.50 \times 6\%$.

principal balance of a pool of new mortgage loans. A 100% prepayment assumption for loan group 1 (the "prepayment assumption") assumes a CPR of 8.0% per annum of the then outstanding principal balance of the applicable mortgage loans in the first month of the life of the mortgage loans and an additional approximately 1.0909090909% (precisely 12%/11) per annum in the second through 11th months. Beginning in the 12th month and in each month thereafter during the life of the mortgage loans, a 100% prepayment assumption assumes a CPR of 20.0% per annum each month.

Note that the prospectus supplement does not directly refer to a "PPC," but rather defines the prepayment ramp as "100% Prepayment Assumption."

Prepayment Conventions for Securities Backed by Home Equity and Manufactured Housing Loans

While the expression of prepayments in the MBS market is fairly standardized and comprises a combination of PSA curves and CPR calculations as just described, a variety of descriptions are used to express the paydown behavior of securities backed by home equity and manufactured housing loans. Despite the diversity in terminology, most of the concepts used to indicate prepayments for these two sectors of the mortgage market use the CPR concept as the numeraire while incorporating the PSA ramping methodology.

Home Equity Prepayment Speeds

In the early stages of the development of the securitized market for home equity loans, the majority of the loans were fixed rate, closed-end loans. Over the years, the balance has slowly shifted in favor of adjustable rate loans, particularly subprime ARMs. The earliest definition of prepayment speeds in the home equity market was the *home equity prepayment* (HEP) *curve*.[4] The primary motivation for using a different prepayment methodology for home equity loans was to capture the faster seasoning ramp observed for prepayments. Typically, home equity loans season faster than traditional single-family loans, making the PSA ramp an inappropriate description of the behavior of prepayments.

The HEP curve reflects the observed behavior in historic HEL data—it has a ramp of 10 months and a variable long-term CPR to reflect individual issuer speeds. A faster long-term speed means faster CPRs on the ramp because the ramp is fixed at 10 months regardless of the long-term speed. For example, a 20% HEP projection would mean a 10-month ramp going to 20% in the 10th month from 2% in the first month and a constant 20% thereafter. Exhibit 3.6 shows several HEP curves at 20% HEP and 24% HEP, where month 1 speeds of 2.4% CPR increase over 10 months to 24% CPR.

In addition to utilizing the HEP curve, a PPC ramp is also commonly used to define the base-case prepayment assumption. As with other mortgage products, the specification of the ramp will be dependent on the attributes of the underlying loan collateral, with respect to both the beginning and terminal speeds as well as the duration of the ramp. Occasionally, deals are also priced to a constant CPR assumption, ignoring the impact of seasoning in generating the deal's cash flows.

---

[4] The HEP curve was developed by Prudential Securities based on the prepayment experience of $10 billion home equity loan deals.

EXHIBIT 3.6   HEP Curves

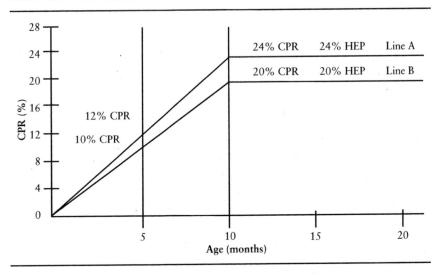

Manufactured Housing Prepayment Curve

The *manufactured housing prepayment* (MHP) curve is a measure of prepayment behavior for manufactured housing, based on the Green Tree Financial manufactured housing prepayment experience. MHP is similar to the PSA curve, except that the seasoning ramp is slightly different to account for the specific behavior of manufactured loans. 100% MHP is equivalent to 3.6% CPR at month zero and increases 0.1% CPR every month until month 24, when it plateaus at 6% CPR. Exhibit 3.7 shows the prepayment speeds at 50% MHP, 100% MHP, and 200% MHP.

DELINQUENCY, DEFAULT, AND LOSS TERMINOLOGY

Since all credit-sensitive MBS structures rely on some form of credit enhancement, the measurement of defaults and losses is very important. The importance of these measurements stems from the fact that in addition to the relevance of these measures to assess the relative value of lower rated tranches, the issuer typically retains the unrated and residual components of securitized deals. Therefore, any differences in the actual loss and default experience from expectations at pricing may lead to significant writedowns and adversely affect firm valuation. Despite the importance of delinquencies, losses and defaults in the mortgage-related markets, the terminology is not standardized. For instance, static pool losses may be reported on a

EXHIBIT 3.7 MHP Curves

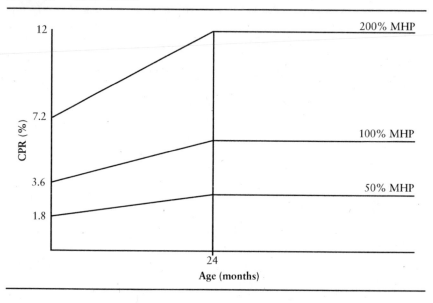

monthly or annualized basis as a percentage of either current or original balance with the metric based upon current balance being the preferred method to ensure consistency with prepayment reporting.

Before we discuss the measurement of defaults and losses, it is instructive to briefly review the various outcomes of a loan when the obligor ceases making scheduled payments. A loan becomes delinquent when the obligor fails to make the contractual payment on the stated date. Typically, when all collection efforts have failed while the loan is in delinquent status the loan is declared to be in default. At that point, the issuer (or the servicer) has several options. There may either be a short sale, where the borrower sells the property in a negotiated transaction subject to approval by the servicer or the property may go into the foreclosure or repossession process and be eventually sold by the servicer. Therefore, the process chain is delinquency to default to foreclosure or repossession to liquidation, at which time the severity of loss will be assessed.

Delinquency Measures

As mentioned above, when a borrower fails to make one or more timely payments, the loan is said to be *delinquent*. Delinquency measures are designed to gauge whether borrowers are current on their loan payment as well as stratifying unpaid loans according to the seriousness of the delinquency. The calculation method used is determined by the servicer.

When the underlying pool of assets is mortgage loans, the two commonly used methods for classifying delinquencies are those recommended by the Office of Thrift Supervision (OTS) and the Mortgage Bankers Association (MBA).

The OTS method uses the following loan delinquency classifications.

- Payment due date to 30 days late: *Current*
- 30–60 days late: *30 days delinquent*
- 60–90 days late: *60 days delinquent*
- More than 90 days late: *90+ days delinquent*

The MBA method is a somewhat more stringent classification method, classifying a loan as 30 days delinquent once payments are not received after the due date. Thus, a loan classified as "current" under the OTS method would be listed be as "30 days delinquent" under the MBA method. The two methods can report significantly different delinquencies.[5]

Default Measures

The conditions that result in classification of some loans as delinquent (such as the loss of a job or illness) may change, resulting in the resumption of timely principal and interest payments. However, some portion of the loans classified as delinquent may end up in default. By definition, default is the point where the borrower loses title to the property in question. Default generally occurs for loans that are 90+ days delinquent.[6] Default is generically defined as the event when a loan no longer makes contractual payments and remains in this status till liquidation.

Three measures for quantifying default are the conditional default rate, the cumulative default rate, and the charge-off rate. The *conditional default rate* (CDR) is the annualized value of the unpaid principal balance of newly defaulted loans over the course of a month as a percentage of the unpaid balance of the pool (before scheduled principal payment) at the beginning of the month. It is computed by first calculating the default rate for the month as shown below:

Default rate for month t

$$= \frac{\text{Default loan balance in month } t}{\text{Beginning balance for month } t - \text{Scheduled principal payment in month } t}$$

---

[5] For example, a June 9, 2000 report by Moody's titled, "Contradictions in Terms: Variations in Terminology in the Mortgage Market," shows that the reported delinquencies can differ dramatically when the different conventions are used.

[6] Loans where the borrower becomes bankrupt may be classified as having defaulted at an earlier point in time.

Then this is annualized as follows to get the CDR:

$$CDR_t = 1 - (1 - \text{Default rate for month } t)^{12}$$

Note that the CDR metric measures only the amount of defaults and not the amount of losses because the actual amount of losses depend upon the amounts that can be recovered on loans in default, adjusted for the costs of collection, and servicer advances, if applicable. In the extreme case, if there is full recovery of the unpaid principal balance of the defaulted loans, the losses will be zero with the exception of the costs of recovery. However, depending upon the timing of the recovery of the defaulted loan balances, the cash flows to certain bondholders may be interrupted.

The second default measure is the *cumulative default rate* which is denoted by CDX in order to avoid confusion with CDR. CDX is the proportion of the total face value of loans in the pool that have gone into default as a percentage of the total face value of the pool.

The *charge-off rate* (COR) is the annualized rate of loan liquidations.[7] The calculation begins with the following for the month:

Liquidation rate for month t

$$= \frac{\text{Liquidated loan balance in month } t}{\text{Beginning balance for month } t - \text{Scheduled principal payment in month } t}$$

and then annualized as follows:

$$COR_t = 1 - (1 - \text{Liquidation rate for month } t)^{12}$$

There are, however, disadvantages to using constant CDRs that tend to distort credit analysis. A constant CDR assumption is not necessarily consistent with the actual behavior of defaults, and also does not allow the analysis to take variations in the timing of defaults into account. As with prepayments, credit problems tend to be very low immediately after the loans are closed, but generally increase with time as the pool in question ages.

One time-honored methodology is to utilize the Standard Default Assumption (SDA) model, which assumes that defaults (as measured in annual terms using CDRs) have a fairly consistent pattern over the life of the pool. The model is similar in concept to the PSA model used in prepayment analysis, and is specified as follows:

---

[7] See Joel W. Brown and William M. Wadden, "Mortgage Credit Analysis," Chapter 18 in Frank J. Fabozzi (ed.), *Investing in Asset-Backed Securities* (Hoboken, NJ: John Wiley & Sons, 2000).

EXHIBIT 3.8   100% SDA Without Effects of Prepayments

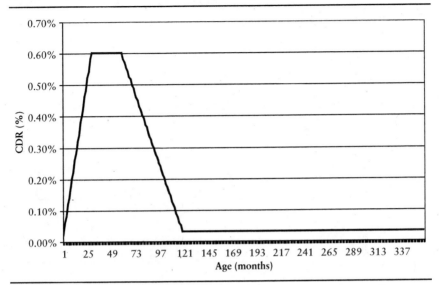

- 0.02% initial CDR, rising 0.02% CDR until reaching 0.6% CDR in month 30.
- A constant 0.6% CDR from months 30 to 60.
- A linear decline of 0.0095% between months 61 and 120, reaching 0.03% in month 120.
- A constant 0.03% CDR for the remaining term.

The base SDA curve is shown in Exhibit 3.8.

However, the SDA model is constructed to account for the effects of prepayments, which profoundly impact credit performance in a number of ways. Fast prepayment of principal improves the overall credit performance of a pool of mortgages, in that outstanding principal is returned to the investor faster. However, as loan populations experience prepayments, the credit quality of the remaining loans becomes increasingly questionable. (The assumption is that the better credits are able to prepay their loans, leaving only the weaker loans to remain. This is referred to as "adverse selection.")

In addition to the prescribed CDR curve described above, the base SDA model assumes a prepayment speed of 150% PSA. One hundred percent SDA at 150% PSA results in cumulative defaults of around 2.80%, and vary significantly when different assumptions are used. The actual level of monthly defaults is calculated as the product of monthly default rates or MDRs (i.e., the deannualized CDR) and the monthly balance factor at the projected prepayment speed. Cumulative defaults are the sum of this vector. Exhibit 3.9 shows how 100% SDA would be calculated, assuming a 6.0% coupon pass-through (as in the prior examples). A depiction of monthly defaults using the base assumptions of the SDA model at 15% PSA is shown in Exhibit 3.10. Note that this example results in cumulative defaults of roughly 2.73%.

EXHIBIT 3.9 Calculation of Monthly Defaults Using 100% SDA at 150% PSA for a Pass-Through with a 5.5% Pass-Through Rate, a WAC of 6.0%, and a WAM of 357 Months

(1)	(2)	(3)	(4)	(5)
Month	100% SDA (in CDRs)	100% SDA (in MDRs)[a]	Bond Factor (@ 150% PSA)	Factor-Adjusted MDR[b]
1	0.080%	0.007%	0.99798	0.0067%
2	0.100%	0.008%	0.99571	0.0083%
3	0.120%	0.010%	0.99318	0.0099%
4	0.140%	0.012%	0.99041	0.0116%
5	0.160%	0.013%	0.98738	0.0132%
6	0.180%	0.015%	0.98410	0.0148%
7	0.200%	0.017%	0.98057	0.0164%
8	0.220%	0.018%	0.97680	0.0179%
9	0.240%	0.020%	0.97278	0.0195%
10	0.260%	0.022%	0.96853	0.0210%
11	0.280%	0.023%	0.96403	0.0225%
12	0.300%	0.025%	0.95930	0.0240%
13	0.320%	0.027%	0.95433	0.0255%
14	0.340%	0.028%	0.94914	0.0269%
15	0.360%	0.030%	0.94372	0.0284%
16	0.380%	0.032%	0.93807	0.0298%
17	0.400%	0.033%	0.93220	0.0311%
18	0.420%	0.035%	0.92612	0.0325%
19	0.440%	0.037%	0.91982	0.0338%
20	0.460%	0.038%	0.91332	0.0351%
21	0.480%	0.040%	0.90661	0.0363%
22	0.500%	0.042%	0.89970	0.0376%
23	0.520%	0.043%	0.89260	0.0388%
24	0.540%	0.045%	0.88531	0.0399%
25	0.560%	0.047%	0.87783	0.0411%
26	0.580%	0.048%	0.87017	0.0422%
27	0.600%	0.050%	0.86233	0.0432%
28	0.600%	0.050%	0.85456	0.0428%
29	0.600%	0.050%	0.84685	0.0425%
30	0.600%	0.050%	0.83920	0.0421%

EXHIBIT 3.9   (Continued)

(1)	(2)	(3)	(4)	(5)
Month	100% SDA (In CDRs)	100% SDA (In MDRs)[a]	Bond Factor (@ 150% PSA)	Factor-Adjusted MDR[b]
100	0.192%	0.016%	0.43487	0.0069%
101	0.182%	0.015%	0.43064	0.0065%
102	0.173%	0.014%	0.42644	0.0061%
103	0.163%	0.014%	0.42228	0.0057%
104	0.154%	0.013%	0.41815	0.0054%
105	0.144%	0.012%	0.41406	0.0050%
200	0.030%	0.003%	0.14894	0.0004%
201	0.030%	0.003%	0.14715	0.0004%
202	0.030%	0.003%	0.14538	0.0004%
203	0.030%	0.003%	0.14363	0.0004%
204	0.030%	0.003%	0.14188	0.0004%
205	0.030%	0.003%	0.14016	0.0004%
300	0.030%	0.003%	0.03093	0.0001%
301	0.030%	0.003%	0.03022	0.0001%
302	0.030%	0.003%	0.02952	0.0001%
303	0.030%	0.003%	0.02882	0.0001%
304	0.030%	0.003%	0.02814	0.0001%
305	0.030%	0.003%	0.02745	0.0001%
350	0.030%	0.003%	0.00289	0.0000%
351	0.030%	0.003%	0.00247	0.0000%
352	0.030%	0.003%	0.00204	0.0000%
353	0.030%	0.003%	0.00163	0.0000%
354	0.030%	0.003%	0.00121	0.0000%
355	0.030%	0.003%	0.00080	0.0000%
356	0.030%	0.003%	0.00040	0.0000%
357	0.030%	0.003%	0.00000	0.0000%
			Cumulative Defaults	2.75%

[a] CDRs are converted to MDRs by using the following formula:

$$MDR = 1 - (1 - CDR)^{1/12}$$

[b] Column (3) × (4)

Loss-Severity Measures

Where the lender has a lien on the property, a portion of the value of the loan can be recovered through the legal recovery process (i.e., through foreclosure and repossession) and subsequent sale of the asset. The difference between the proceeds received from the recovery process (after

EXHIBIT 3.10   Monthly CDRs for 100% SDA Using 150% PSA

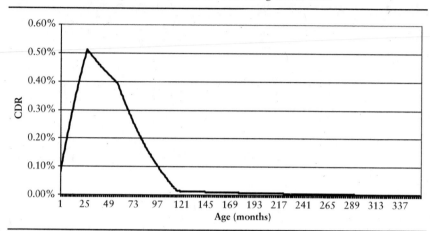

all transaction costs) and principal balance of the loss is the loss in dollars. The *loss-severity rate* is

$$\text{Loss-severity rate} = \frac{\text{Liquidation balance in month } t - \text{Liquidation proceeds}}{\text{Liquidation balance in month } t}$$

The loss-severity rate ranges from 0 to 1 (or 0% to 100%). If the loss severity rate is zero, then liquidation proceeds are equal to the liquidated loan balance. A loss-severity rate of 1 (or 100%) means that there are no liquidation proceeds. The *loss rate* is equal to the annual default rate multiplied by the loss assumption severity.

Default and loss severity assumptions (which translate into expected losses) are critical metrics for holders of mortgages and MBS that have exposure to mortgage credit performance. From the viewpoint of issuers, the assumptions used to value and capitalize investments in retained tranches are critical for assessing firm value, as any deterioration in the performance of retained tranches can negatively impact overall corporate valuations. Investors in whole-loan mortgages and subordinate MBS routinely use the credit metrics discussed above to analyze the relative value of different alternatives by generating default- and loss-adjusted returns and valuations.

CHAPTER 4

Prepayment Behavior and Performance

A critical component in the valuation, risk management, and trading of mortgage-backed securities (MBS) is prepayments. The rate of prepayments, or prepayment "speed," impacts MBS values in a number of ways. Because of this, large amounts of resources and many personnel hours are expended by investors and dealers in understanding and modeling prepayment behavior. However, refinancing behavior and prepayment performance are not static, and have changed significantly since the first prepayment waves were experienced in the early 1990s. This is due to a number of factors: rapid real estate appreciation in the United States, the growth of the adjustable rate mortgage (ARM) market, and the development of a more consumer-friendly mortgage industry. While not intended to be a comprehensive study of prepayment behavior, this chapter addresses the underlying factors driving prepayment and refinancing behavior, while also addressing why prepayment behavior has changed from the early 1990s to the current period. We will also attempt to identify additional factors affecting prepayment speeds, including loan size, credit performance and geography, as well as factors unique to different mortgage products and product sectors.

PREPAYMENT BEHAVIOR

Traditionally, prepayment behavior has been ascribed to two different and mutually exclusive phenomena. One is "turnover," which involves transactions where a property is sold or liquidated. Turnover can occur when:

71

- The homeowner moves or trades up to a larger house.
- The obligor relocates as part of changes in their job or employment.
- The property is sold subsequent to the death of the homeowner, or as part of a divorce settlement.
- The property is destroyed by a fire or other natural disaster.

The resulting proceeds (from either the property's sale or an insurance settlement) are passed on as prepaid principal to the holder of the mortgage.

The second phenomenon can be broadly characterized as "refinancing." Strictly defined, a refinancing occurs when obligors prepay their loans in the absence of the sale or destruction of the underlying property. Refinancings are often undertaken by borrowers in order to lower the loan's note rate and reduce the monthly payment on their mortgage. This type of transaction, referred to as a *rate-and-term refinancing*, has normally taken place when borrowers perceive that they can reduce their interest costs or their monthly mortgage payment by taking out a new loan. To borrow a term from the option market, the borrower's existing loan in this case is considered "in-the-money." Loans where borrowers are not able to improve their monthly cash flow situation are considered "out-of-the-money."

Another related form of refinancing occurs when borrowers refinance in order to liquefy their home's equity. Such transactions, referred to as "cash-out refinancings," typically are taken as an alternative to second-lien loans. Borrowers have historically utilized cash-out refinancings when the prevailing level of rates is low enough to create a refinancing incentive for their existing loan. This makes it economical for the borrower to liquefy equity by refinancing the entire loan, rather than by taking a second lien for the amount of equity to be liquefied. Before 2002, the proportion of cash-out refinancings had varied with the level of mortgage rates and the amount of refinancing activity. As we will see, however, cash-outs have been strongly correlated with home price appreciation and the growth in overall homeowner equity since the beginning of 2002.

The combination of refinancing activity and housing turnover dictates the level of prepayments. Prepayment speeds can be illustrated by the means of prepayment "S-curves," which show prepayment rates for different levels of rates and refinancing incentives. S-curves can be created using a number of different methodologies and data sources. Either projected or historical prepayment speeds can be shown; additionally, the level of prepayments can be compared to either the absolute level of rates or to some measure of refinancing incentive.

An example of S-curves for different periods is shown in Exhibit 4.1. The chart shows historical prepayment speeds for 30-year conventional loans exhibited by refinancing incentive (defined as the cohort's note rate

EXHIBIT 4.1 Prepayment S-Curves for Different Periods for 30-Year, Fixed Rate Conventional Loans

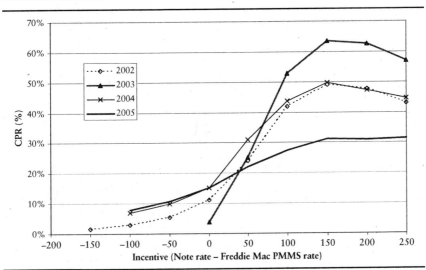

less the Freddie Mac fixed 30-year survey rate[1]) for different years. The S-curves shown in the chart have a number of different aspects:

- The fastest in-the-money prepayment speeds (i.e., speeds for positive refinancing incentives) occurred in 2003. Additionally, the lowest incentive for the 2003 data is zero; rates were so low for most of the year that there were very few loans that had a negative incentive.
- The earlier periods (2002 and 2003) had very steep S-curves. By contrast, the S-curve for 2005 was extremely flat, a positive development for mortgage products. (A flat S-curve indicates relatively fast prepayment speeds for discount mortgages, and relatively slow speeds for premium securities.)

Traditionally, prepayment speeds for out-of-the-money coupons (typically those coupons trading at a discount, where no refinancing incentive was apparent) were consistently around the level of housing turnover, while prepayment rates for premium or in-the-money coupons were the sum of turnover- and refinancing-based prepayments, where borrowers refinanced primarily from one fixed rate loan into another. This is

---

[1] Since 1972, Freddie Mac has surveyed a large number of lenders and published the average rate for a variety of fixed and adjustable rate products. The results can be accessed on Freddie Mac's Web Site, www.freddiemac.com.

reflected in the steep S-curves for 2002 and 2003 in Exhibit 4.1. While the two primary dynamics of turnover and refinancing continue to drive prepayment behavior, more recent behavior have demonstrated that additional factors are influencing prepayment speeds. There have been two primary changes to the prepayment landscape since the late 1990s:

- The evolution of the real estate markets, the mortgage industry, and borrower preferences to change the nature of borrower's refinancing choices and decisions.
- The recognition that borrower- and loan-level factors influence prepayment behavior both directly and indirectly.

Some of these factors have fundamentally altered refinancing behavior and distorted the concept of "in-the-money-ness," as reflected in the changing shape of the S-curves noted in Exhibit 4.1. Other factors, while not having as dramatic an impact on prepayments, have exhibited a more subtle influence on prepayment behavior. These factors have forced investors and dealers to revisit their models in order to accurately forecast and project prepayment speeds in different rate and home price appreciation regimes.

DRIVERS OF PREPAYMENT ACTIVITY

As noted previously, the two key drivers of prepayment activity are turnover and refinancing. We discuss each next.

Turnover

As previously described, turnover refers to activity where the underlying property is sold or liquidated, and the proceeds of the sale are subsequently passed through to the holder of the mortgage (either outright or as part of a mortgage-backed security) as a prepayment. Casual observers of prepayment speeds will note that speeds for out-of-the-money MBS have, since roughly 2002, been faster than historical norms. Much, but not all, of this increase can be attributed to faster turnover. There is no doubt that speeds on discount securities and loans have been faster since the beginning of 2002 than during earlier periods. However, only part of this evolution can be attributed to turnover in its true economic sense, even though turnover rates have certainly increased in the ten-year period after 1996.

A truer estimate of housing turnover can be created by calculating existing home sales for single-family homes as a percentage of the number of such homes owned. Existing home sales data are published monthly by the National Association of Realtors, while the number of single-family

EXHIBIT 4.2   Implied Turnover Rate (single-family existing home sales/total single-family homes)

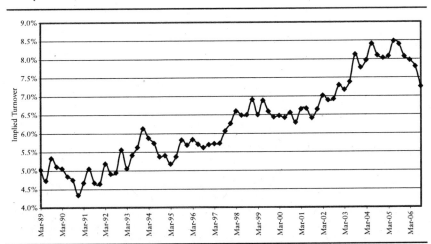

Source: Constructed from data obtained from the National Association of Realtors and the Census Bureau.

homes outstanding is published by the Census Bureau on a quarterly basis, subject to periodic adjustments. Exhibit 4.2 shows housing turnover over time, calculated by dividing existing home sales into the total number of single-family homes. As the chart indicates, this estimate of turnover has increased over time, reflecting both the strength of U.S. real estate markets and the growth in the number of real estate transactions.

In the same vein, Exhibit 4.3 shows a scatterchart of turnover rates versus the level of the Freddie Mac 30-year fixed survey rate, expressed as a quarterly average. The exhibit suggests a fairly consistent long-term relationship between turnover and rates. In a broad sense, turnover and rates have been inversely correlated; arguably, some of the strength in housing turnover is attributable to the impact of low mortgage rates on residential real estate. However, the exhibit also suggests that mortgage rates and turnover have not moved in lockstep. An interpretation of the data suggests that turnover has undergone a number of different regimes:

- A relatively slow period from the beginning of 1989 until the middle of 1997, when turnover ranged from the area of 4.25% to approximately 6%.
- A faster period that began in late 1997 until mid-2002, when turnover was between 6% and 7%.
- Another increase beginning toward the end of 2002 until mid-2006, with turnover ranging from roughly 7% to more than 8.5%.

EXHIBIT 4.3   Housing Turnover versus Freddie Mac 30-Year Fixed Survey Rate

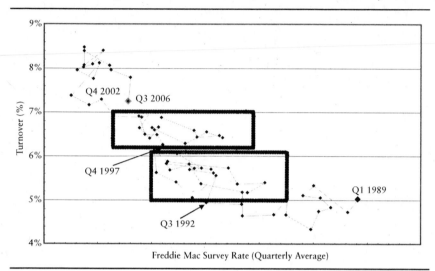

Source: Constructed from data obtained from the National Association of Realtors and the Census Bureau.

It is tempting to associate elevated housing turnover with robust growth in home prices. Purely speaking, however, housing turnover is not directly associated with real estate price appreciation, but rather with the level of home sales activity and the number of completed transactions. While home prices and sales are highly correlated, it is conceivable that home prices could stagnate while sales activity remains firm, and vice versa.

In addition, prepayment speeds can be influenced by home price appreciation (or "HPA") through effects that are commonly attributed to "turnover" but in fact represent other phenomena. As discussed later in this chapter, for example, rising home prices have been associated with high levels of cash-out refinancings since 2002. Since cash-out refinancings often are taken by borrowers when the loan has no apparent refinancing incentive, it is tempting to lump it in with "turnover," although in actuality no sale or disposition of the properties in question took place.

Refinancing

Rational borrowers will always seek to lower their borrowing costs by refinancing their debts. This typically occurs when the prevailing level of interest rates declines to the point where the borrower can, after accounting for transaction costs and potential penalties, take out a new loan and use the proceeds to pay off the preexisting loans. Changes in the lending environment, such as high rates of home price appreciation and the introduction and popularization of new products, can also create opportunities for borrowers to reduce their monthly payments and/ or improve their cash flow situation. Therefore, refinancing activity is an increasingly dynamic phenomenon, where the response of borrowers to changes in rates and product choices can evolve rapidly.

Refinancing opportunities present themselves to both institutional and individual borrowers. Unlike corporations and municipalities, however, residential borrowers are relatively inefficient in capitalizing on refinancing opportunities. This manifests itself in the very existence of so-called in-the-money mortgage loans (i.e., those loans with a note rate that is clearly above-market), since borrowers would have availed themselves of the opportunity to refinance if they were uniformly efficient and rational. For example, in June of 2005 almost $200 billion of conventional 30-year agency pools with coupons of 6.5% and higher were outstanding. Since Freddie Mac's 30-year survey rate had averaged around 5.75% for the prior three months, a large number of loans with above-market rates remained outstanding despite having at least 125 basis points of incentive. This assumes that the weighted average coupon (or WAC) for this cohort is 50 basis points higher than the coupon.

This type of borrower inefficiency exists for a number of reasons. Borrowers have varying degrees of awareness of conditions in the financial markets, and are not always cognizant of refinancing opportunities. Borrowers often hear about declines in rates from their friends and co-workers; they also may read about it in the financial press or see it discussed on news programs. These are collectively referred to as "media effects." It often takes a significant and noteworthy drop in rates to generate conversation and media "buzz," which explains the tendency for refinancings to occur in waves. Exhibit 4.4 demonstrates this behavior over time. The chart shows mortgage rates (again using Freddie Mac's 30-year survey rate as a proxy) versus refinancing activity, using the Mortgage Bankers Association's Refinancing index. The chart indicates that refinancing activity often remains tepid for long periods of time, but spikes when mortgage rates move significantly slower. The biggest surge in activity occurred in mid-2003, when the refinancing (or "refi") index surged to around 10,000 as rates moved to an all-time low of about 5.25%. During other periods, however, the refi index remained relatively low even though mortgage rates were also low by historical standards.[2]

---

[2] The refi index is part of a weekly applications survey taken by the MBA of the number and composition of applications reported by major lenders. The refi index accounts only for applications for loan refinancings.

EXHIBIT 4.4   MBA Refinancing Index (March 1990 = 100) versus Freddie Mac 30-Year Survey Rate

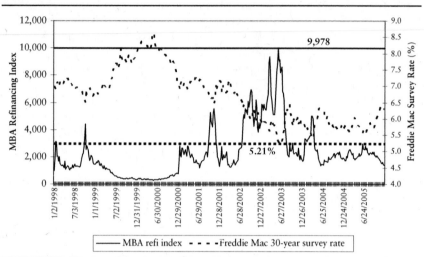

Source: Constructed from data obtained from the Mortgage Bankers Association and Freddie Mac.

In addition, most refinancing transactions are accompanied by a series of costs that are largely fixed (e.g., application fees and the costs of appraisals and credit reports). However, the monetary value associated with the borrower's rate savings is variable, and largely a function of the size of the loan. This suggests that borrowers with larger loan balances have a greater incentive to refinance. By contrast, the rate savings on a smaller loan generally must be greater, all things equal, to allow the borrower to overcome the fixed cost hurdle over a reasonable period of time. For example, a 50 basis point rate savings on a $100,000 loan would reduce the borrower's payment by $32 per month. If refinancing the loan entails $1,000 in costs, it would take more than 31 months for the borrower to recover his/her costs and begin saving money. On a $350,000 loan, by contrast, the borrower's costs are recovered in nine months. Therefore, the borrower with the smaller loan needs a greater rate savings to be enticed into a refinancing.

Refinancing efficiency has, however, improved over time. One factor is the growing presence of the financial press, especially on television and the Internet, which serves to disseminate financial data and conditions more efficiently. The mortgage industry has also become more adept at generating refinancing volume through marketing activities. Some of these activities involve directly contacting existing customers, while others involve mass marketing through television commercials, print advertisements, and direct mail solicitations. Also contributing to the marketing efforts is a growing cadre of mortgage brokers, who act as agents linking lenders and borrowers. While lenders do attempt to use their preexisting relationships with realtors to generate purchase-loan activity, an important objective of their marketing efforts is to generate refinancing business by notifying clients and contacts of potential opportunities.

Changes in Refinancing Activity and Behavior

In light of the above discussion, the analysis of refinancing activity traditionally has focused on activity generated by a decline in the prevailing level of interest rates. Declines in rates present refinancing opportunities for borrowers whose current loan has a rate higher than that available in the market to reduce their monthly payment (after accounting for fixed costs). This business model suggests that refinancing is binary in nature, and borrowers either have, or don't have, an incentive to refinance.

A recent evolution in the market has been the growth in so-called product transitions, where borrowers refinance out of one product into a different sector. This type of activity is exemplified by refinancings between fixed and adjustable rate products. A time-honored transition was that borrowers with adjustable rate loans would refinance into new fixed rate loans when fixed mortgage rates declined. This type of activity was especially prominent during times when the yield curve was relatively flat, since the rate on ARM loans after the coupon resets were often higher than the current level of fixed mortgage rates. In addition, borrowers with 30-year loans that sought to shorten their loan term took advantage of declines in mortgage rates to refinance into 15-year products (hence the nomenclature rate-and-term refinancing introduced previously).

More recently, however, large numbers of borrowers having fixed rate loans have refinanced into ARMs. This phenomenon first became evident in mid- to late-2003, and coincided with the increased acceptance of the ARM product (particularly the hybrid ARM) on the part of borrowers, very low-short interest rates, and a steep yield curve. The sudden and dramatic change in behavior is illustrated in Exhibit 4.5. The exhibit shows a scatterchart of the MBA's refi index on the horizontal axis and the percentage of ARM applications by dollar amounts (which is reported as part of the weekly applications survey) on the vertical axis. Prior to August 2003, the percentage of ARM applications was high when refinancing activity was muted, and dropped when the refi index was greater than 900. The ARM percentages after July 2003, however, have been consistently higher, implying that its relationship to refinancing activity has clearly changed.

EXHIBIT 4.5 MBA Refinancing Index versus Percentage of ARM Applications (by dollars)—March 1998 to November 2005

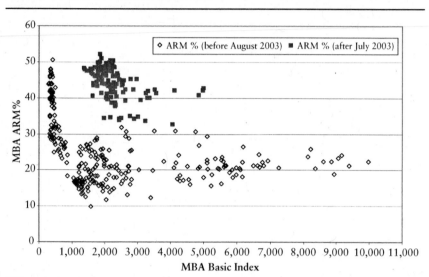

Source: Constructed from data obtained from the Mortgage Bankers Association.

A different way to demonstrate changing refinancing behavior is through the use of transition data. This data tracks the original loan (i.e., the loan being refinanced) along with the new (or "destination") product being taken. The increased proportion of refinancing out of fixed rate loans into ARMs after mid-2003 is clearly shown in Exhibit 4.6. The exhibit shows the monthly percentage of fixed and adjustable rate loans being taken by borrowers refinancing out of fixed rate loans. The chart indicates that fixed-to-ARM refinancings took place in very small amounts until August 2003; after that point, borrowers refinanced out of fixed rate loans and into ARMs in increasingly large numbers.

There are a number of potential reasons for this pronounced change in borrower behavior. The sudden growth in fixed-to-ARM refinancing activity was associated with a sharp rise in fixed interest rates over summer 2003 after having been at very low levels for the previous two to three months. While purely conjectural, it may be that the desire of large numbers of borrowers to refinance who missed the opportunity when fixed rates were low coincided with marketing efforts by the mortgage industry to increase the utilization of ARMs by borrowers. This also was a period where the "hybrid" or fixed period ARM became a prominent product. The combination of an initial fixed rate period with an adjustable rate "tail" appealed to borrowers that were willing to accept incre-

EXHIBIT 4.6   "Destination" Product for Refinancings Out of Fixed Rate Loans

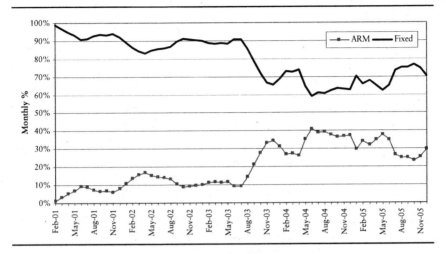

Source: Constructed from data obtained from Countrywide Home Loans.

mentally more interest rate risk in the future in order to obtain lower rates, albeit with less exposure to rising rates than that of more traditional ARM products. Whatever the reasons, it is clear that borrower preferences and behavior changed dramatically in August 2003.

The growing importance of product transitions, particularly fixed-to-ARM refinancings, has introduced new elements to refinancing behavior. The most important factor is that rates across the entire yield curve affect borrowers' refinancing decisions, and must be taken into account when evaluating prepayment behavior. The initial rate for most ARM products (which dictates the monthly payments prior to the point when the loan resets) is based off short-duration interest rates; the start rate for 5/1 hybrid ARMs, for example, has a strong correlation with the three-year swap rate. Since short interest rates are generally lower than long rates and the yield curve is typically upward-sloping, many borrowers have the incentive to refinance into ARM products irrespective of the level of 30-year mortgage rates. However, the incentive to refinance into many types of ARMs is mitigated during periods when short interest rates are rising, as they did throughout 2005. When refinancing out of fixed rate loans into ARMs was less common, changes in the shape of the yield curve did not impact refinancing activity to the same degree; the refinancing incentive was driven largely by the 30-year fixed mortgage rate, which in turn is a function of 10-year yields.

An additional element came into play when alternative amortization schemes became increasingly prevalent. Products such as interest-only loans have become increasingly popular among borrowers in both the ARM and fixed rate sectors. These products require only the payment of interest during a predefined initial period; after the expiration of the interest-only period, the borrower makes a fully amortizing payment based on the remaining term of the loan. In fact, some loans (called *negative amortization* or *payment-option loans*) allow the borrower to make a payment less than the interest amount due that month; the shortfall is treated as deferred interest and added to the loan's principal balance. The availability of interest-only and negative-amortization loans has led borrowers to measure the benefits from refinancing in terms of reducing their monthly cash lays, rather than strictly through the vehicle of a lower interest rate.

The changing nature of borrowers' refinancing incentives and decisions is illustrated in Exhibit 4.7. Panel A of the exhibit shows a borrower's refinancing decision in a world where the only refinancing option is into a new 30-year loan. In the example, the borrower's current loan has a 6.25% rate, and the 30-year fixed rate available in the market is 5.75% (before points and costs). The refinancing decision here is very simple. The borrower's decision is based on (1) the current level of rates relative to the borrower's existing loan; and (2) the amount of rate savings required to justify the expense and paperwork involved with the transaction. This example assumes a "savings threshold" of 50 basis points; in reality, the required threshold depends on both the preferences of the borrower as well as other loan-level factors, such as loan size, that influence the perceived savings.

Panel B of Exhibit 4.7 shows the same decision when ARM refinancing alternatives exist. For simplicity's sake, we limit the available refinancing choices to amortizing hybrid ARMs with a variety of fixed rate periods. In the exhibit, the fixed-to-fixed refinancing incentive is only 25 basis points. However, a borrower going into the ARM alternatives can save anywhere from 50 to 150 basis points by refinancing into an ARM.

EXHIBIT 4.7
Panel A: Example of Simple Refinancing Incentive: Fixed-to-Fixed Refinancings

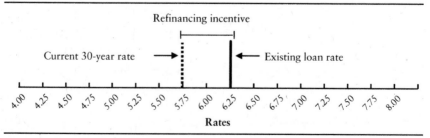

EXHIBIT 4.7   (Continued)

Panel B: Example of Refinancing Incentive with Additional Fully Amortizing Alternatives

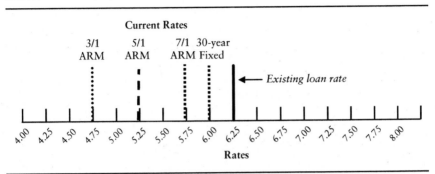

Panel C: Hypothetical Monthly Payments on $300,000 Loan for Different Products

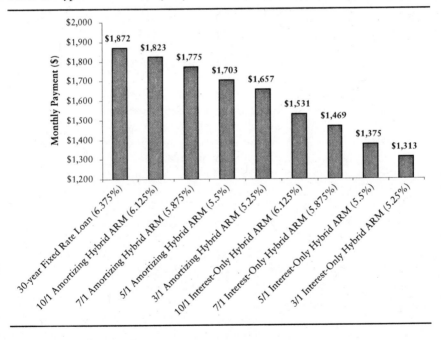

The increased availability and popularity of fixed-to-ARM refinancings has several implications. Because of the generally upward slope in the yield curves, ARM rates are typically lower than fixed rates; therefore, more borrowers can now profitably refinance than in the past. This includes borrowers that, under the earlier regime (i.e., prior to mid-

2003), would not have had a refinancing option. This suggests that prepayments on lower-coupon mortgages that would previously have been considered "out of the money" are faster than they have been in the past, all things equal. However, when short rates rise and push ARM rates higher, the fixed-to-ARM refinancing incentive is reduced. Therefore, the shape of the yield curve and the level of short and intermediate interest rates have a much greater impact on refinancing activity than in the past.

The aforementioned popularity of loans with alternative amortization schemes has further altered the refinancing calculus for borrowers. Panel C of Exhibit 4.7 illustrates this development by showing the monthly payments on a $300,000 loan for a variety of products with different rates and amortization schedules. Note that the rates utilized, while purely hypothetical, are generally representative of periods (such as much of 2004) when the yield curve was fairly steep and hybrid ARM rates were significantly lower than those of fixed rate loans. During periods when the yield curve was flat (such as in late 2005), ARM rates often increase enough to be comparable to those offered by fixed rate products. In these cases, 30-year, fixed rate borrowers can only economically refinance into products with alternative amortization schedules, such as interest-only loans or products with negative amortization features.

However, there remains a portion of the borrower population that continues to eschew adjustable rate loans, presumably because they do not wish to accept the interest rate risk associated with an ARM. Therefore, while fixed-to-ARM activity acts to push the overall level of prepayment speeds higher, it has not been associated with the explosive levels of refinancing activity observed during periods such as the spring of 2003. To this point, the levels of refinancing and prepayment activity associated with a "refinancing wave" (i.e., a refi index of 10,000 and 50+% annualized prepayment rates) have occurred when fixed rates declined enough to give large numbers of borrowers a fixed-to-fixed refinancing incentive, as well as create a media "buzz."

The continued willingness of borrowers to utilized loans with alternative amortization schedules may be contingent on rising home prices. This may be because real estate appreciation, and the increase in wealth generated by rising home equity, reduces the loan-to-value (LTV) ratios of borrowers, making them more willing to enter transactions where equity is not generated through amortization. Alternatively, borrowers accustomed to strong growth may seek to subsidize their lifestyle by reducing their monthly mortgage payment and eliminating the portion of the payment made to reduce their balance. This phenomenon represents another case where real estate appreciation impacts prepayment speeds by affecting refinancing activity, instead of through enhanced turnover.

Aggregate Refinancing and Prepayment Behavior

A better understanding of how the new refinancing environment impacts aggregate levels of prepayments can be achieved by gauging the refinanceability of the overall market, in a fashion similar to that shown in the three panels in Exhibit 4.7. This can be accomplished by examining the distribution of note rates within the population of the fixed rate universe at different points in time. Using pool WACs as a proxy, we can create and chart cumulative balance percentages of the outstanding mortgage market. (These exhibits use data from the agency fixed rate market, although other markets can also be evaluated in this fashion.) Using the balances outstanding at any point in time, the cumulative balance percentages are calculated as follows:

- Divide the outstanding market balances into discrete segments or "buckets" by WAC. (The following analysis uses 12.5 basis point WAC buckets.)
- For each WAC bucket, calculate the percentage of the remaining balances with note rates equal to and below that bucket. For example, if the lowest WAC bucket is 5.0% to 5.124% and it represents 2% of the remaining balance, its cumulative percentage is 2%. If the next WAC bucket (5.125% to 5.249%) comprises 6% of the unpaid balance of the market, its cumulative balance is therefore 8%. This process is completed for all WAC buckets.

Exhibit 4.8 shows a chart of the cumulative balances outstanding as of January 2003 and January 2004. Note that the cumulative balances changed fairly dramatically during 2003, reflecting lower fixed mortgage rates for that period of time. This change resulted from both fast prepayments of higher-rate loans, along with a commensurate increase in issuance of loans with lower note rates.

To interpret and utilize Exhibit 4.8, keep in mind that this shows the percentage of the market with a note rate equal to or lower than each note rate bucket. Therefore, the loans with a refinancing incentive are the loans above the note rate bucket, that is, the remaining percentage calculated by subtracting each percentage from 100%. For example, the curve for January 2003 shows that roughly 33% of the market had a note rate in, or lower than, the 6.5% bucket, leaving approximately 67% of the outstanding balances at that point above that bucket. The balances above the rate bucket can be considered to have a refinancing incentive (or be in-the-money) at that level of rates. The actual degree of incentive depends on the refinancing threshold necessary to undertake a rate-and-term refinancing transaction. The general assumption is that 25 to 50 basis points of incentive is necessary to trigger rate-driven refi-

EXHIBIT 4.8   Cumulative Percentage of 30-Year, Fixed Rate Conventional Market by Note Rate Bucket for Different Months

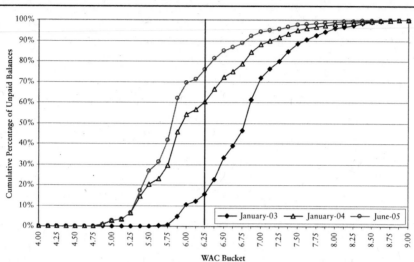

Source: Constructed from data obtained from eMBS.

nancings. This suggests that if fixed mortgage rates were 6.25% (indicated by the vertical line, and assuming a 25 basis point threshold), more than 85% of the outstanding fixed rate market would have a fixed rate refinancing incentive. (The required incentive, however, varies depending on the characteristics of both the individual borrower and the subject loan. As noted previously, for example, borrowers have a greater incentive to refinance larger loans.)

Exhibit 4.8 also demonstrates the impact of changes in the composition of the market on overall refinanceability. The change in composition of the market over the course of 2003 (a period of historically low rates and high refinancing activity) means that by January of 2004 loans with rates of 6.5% and higher now constituted 72% of the outstanding market. Assuming a 25 basis point threshold, only 40% of the market would have had a refinancing incentive if fixed rates were 6.25%. Therefore, a decline in rates to the 6.25% level would have had a much greater impact on refinancing activity and prepayments at the beginning of 2003 than by the end of the same year. Along with the presence (or lack of) a media effect, this illustrates why prepayment activity and speeds can vary greatly for similar levels of mortgage rates at different points in time.

Finally, Exhibit 4.9 illustrates the impact of the availability of different products on the incentive to refinance. The chart shows the cumulative 30-year percentage balances of the 30-year conforming market as

EXHIBIT 4.9 Cumulative Percentage of 30-Year, Fixed Rate Conventional Market by Note Rate Bucket for June of 2005 with Different Market Rates

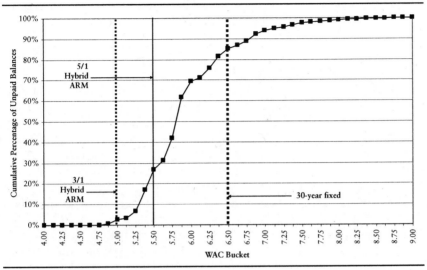

Source: Constructed from data obtained from eMBS.

of June 2005. It also shows, denoted as vertical lines, the following series of hypothetical one-point rates for different conventional loan products:

- 30-year fixed—6.5%
- 5/1 hybrid ARM—5.5%
- 3/1 hybrid ARM—5.0%

Using the simplifying assumption of no necessary rate incentive, the chart shows that roughly 15% of the market would have had an incentive to refinance into a fixed rate loan at that point. If 30-year fixed rate loans were virtually the only refinancing option considered by borrowers, refinancing activity would have declined sharply. However, at the same time roughly three-quarters of the market had an incentive to refinance into a new 5/1 hybrid ARM, and virtually all of the existing 30-year fixed market would have had an incentive to refinance into a 3/1 hybrid ARM. Therefore, the increased acceptance of the ARM product as a refinancing vehicle has altered the traditional view of when a loan is considered in-, at-, or out-of-the-money. At the same time, the growth of refinancing activity into ARMs makes the level of ARM rates (which in turn are pegged off the short end of the yield curve) much more important in dictating the overall level of refinancing activity than it was in the past. Finally, this change in the behavior of the market partially explains why out-of-the-money prepayments rose after 2003; the refinancing S-curves for these years are much flatter than that experienced during periods when fixed-to-ARM refinancing activity was less prevalent.

Types of Refinancing Transactions

As noted earlier in this chapter, there are two different types of refinancing transactions. If a refinancing loan is the same size as the original loan and no cash is taken out of the property, it is referred to as a rate-and-term refinancing. A refinancing where the new loan's balance is larger than that of the original loan is called a "cash-out loan," since the borrower takes cash out of the property by liquefying their equity.

As with general refinancing behavior, the factors driving cash-out refinancing activity have varied over time. At times, the proportion of cash-out refinancings has been strongly correlated with the level of mortgage rates, since refinancings during periods of higher rates typically are uneconomical except to liquefy equity. Exhibit 4.10 shows cash-out refinancings as a percentage of total refinancing transactions, along with the Freddie Mac 30-year, fixed survey rate, beginning with

EXHIBIT 4.10   Freddie Mac Cash-Out Percentage versus Survey Rate

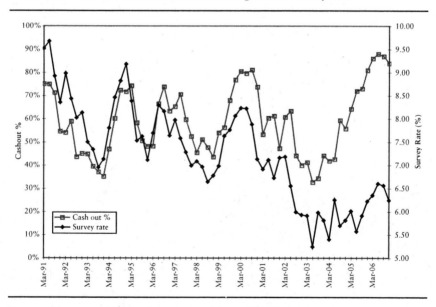

Source: Constructed from data obtained from Freddie Mac.

the first quarter of 1998. While the exhibit indicates a very strong correlation between the two factors, the relationship between mortgage rates and the percentage of cash-out loans has actually varied over time. For example, the two factors had a correlation of roughly 44% between the first quarter of 1985 and the fourth quarter of 1997. The correlation between the two factors from the first quarter of 1998 to the fourth quarter of 2002, however, was a very strong 80%. Since the end of 2002, however, the relationship between mortgage rates and the proportion of cash-out activity has been weaker. As Exhibit 4.10 indicates, equity withdrawal has grown despite the relatively low level of rates.

The strength in cash-out activity since the beginning of 2003 was coincidental with the robust housing market and strong levels of real estate appreciation over the period in question. Exhibit 4.11 shows the same percentage of cash-out activity reported by Freddie Mac, accompanied by the aggregate quarterly dollar change in U.S. residential real estate values. The chart shows that the post-2002 growth in cash-out activity as a percentage of total refinancings coincides with the strong growth in home prices. This development is fairly unique to this period of time, however. In fact, from the beginning of 1985 through the end of 2001 the two factors exhibited virtually no relationship (the correlation

EXHIBIT 4.11   Cash-Out Percentage versus Quarterly Change in Aggregate Value of Real Estate

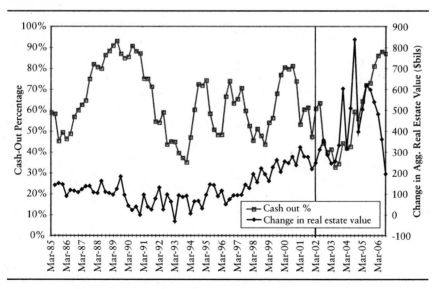

Source: Constructed from data obtained from Freddie Mac and the Federal Reserve.

was −6%); between the first quarter of 2002 and the second quarter of 2005, the correlation was a much stronger 44%. While the two factors have diverged since that point, the proportion of cash-out refinancings has remained strong, arguably reflecting the cumulative growth in borrower equity since the late 1990s.

ADDITIONAL FACTORS AFFECTING PREPAYMENT SPEEDS

As the previous discussion indicates, prepayment behavior can be highly complex, as it is subject to both market forces and changing consumer tastes. Ultimately, both turnover- and refinancing-based prepayments occur due to individual actions taken by or on behalf of the borrower. The earlier sections of the chapter highlighted the critical factors driving prepayment behavior, namely the level of interest rates, changes in home prices and price appreciation rates, and the level of real estate activity and sales. However, other factors related to either the borrower or the obligation itself can also impact prepayment behavior. We previously described the effect of loan size on the refinancing decision, but other borrower- and loan-level factors also influence how specific loans and securities prepay.

Credit

The effect of creditworthiness and borrower wealth on prepayments is complex and somewhat contradictory. Evidence suggests that both very high and very low credit borrowers tend to prepay somewhat faster than the "average" borrower. Borrowers with very high credit scores and significant financial resources tend to respond to refinancing opportunities very actively, in large part due to their greater financial acumen and resources. In addition, their homes and loan sizes tend to be larger, all things equal, which creates a greater savings in monetary terms for the borrower.

However, loans made to borrowers with very low credit scores also tend to prepay somewhat faster than average. This is mainly because these borrowers have higher incidences of delinquencies and defaults, caused by either the inability or unwillingness to make timely loan payments. When loans go into default and foreclosure, they eventually are pulled out of the pool and the recovered principal is passed on to investors. These actions create a so-called involuntary prepayment.

In addition, loans to borrowers with low credit scores and weak payment histories often prepay due to other factors short of foreclosure. These include:

- Borrowers that lose their jobs and become unemployed may sell the property before going into default in what might be called a "semivoluntary" prepayment.
- Lenders may proactively approach delinquent borrowers offering products that will reduce their monthly financial burden in what is often described as "lender aid."
- Borrowers whose credit has improved may take advantage of the increased options available to refinance into a product with a lower rate or reduced payment in a transaction referenced as "credit curing."

The impact of credit-related prepayments depends on the credit quality of the product in question. Products such as subprime and government-backed loans, which typically are made to borrowers with limited resources and/or weak credit histories, have elevated levels of delinquencies and defaults and thus higher levels of credit-induced prepayments.[3]

Geography

Region- and state-specific factors impact prepayments in a number of different ways. Variations in home price appreciation and housing turnover clearly impact refinancing and turnover activity. The lack of a competitive mortgage industry in some regions has historically slowed their prepayment speeds; for example, this explains the slow speeds associated with loans originated in Puerto Rico. Finally, certain states (including New York and Florida) have the equivalent of "refinancing taxes." While the cost can sometimes be avoided, these transaction taxes significantly increase the costs associated with refinancings, which in turn results in slower prepayment speeds for loans issued in those states.

Loan-to-Value Ratios

Loan-to-value ratios (or LTVs) have had a clear affect on prepayments historically, although the impact has varied over time. Early historical data suggested that high-LTV loans (e.g., loans with LTVs of 90% or higher) prepaid more slowly than loans with lower LTVs; however, this behavior changed after 2000, where high-LTV loans became faster than the rest of the population.

---

[3] While beyond the scope of this chapter, government loans pooled in Ginnie Mae securities can be "bought out" of the pool by the servicer when they are more than 90 days delinquent. This activity is generally economical only for loans trading at significant premiums. Therefore, premium Ginnie Mae speeds can be somewhat erratic, and subject to spikes due to buyout activity.

The most plausible explanation for this phenomenon, which is also consistent with the overall behavior of prepayments vis-à-vis LTV, is that the impact of LTV on prepayment speeds is linked to both real estate prices and technical factors associated with the products. The slower speeds associated with high-LTV loans are fairly typical of speeds associated with borrowers that have reduced financial resources and are more "stretched" to make their loan payments; these borrowers typically are slower to respond to refinancing opportunities, and often require a greater incentive in order to absorb the up-front costs of refinancings.

As noted previously in Chapter 1, however, lenders generally required loans with LTVs over 80% to have mortgage insurance (or "MI"), which insures the amount of the loan in excess of the 80% LTV mark. (If a $90,000 loan is taken to finance the purchase of a $100,000 home, for example, mortgage insurance would have to be paid on the amount of the loan greater than $80,000, or $10,000.) Mortgage insurance is effectively an insurance premium added to the borrower's monthly payment. This incremental payment can be eliminated for most loans, however, if the home appreciates to the point where the effective LTV of the transaction is 80% or less, if the borrower gets a new appraisal that confirms an LTV below 80%. Therefore, rapid home price appreciation creates an opportunity for the borrower to eliminate the MI payment. However, the borrower must contact the lender to affect this change. Such interaction between borrowers and lenders typically results in a new loan or product being marketed to the borrower, which in turn often culminates in the borrower prepaying their existing loan and taking out a new obligation. In addition, loans where the MI payment is made directly to the lender through "lender-paid" MI (LPMI) can only have the MI payment eliminated by refinancing the loan.

The example of LTV is instructive. It suggests that assessing and understanding prepayment behavior based on loan-level factors is more complex than merely applying a dogma to the attribute in question. Rather, it requires an understanding of why the observed behavior is occurring, and how different factors are interacting in the prevailing economic and lending environment, in order to gauge how persistent the effect may be and understand how prepayment behavior may evolve.

PREPAYMENT BEHAVIOR OF "NONFIXED-PAYMENT" PRODUCTS

In an earlier section of this chapter, we reviewed the impact of the increased popularity of ARMs on prepayment speeds for fixed rate loans.

The changing market for mortgage products has also impacted the prepayment behavior of adjustable rate loans, as well as loans with nonconstant payments such as interest-only products. In addition to the aversion to adjustable rate loans exhibited by a segment of the population, prepayments on loans with variable payment structures (which can be referenced as *nonfixed-payment products*, for the purposes of this discussion) are highly dependent on factors related to the timing of payment changes.

The change in monthly payment for nonfixed products after a loan "recasts" depends on a number of interacting factors. (The term *reset* typically indicates when the rate of the subject loan changes; a *recast* indicates that the payments on the loan are recalculated, based on the new rate and remaining term.) Clearly, the level of the reference index is an important driver of the ARM payment after the loan recasts. However, whether the loan has an interest-only feature, and how long the interest-only part of the loan remains in effect, are also significant in dictating the post-recast payments required on the loan.

To illustrate this phenomenon, Exhibit 4.12 shows the necessary payments on hypothetical amortizing and interest-only hybrid ARM loans with 6.0% original note rates. For both products, the payments are shown assuming LIBOR at 3.5% and 5.5% for the life of the loans. Assuming 3.5% LIBOR, the payment on the amortizing product drops roughly 2.5% after the recast in month 60, when the interest rate declines to 5.75%. With a 5.5% LIBOR assumption, however, the payment at the recast increases by more than 17%, as the postreset payment is assumed to increase to 7.75%.

For an adjustable rate loan, this so-called payment shock is almost entirely a function of the level of the index. However, the results are more pronounced when an adjustable rate is combined with an interest-only period, as shown for the hybrid ARM with a 60-month interest-only period in Exhibit 4.12. In this case, the payment increases in month 61 by more than 25% even at 3.5% LIBOR (which implies a 25 basis point drop in the loan's note rate). If a 5.5% LIBOR is assumed, the borrower's payment increases by more than 50% (from $2,000 per month to a monthly payment of more than $3,000). The payment increases substantially for the interest-only loan at the recast, even if the note rate remains unchanged or drops, because the balance of the loan must be amortized over a shorter term. Assuming that the loan's overall term is 360 months, a loan with an interest-only payment for five years is subsequently amortized over a 25-year remaining term. In this case, a borrower receives a lower payment for a period early in the life of the loan, at the cost of a higher payment after the loan recasts. In addition, a longer interest-only period will result in a greater payment shock at the recast; a 30-year loan with a 10-year interest-only period must amortize the remaining principal over a 20-year term.

EXHIBIT 4.12 Monthly Borrower Payments on Hypothetical Amortizing and Interest-Only 5/1 Hybrid ARMs (6.0% initial note rate, $400k loan balance, 225 basis point gross margin)

	Amortizing		5-Year Interest Only	
	3.5% LIBOR	5.5% LIBOR	3.5% LIBOR	5.5% LIBOR
1	2,398	2,398	2,000	2,000
2	2,398	2,398	2,000	2,000
3	2,398	2,398	2,000	2,000
4	2,398	2,398	2,000	2,000
5	2,398	2,398	2,000	2,000
6	2,398	2,398	2,000	2,000
7	2,398	2,398	2,000	2,000
8	2,398	2,398	2,000	2,000
9	2,398	2,398	2,000	2,000
10	2,398	2,398	2,000	2,000
11	2,398	2,398	2,000	2,000
12	2,398	2,398	2,000	2,000
55	2,398	2,398	2,000	2,000
56	2,398	2,398	2,000	2,000
57	2,398	2,398	2,000	2,000
58	2,398	2,398	2,000	2,000
59	2,398	2,398	2,000	2,000
60	2,342	2,811	2,516	3,021
61	2,342	2,811	2,516	3,021
62	2,342	2,811	2,516	3,021
63	2,342	2,811	2,516	3,021
64	2,342	2,811	2,516	3,021
355	2,342	2,811	2,516	3,021
356	2,342	2,811	2,516	3,021
357	2,342	2,811	2,516	3,021
358	2,342	2,811	2,516	3,021
359	2,342	2,811	2,516	3,021
360	2,342	2,811	2,516	3,021

EXHIBIT 4.13 Hypothetical Prepayment Ramp for an At-the-Money Amortizing 5/1 Hybrid ARM

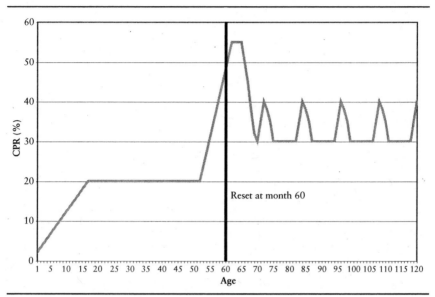

The prepayment behavior for loans with variable payment structures is strongly influenced by the amount and timing of payment changes. A hypothetical example of the prepayment behavior of an at-the-money 5/1 hybrid ARM, by loan age, is shown in Exhibit 4.13. The example shows the following stages in the life of the 5/1 hybrid ARM (and, by implication, other products with variable payments):

- An initial ramp over the first 16–17 months to around 20% CPR.
- Stable prepayments until roughly eight months prior to the recast.
- A spike in prepayments to approximately 55% CPR until roughly three to four months after the recast.
- A decline in speeds to roughly 30% CPR until the next reset in month 72.
- Annual spikes in prepayments associated with the annual reset of the loan's rate and recast of its payment.

Note that for a hybrid ARM, the loan resets annually after the first recast in month 60, which is why prepayments experience an annual short-term increase.

A similar logic drives prepayment behavior for a variety of nonfixed-payment products. Because of the increased payment shock on an interest-only hybrid ARM, it is reasonable to believe that the prepayment spike at the recast would be exacerbated. A spike speed approaching 70% CPR may occur on an interest-only hybrid ARM if LIBOR rates are high enough and the interest-only period is extended. (For example, this could occur for a 10/1 interest-only ARM at the reset.) The prepayment speed for fixed rate interest-only loans is also expected to accelerate at the recast, because of the payment-shock effect. Finally, prepayment speeds for hybrid ARMs with noncontiguous resets (i.e., a 5/1 hybrid ARM with a 10-year interest-only period) can be expected to have two smaller peaks in speed, coinciding with multiple payment shocks.

While the prepayment behavior of all mortgage products evolves over time, the prepayment speeds associated with nonfixed payment products exhibit significant changes as the loans age. There are a number of implications to this notion. Some products, such as fixed rate interest-only loans, are relatively new; historical prepayment data on these products are quite thin. Understanding how the borrowers' incentives evolve over time allows investors to develop some expectations for how prepayments speeds might behave, even in the absence of robust historical data.

In addition, the variability of prepayments on these products over time means that quoted prepayment speeds can be nebulous; their prepayments are highly dependent on the products' age and the time to recast. This means that simple comparisons across products or securities, such as "life CPRs," are not meaningful unless the prepayment changes due to approaching recasts are taken into account.

SUMMARY

Prepayment behavior has evolved greatly over time, impacted by changes in both the consumer mortgage and real estate markets. Since 2002, baseline prepayment speeds have been elevated by faster turnover and equity withdrawal, while refinancing activity has been boosted by a growing assortment of mortgage products into which borrowers can refinance and cut their monthly cash outlay. Understanding prepayment behavior requires a flexible approach; rather than rote memorization of the impact of different attributes on prepayment speeds, the relevant characteristics must be viewed in the context of the current environment for consumer financing and real estate.

Three
PART

Structuring

CHAPTER 5

Introduction to MBS Structuring Techniques

The mortgage-backed securities (MBS) market has, over the past two decades, exemplified the development and evolution of the structured transaction market. Structuring has expanded from its simplest form (a pass-through security, which "passes through" principal and interest to investors) to include techniques that allow investors to meet maturity and duration targets while choosing from different risk/reward trade-offs. Arguably, the ability to carve up and redirect mortgage cash flows to meet the needs of different investor clienteles has contributed strongly to the growth of the MBS market, which, at this writing, is the largest securities market in the world.

Many types of securitized and nonsecuritized assets can be used as the "collateral" (i.e., the assets providing the principal and interest cash flows) for structured deals. However, mortgages and MBS are the most interesting asset group around which to frame a discussion of structuring ideas and techniques. This is attributable to a number of factors:

- Mortgages are typically amortizing assets that generate principal cash flows throughout much of the loan's term.
- The product has varying degrees of credit risk, depending on the characteristics of the obligors.
- Mortgages have the unique dimension of prepayment risk, impacting returns in ways often difficult to foresee.

The interplay of these factors, and the varying appetites for each of the associated risk parameters, has resulted in a large variety of structuring variations. While this book is dedicated to discussing mortgage products and MBS structures, the techniques addressed in the remainder of the text are applicable to a growing number of asset classes, including consumer and commercial debt.

UNDERLYING LOGIC IN STRUCTURING CASH FLOWS

The goal of structuring is to maximize the proceeds received for the sale of any loans through the mechanism of securitization. Dealers, either acting as agents for an originator or as principals, seek to create structures that can be sold at the highest price, given market conditions, demand for various structured products, and the cost of creating such securities.

There are two primary ways that structuring cash flows maximizes deal proceeds and thus improves execution. Splitting and tranching cash flows allows bonds to be created to better match the specific risk-and-return profiles of different investor clienteles. As noted earlier in this book, the different segments of the fixed income markets have fairly standard duration and convexity preferences. In addition, investors within a market segment may vary in terms of their investment needs. For example, while banks typically invest in short-duration assets, each institution will have its own investment guidelines and performance measures. Cash flow structuring allows bonds to be created that more closely adhere to the investment objectives of a variety of investors and institutions.

The type of structuring described above typically takes place in agency deals and the senior (i.e., triple-A) bonds created off a private label structure. Many of the techniques discussed in later chapters are used to modify the return-and-risk profiles of the senior bonds by altering how principal and/or interest can be allocated to the bonds in question. The goal of the dealer is to create a combination of bonds that maximize the proceeds received once all the tranches are sold.

Structuring also allows dealers to create more cost-efficient structures, particularly with respect to private label structures where the cost of credit enhancement is embedded in the transaction through the mechanism of subordination. (In agency deals, by contrast, credit enhancement is obtained through the mechanism of the guaranty fee, which is obtained at the pool level and does not factor into a deal's costs.) In general terms, cost efficiency involves creating the largest possible amount of senior bonds while simultaneously obtaining the greatest possible proceeds for the resulting subordinated bonds and interests. The latter can often be complex, particularly for mortgage ABS deals that utilize both subordination and overcollateralization as credit enhancement techniques.

Note that for a nonagency private label deal, the transaction is the sole mechanism used to liquefy loan production into the capital markets. Typically, transactions take place in two ways; either dealers bid for loan packages in whole loan form from originators (through so-called conduits), or bid for parts of the deals to be marketed under the originator's deal name or "shelf." In the latter case, the senior bonds are generally bid as an unstructured senior pass-through with initial subordination assumed to be sufficient to provide it with a triple-A rating; the subordinates are sold as a package, with subordination percentages (or "splits") subject to the availability of the final loan pool. (In both cases, the final sizes are subject to an adjustment when the loan pool collateralizing the deal is assembled.) In either scenario, such bids are dictated by the execution the dealers can obtain by selling the resulting structure to investors. In contrast to an agency transaction (in which the transaction can be viewed as an arbitrage), the private label deal is an intrinsic part of the process of funding and distributing loan production; therefore, the efficiency of the structure has implications not only for the profitability of the deal, but ultimately affects how loans are priced to the consumer.

STRUCTURING DIFFERENT MORTGAGE PRODUCTS

The mortgage market can be broadly classified into two "kingdoms" from the perspective of borrower credit. The larger and more traditional sector is generally referenced as "prime" mortgages, in that the loans are considered to have a high degree of credit quality and are expected to exhibit a low incidence of defaults and principal losses. The primary focus of structuring is to improve the overall deal execution by creating bonds that appeal to different segments of the investor community, targeting both different average life and duration "buckets" and different degrees of exposure to prepayment and duration uncertainty.

Due to the high quality of the loans, credit enhancement in the prime sector is generally straightforward. As discussed above, credit support for prime deals is generally provided either through the auspices of government agencies or through senior/subordinate structures that create sectors within a structure that have different degrees of priority with respect to both cash inflows and loss writeoffs. While structurers have some flexibility with respect to creating the most efficient credit enhancement in private label structures, the credit support levels are typically dictated by the rating agencies, and the subordination structures are fairly straightforward. Thus structuring the senior portion of the deal (i.e., the triple-A bonds in the structure) has the greatest impact on the execution of the deal.

While there can be profound differences in borrower creditworthiness, loan-to-value (LTV) ratios, and degrees of documentation across the loan population, the incidence of credit losses in the prime sector is relatively low. The high quality of these loans allows the creation of senior/subordinate structures where the subordinate sector is fairly small, and the allocation of cash flows and losses is simple. In senior/subordinate (or "senior/sub") structures, multiple classes of bonds are created that have different priorities with respect to allocation of both cash flows and losses. The most senior bonds are typically structured to obtain a triple-A rating, and trade at relatively low yields; the more junior classes can have both investment-grade and noninvestment-grade ratings, and are traded at higher yields and spreads, depending on their exposure to potential losses.

The smaller "subprime" sector, by contrast, consists of loans that are made to less creditworthy borrowers. These borrowers may have a history of late or missed payments, or have less income or assets than required for prime lending. Subprime loans (along with other products such as second liens) are securitized in so-called mortgage ABS deals. As with private label structures in the prime sector, mortgage ABS deals have bonds with a range of cash flow priorities and ratings. However, the inherent riskiness of the loans, and the large amount of credit enhancement necessary in order to create senior bonds, means that the primary objective of mortgage ABS structuring is efficient credit enhancement, with the overriding goal of protecting the deal's senior tranches. While there are similarities between private label and mortgage ABS deals, the credit enhancement techniques utilized in the private label prime sector would be very inefficient if applied to subprime loans, especially if utilized as the sole means of credit support. For example, using subordination as the only form of credit enhancement would be inefficient for two reasons: The subordinate classes would be extremely large, and the incremental interest paid by the borrowers on these loans (which typically carry high rates due to their inherent riskiness) cannot be optimally utilized toward providing credit support for the senior tranches. As a result, mortgage ABS structures use a combination of subordination, overcollateralization (either by issuing less bonds than loans, or by using interest to pay down the bonds more rapidly than the loan collateral backing the deal), and "excess spread" (i.e., the aggregate note rate overaggregate bond coupon) to support the senior bonds. The direction of cash flows within the structure is also subject to a series of tests designed to protect the senior securities. Therefore, both the structuring of credit enhancement and the structuring trade-offs in a mortgage ABS structure are quite different than those in prime private label structures. (The techniques utilized in mortgage ABS structures will be addressed in Chapter 9.)

In all types of private label transactions, the overall size of the deal's subordinate sector depends both on the type of the underlying collateral and the unique attributes of the loan pool. Initial subordination levels (i.e., the deal's subordinate interest as a percentage of the total dollar amount of the pool at issuance) are determined by rating agencies, and currently range from the area of around 1% (for products such as 15-year loans with low incidence of credit losses) to levels exceeding 20% (for subprime loans). Required initial enhancement levels also change over time. For example, enhancement levels can be high for new products or product attributes where the historical credit data are relatively thin. As additional data become available over time and rating agencies become more comfortable with the quality of the collateral, it is possible that subordination levels may trend lower.

Additionally, as deal ages and the senior classes pay down, the effective level of subordination may also increase over time. This deleveraging effect occurs as the ratio of senior to subordinate classes decreases, due to structuring techniques designed to pay the senior classes more than their pro rata share of principal. This has the effect of enhancing the credit worthiness of the senior classes as time passes and the deal ages or "seasons."

As mentioned in Chapter 2, the straightforward senior/sub deals typically used in the prime sector are often called *shifting interest structures*, while structures used to securitize subprime loans are sometimes referenced as *overcollateralization* or *OC structures*. While there are numerous differences between them, there are also many similarities between the two forms of structures. In addition to utilizing subordination, for example, both types of deals employ a means of directing cash flows within the structure based on cash flow priorities called the "waterfall." This mechanism dictates the allocation of principal and interest on a monthly basis. In addition, all structured deals have residual tranches, which serve as the equity interest of the deal. In prime deals, however, residuals are almost always "noneconomic" in nature, in that such interests do not receive any cash flows. The only value of a noneconomic residual is that of the associated tax situation, which is negative at issuance (meaning that investors are paid to take the liability). However, in the subprime sector, the residual has economic value, since it is structured to receive cash flows if the collateral meets basic performance standards.

It is also noteworthy that deals securitizing prime loans are increasingly utilizing the OC structure. In part, this reflects the blurring of the lines between the prime and subprime "kingdoms." The growth of the alt-A sector, for example, reflects the growing proportion of loans made to borrowers with nontraditional credit attributes and reduced ability (or willingness) to document their income and assets. In 2005, deals backed by alt-A loans (particularly ARMs) increasingly began to be securitized using OC structures rather than the more straightforward senior/subordinate mechanism, as the techniques traditionally used to structure subprime deals provided more cost-efficient credit enhancement.

FUNDAMENTALS OF STRUCTURING CMOs

The following four chapters cover some of the fundamental concepts in structuring tranches within deals backed by prime loans. The various concepts can be broadly categorized as follows:

- Credit tranching
    - Senior/subordinate structures
    - Over-collateralization/excess spread structures
- Divisions of principal
    - Time tranching
    - Prepayment prioritization
    - Accretion direction
    - Non-accelerated seniors (or NAS) bonds
- Divisions of Interest
    - Coupon adjustment (or IO stripping)
    - Floater/inverse floater/two-tiered index (or TTIB) combinations
    - Floater/inverse IO combinations

While each of these concepts is addressed separately, it is important to note that the concepts are not mutually exclusive. For example, a form of coupon stripping involves a variation on the floater/inverse floater combination called an *inverse IO*. In addition, multiple techniques can be used to structure cash flows. As noted in the next chapter, an example may be the creation of a PAC/Support structure, which further involves time-tranching the PAC cash flow. In this context, the main PAC cash flows would be considered the "parent" bond with the resulting tranched PACs labeled as the "children." Most concepts are utilized in both agency and private label structures, although some are the exclusive purview of certain sectors. (NAS bonds, for example, are almost exclusively a nonagency phenomenon.)

Chapters 6 and 7 explain how to use fundamental structuring techniques for redirecting principal and interest, respectively, within agency CMO structures. Chapter 8 focuses on structuring techniques used for private label deals in the prime sector. While many of the structuring techniques are identical with those used in agency deals, there are some noteworthy differences between private label and agency structures. These differences stem from a number of sources, including both the necessity for credit enhancement in private label structures, as well as differences in the assumed prepayment behavior of the collateral backing these structures. Finally, Chapter 9 will focus on the overcollateralization structures typically used in mortgage ABS deals.

CHAPTER 6

Fundamental MBS Structuring Techniques: Divisions of Principal

Directing principal cash flows to different tranches within a deal is a primary method of creating bonds to meet the varying needs of different investor classes. Viewing a *collateralized mortgage obligation* (CMO) deal as a cash flow allocation mechanism, as described in the previous chapter, means that the allocation of principal is accomplished by the creation of a set of payment rules. The rules specify how cash flows are allocated for each month's payments and will vary depending on what type of bond is being created. For example, a deal's pay rules may state that a bond in the structure receives all principal paid by the collateral until the bond is fully paid; at that point, principal is directed to a different tranche. In this and the following chapter, we describe fundamental structuring techniques used in agency CMO deals, in which no credit enhancement is necessary due to the agency guaranty at the pool level. In both chapters, payment rules are shown for each structuring example, in order to demonstrate how different structuring techniques allocate principal and interest cash flows.

It is important to remember that a deal represents a "closed universe" of principal. A deal with a principal face value of $400 million means that the total amount of principal available to be paid is $400 million—not a penny more. At faster prepayment speeds, for example, principal cash flows are paid to the investor sooner, leaving less cash flow available later in the deal's life. Particularly in discussing the more complex structures, the question becomes not how much principal but *when* principal is paid to the investor. Interest, however, is not fixed; rather, it is a function of the outstanding principal balance at any particular point in time.

TIME TRANCHING

The most fundamental form of structuring is time tranching, which creates a series of bonds with different average lives and durations from either a collateral group or a preexisting parent bond. Basically, principal cash flows are allocated sequentially to a series of tranches. All principal payments are directed to the shortest maturity bond until it is fully amortized. Principal is then directed to the second bond until it is fully amortized, and so on until the principal source is fully amortized. A simple representation of the concept is shown in panels A and B of Exhibit 6.1, where passthroughs are structured into short, intermediate, and long classes. Note that the collateral does not have to be pass-throughs; as noted above, other tranche types can be created and subsequently time-tranched.

In structuring a set of sequentials, the first step involves the specification of the number of sequential tranches and the associated average lives. One bond (typically the long or "last cash flow" bond) acts as a "plug" that receives cash flows after the other bonds receive the principal allocation necessary to achieve their average life target. Using the prepayment pricing speed, the beginning and ending date are calculated such that the average life target of each tranche is met, with the remain-

EXHIBIT 6.1   Sequential Tranching
Panel A: At Issuance

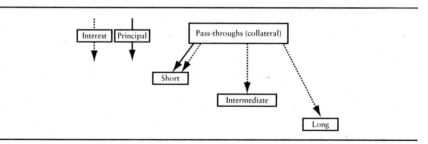

Panel B: First Tranche Paid Off

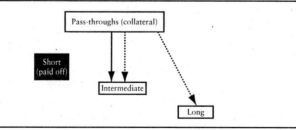

ing cash flows directed to the plug bond. In some cases, other parameters may also be targeted in the structuring exercise. For example, sequential tranches can be structured to pay off in a particular month, with the average lives being subject to the attributes of the resulting tranche (or "falling out"). Note that since structuring models use cash flows from the collateral, the structuring exercise depends heavily upon the availability of the relevant cash flows. Put differently, not all structures are creatable; the ability to create a structure that meets a series of average life or maturity targets is contingent on the availability of cash flows sufficient to create the desired structure.

To illustrate a sequential-pay CMO, we discuss Deal-01, a hypothetical deal made up to illustrate the basic features of the structure. The collateral for this hypothetical CMO is a hypothetical pass-through with a total par value of $400 million and the following characteristics: (1) the pass-through coupon rate is 5.5%; (2) the weighted average coupon (WAC) is 6.0%; and (3) the weighted average maturity (WAM) is 357 months. This is the same pass-through that we used in Chapter 3 to describe the cash flows of a pass-through based on different prepayment assumptions.

From this $400 million of collateral, four bond classes or tranches are created. Their characteristics are summarized in Exhibit 6.2. The total par value of the four tranches is equal to the par value of the collateral (i.e., the pass-through pool or pools). In this simple structure, the coupon rate is the same for each tranche and also the same as the collateral's coupon

EXHIBIT 6.2   Deal-01: A Hypothetical Four-Tranche Sequential-Pay Structure

Tranche	Par Amount	Coupon Rate (%)	Average Life
A	194,500,000	5.5	3.4
B	36,000,000	5.5	7.3
C	96,500,000	5.5	10.9
D	73,000,000	5.5	19.8
Collateral	400,000,000	5.5	8.6

Payment rules:
1. *For payment of periodic coupon interest.* Disburse periodic coupon interest to each tranche on the basis of the amount of principal outstanding at the beginning of the period.
2. *For disbursement of principal payments.* Disburse principal payments to tranche A until it is completely paid off. After tranche A is completely paid off, disburse principal payments to tranche B until it is completely paid off. After tranche B is completely paid off, disburse principal payments to tranche C until it is completely paid off. After tranche C is completely paid off, disburse principal payments to tranche D until it is completely paid off.

rate. (Note that this is often not the case, as bond coupons are often reduced or "stripped" in order that they trade close to par. This is especially true for the bonds in the structure with short average lives during regimes when the yield curve is steep and short rates are relatively low, as it would tend to make the dollar prices of these bonds unacceptably high. We discuss techniques for coupon stripping in the subsequent chapter on structuring interest.)

As discussed previously, a CMO is created by redistributing the cash flow—interest and principal—to the different tranches based on a set of payment rules. The payment rules at the bottom of Exhibit 6.2 set forth how the monthly cash flow from the collateral is to be distributed to the four tranches. There are separate rules for the payment of the coupon interest and the payment of principal, the principal being the total of the regularly scheduled principal payment and any prepayments.

In Deal-01, each tranche receives periodic coupon interest payments based on its outstanding balance. The disbursement of the principal, however, is made subject to the deal's payment rules. A tranche is not entitled to receive principal until the entire principal of the tranche before it has been paid off. More specifically, tranche A receives all the principal payments until the entire principal amount owed to that tranche, $194,500,000, is paid off; then tranche B begins to receive principal and continues to do so until it is paid the entire $36,000,000. Tranche C then receives principal, and when it is paid off, tranche D starts receiving principal payments.

While the payment rules for the disbursement of the principal payments are known, the precise amount of the principal in each period is not. This will depend on the principal cash flows generated by the collateral, which in turn depends on the actual prepayment rate of the collateral. In order to project monthly cash flows, a prepayment assumption must be utilized. In the example, we assumed 165% PSA, which generates the cashflows for the collateral pool shown in the earlier example.

To demonstrate how the payment rules for Deal-01 work, Exhibit 6.3 shows the cash flow for selected months assuming the collateral prepays at 165% PSA. For each tranche, the exhibit shows: (1) the balance at the end of the month; (2) the principal paid down (regularly scheduled principal repayment plus prepayments); and (3) interest. In month 1, the cash flow for the collateral consists of a principal payment of $734,171 and interest of $1.83 million (0.055 times $400 million divided by 12). The interest payment is distributed to the four tranches based on the amount of the par value outstanding. So, for example, tranche A receives $891,458 (0.055 times $194,500,000 divided by 12) of the $1.83 million. The principal, however, is all distributed to tranche A. Therefore, the cash flow for tranche A in month 1 is $1,625,630. The

EXHIBIT 6.3   Monthly Cash Flow for Selected Months for Deal-01 Assuming 165% PSA

	A			B		
Month	Beginning Balance	Principal	Interest	Beginning Balance	Principal	Interest
1	194,500,000	734,171	891,458	36,000,000	0	165,000
2	193,765,829	846,102	888,093	36,000,000	0	165,000
3	192,919,727	957,702	884,215	36,000,000	0	165,000
4	191,962,024	1,068,878	879,826	36,000,000	0	165,000
5	190,893,146	1,179,534	874,927	36,000,000	0	165,000
6	189,713,612	1,289,576	869,521	36,000,000	0	165,000
7	188,424,036	1,398,910	863,610	36,000,000	0	165,000
8	187,025,126	1,507,443	857,198	36,000,000	0	165,000
9	185,517,683	1,615,081	850,289	36,000,000	0	165,000
10	183,902,602	1,721,732	842,887	36,000,000	0	165,000
11	182,180,870	1,827,305	834,996	36,000,000	0	165,000
12	180,353,565	1,931,709	826,621	36,000,000	0	165,000
75	8,508,703	2,190,871	38,998	36,000,000	0	165,000
76	6,317,832	2,170,666	28,957	36,000,000	0	165,000
77	4,147,166	2,150,640	19,008	36,000,000	0	165,000
78	1,996,526	1,996,526	9,151	36,000,000	134,266	165,000
79	0	0	0	35,865,734	2,111,120	164,385
80	0	0	0	33,754,614	2,091,623	154,709
81	0	0	0	31,662,991	2,072,299	145,122
82	0	0	0	29,590,693	2,053,147	135,624
83	0	0	0	27,537,546	2,034,165	126,214
84	0	0	0	25,503,381	2,015,351	116,891
85	0	0	0	23,488,030	1,996,705	107,653
95	0	0	0	4,333,172	1,819,126	19,860
96	0	0	0	2,514,045	1,802,226	11,523
97	0	0	0	711,819	711,819	3,263
98	0	0	0	0	0	0
99	0	0	0	0	0	0
100	0	0	0	0	0	0
101	0	0	0	0	0	0
102	0	0	0	0	0	0
103	0	0	0	0	0	0
104	0	0	0	0	0	0
105	0	0	0	0	0	0

EXHIBIT 6.3 (Continued)

	C			D		
	Beginning Balance	Principal	Interest	Beginning Balance	Principal	Interest
1	96,500,000	0	442,292	73,000,000	0	334,583
2	96,500,000	0	442,292	73,000,000	0	334,583
3	96,500,000	0	442,292	73,000,000	0	334,583
4	96,500,000	0	442,292	73,000,000	0	334,583
5	96,500,000	0	442,292	73,000,000	0	334,583
6	96,500,000	0	442,292	73,000,000	0	334,583
7	96,500,000	0	442,292	73,000,000	0	334,583
8	96,500,000	0	442,292	73,000,000	0	334,583
9	96,500,000	0	442,292	73,000,000	0	334,583
10	96,500,000	0	442,292	73,000,000	0	334,583
11	96,500,000	0	442,292	73,000,000	0	334,583
12	96,500,000	0	442,292	73,000,000	0	334,583
95	96,500,000	0	442,292	73,000,000	0	334,583
96	96,500,000	0	442,292	73,000,000	0	334,583
97	96,500,000	1,073,657	442,292	73,000,000	0	334,583
98	95,426,343	1,768,876	437,371	73,000,000	0	334,583
99	93,657,468	1,752,423	429,263	73,000,000	0	334,583
100	91,905,045	1,736,116	421,231	73,000,000	0	334,583
101	90,168,928	1,719,955	413,274	73,000,000	0	334,583
102	88,448,973	1,703,938	405,391	73,000,000	0	334,583
103	86,745,035	1,688,064	397,581	73,000,000	0	334,583
104	85,056,970	1,672,332	389,844	73,000,000	0	334,583
105	83,384,639	1,656,739	382,180	73,000,000	0	334,583
175				71,179,833	850,356	326,241
176				70,329,478	842,134	322,343
177				69,487,344	833,986	318,484
178				68,653,358	825,912	314,661
179				67,827,446	817,911	310,876
180				67,009,535	809,982	307,127
181				66,199,553	802,125	303,415
182				65,397,428	794,339	299,738
183				64,603,089	786,624	296,097
184				63,816,465	778,978	292,492
185				63,037,487	771,402	288,922
350				1,137,498	132,650	5,214
351				1,004,849	131,049	4,606
352				873,800	129,463	4,005
353				744,337	127,893	3,412
354				616,444	126,338	2,825
355				490,105	124,799	2,246
356				365,307	123,274	1,674
357				242,033	121,764	1,109
358				120,269	120,269	551

principal balance at the end of month 1 for tranche A is $193,765,829 (the original principal balance of $194,500,000 less the principal payment of $734,171). No principal payment is distributed to the three other tranches because there is still a principal balance outstanding for tranche A. This will be true for months 2 through 78.

After month 78, the principal balance will be zero for tranche A. For the collateral the cash flow in month 78 is $3,081,817, consisting of a principal payment of $2,130,792 and interest of $91,025. At the beginning of month 79 (end of month 78), the principal balance for tranche A is $1,996,526. Therefore, $1,996,526 of the $2,130,792 of the principal payment from the collateral will be disbursed to tranche A. After this payment is made, no additional principal payments are made to this tranche as the principal balance is zero. The remaining principal payment from the collateral, $134,266, is disbursed to tranche B. According to the assumed prepayment speed of 165% PSA, tranche B then begins receiving principal payments in month 79.

Exhibit 6.3 shows that tranche B is fully paid off by month 97, when tranche C begins to receive principal payments. Tranche C is not fully paid off until month 172, at which time tranche D begins receiving the remaining principal payments. The maturity (i.e., the time until the principal is fully paid off) for these four tranches assuming 165% PSA is 78 months for tranche A, 97 months for tranche B, 172 months for tranche C, and 357 months for tranche D.

The *principal paydown window* for a tranche is the time period between the beginning and the ending of the principal payments to that tranche. So, for example, for tranche A, the principal paydown window would be month 1 to month 78 assuming 165% PSA. For tranche B it is from month 78 to month 97. The window is also specified in terms of the length of the time from the beginning of the principal paydown window to the end of the principal paydown window. For tranche A, the window would be stated as 78 months, for tranche B 19 months. In confirmation of trades involving CMOs, the principal paydown window is specified in terms of the initial month that principal is expected to be received to the final month that principal is expected to be received.

Let's look at what has been accomplished by creating the CMO. First, in the previous chapter we saw that the average life of the passthrough is 8.6 years, assuming a prepayment speed of 165% PSA. Exhibit 6.4 reports the average life of the collateral and the four tranches assuming different prepayment speeds. Notice that the four tranches have average lives that are both shorter and longer than the collateral, thereby attracting investors who have a preference for an average life different from that of the collateral.

EXHIBIT 6.4 Average Life For the Collateral and Four Tranches of Deal-01 at Different PSA Assumptions

	100	125	165	250	400	500	600	700
Collateral	11.2	10.1	8.6	6.4	4.5	3.7	3.2	2.9
Tranche A	4.7	4.1	3.4	2.7	2.0	1.8	1.6	1.5
Tranche B	10.4	8.9	7.3	5.3	3.8	3.2	2.8	2.6
Tranche C	15.1	13.2	10.9	7.9	5.3	4.4	3.8	3.4
Tranche D	24.0	22.4	19.8	15.2	10.3	8.4	7.0	6.0

Note that the average lives of all the tranches in Deal-01 still have considerable variability. The sequential structure does provide some degree of prepayment protection, in that the longer tranches (i.e., tranches B, C, and D) do not receive any principal until the tranches in front of them in priority (beginning with class A) are paid off. Therefore, even at fast prepayment speeds, the later (or "locked-out") tranches receive some protection due to the presence of the shorter tranche, although their average lives and durations will shorten as prepayment speeds increase.

PLANNED AMORTIZATION CLASSES (PACs) AND THE PAC/SUPPORT STRUCTURE

The PAC/Support structure is designed to create mortgage bonds that have reduced exposure to prepayment risk and cash flow uncertainty, and creates securities targeted to appeal to buyers of bullet structures such as corporate bonds. The structuring process involves dividing the available cash flows within a deal into two or more groups, and assigning one group priority in receiving scheduled amounts of monthly principal payments from the collateral. The result is that the prioritized group (and bonds tranched from it) has average lives, durations, and cash flow windows that are constant within a predesignated range of prepayment speeds. The bonds that are lower in priority, however, have increased cash flow volatility, and typically trade to higher yields to entice investors.

The actual process of structuring PACs involves the following steps:

1. Designating the range of prepayment speeds within which the classes will (at issuance) have unchanged principal cash flows (known as the PAC *band* or PAC *collars*).
2. Generating a schedule of principal payments, using the speeds chosen as the upper and lower limits of the PAC band.

The PAC band at issuance (which is sometimes designated as the "structuring band"), is generally chosen at a range of prepayment speeds above and below the expected prepayment speed of the collateral, given the prevailing interest rate environment. In agency deals, the lower band (quoted as an assumed PSA) is generally somewhere in the area of 100% PSA, while the upper band is generally 250% PSA or higher. (PACs are less common in private label structures, but the range of the bands generally exhibits more variability.) The lower and upper limits of the bands, as well as their width, often reflect the perception of risk in the market. For example, bonds might be structured with a 75% PSA lower band in a rising-rate environment where speeds are expected to slow, or may have a 300% upper band when fast prepayments are a concern.

Once the structuring band is designated, the PAC schedule can be generated. The schedule is calculated from a vector of the principal cash flows generated by the prepayment speeds represented by the lower and upper PAC bands. The schedule is derived as follows:

- Generate principal cash flows for the lower and upper band speeds.
- The lower of the two monthly principal payment derived from the calculations is the cash flow used for the PAC schedule.

The following discussion uses the example of a hypothetical PAC/Support deal collateralized by $400 million 5.5% MBS pass-throughs. The process of creating PACs with a band of 100% and 250% PSA is shown in panels A and B of Exhibit 6.5. Panel A shows the principal cash flows at the two designated speeds. Note that the principal cash flows at 250% PSA are much higher during the early years of the deal than at the slower prepayment speed. However, the principal cash flows in the later years are reduced since the effect of the faster speed is to return principal to the investor sooner. In the example, the smaller amount of monthly principal is generated by the lower band until month 109. This "crossover point" occurs when the upper band generates a smaller amount of principal. The resulting PAC schedule is shown graphically in panel B of Exhibit 6.5. The principal balance of the PACs is the sum of the principal cash flows generated by the schedule, which in panel B is the area below the line. (Note that the "PAC schedule" also refers to the schedule of declining principal balances that are used to allocate the PACs' principal cash flows, as discussed later in this chapter. This schedule, however, is generated by first calculating the monthly principal payments at the lower and upper bands, using the process described above. For the sake of clarity, we will reference the PACs' "balance schedule" separately.)

Once the PAC structure is created, the PAC class can be treated as a parent bond and sequentially time-tranched in the fashion described ear-

EXHIBIT 6.5 Creating a PAC Schedule for 5.5% MBS

Panel A: Generating Cash Flows for $400 Million 5.5% MBS at Different Prepayment Speeds

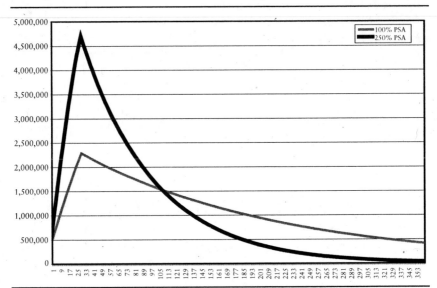

Panel B: The PAC Schedule for 5.5% MBS Pass-Throughs with a 100–250% PSA Band

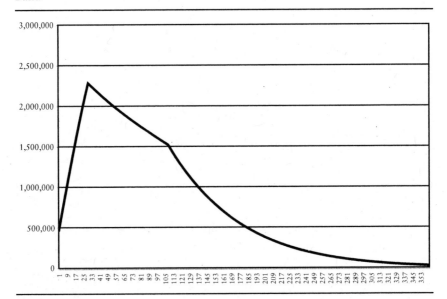

lier, creating bonds with different average lives. Typically, deals might contain short (one- through four-year average life), intermediate (5–10 year) and long (greater than 10-year) PACs, depending on demand from different investor segments. While typical PAC deals create bonds with average lives across the curve, the actual structure is subject to market demand and the extent to which available cash flows can be allocated to create bonds desired by investors.

The cash flows remaining after the PACs are paid their scheduled principal are referred to as *support bonds* or *companion bonds*. The average life and duration profiles of such bonds are more volatile because of the prepayment leverage introduced by the PACs. Put differently, the average life of the support will extend proportionately more at slower prepayment speeds, and contract more at fast prepayment speeds, than the deal's collateral.

A useful analogy is to view the CMO structure as if it were a corporate balance sheet. In a case where a corporation has no debt, its *earnings per share* (EPS) will be no more volatile than its after-tax earnings. Introducing debt means that the EPS are more volatile because of the effects of leverage, as payments must be made to the debt holders (through the equivalent of a schedule) before earnings flow through to shareholders. In this framework, a structure without PACs is the equivalent of the unleveraged corporation. As such, the PACs are the equivalent of debt, and the support bonds act as leveraged equity.

A graphic representation of the structure at issuance is shown in Exhibit 6.6. Note that since the deal is structured using a 165% PSA pricing speed, the size of the support bonds is the difference between principal cash flows generated at the 165% PSA speed and the PAC schedule.

The process of creating PACs through the schedule mechanism has some interesting implications. For example, the width of the structuring band not only dictates the quality of the PACs (i.e., the range of prepayments within which the band offers protection) but also the size of the PAC classes, as illustrated by Exhibit 6.7. The exhibit shows the same PAC schedule as in Exhibit 6.5B, along with a schedule created for PACs with a 75% to 300% PSA band. If this schedule were inserted into Exhibit 6.6, the lower level of the line representing the PAC schedule means that the size of the PACs is smaller. Since the face value of total bonds is the same, the value of support bonds has increased. However, since there are fewer PACs, the support bonds are less leveraged and as such, the average lives and durations are less sensitive to changes in prepayment speeds and thus less volatile. Conversely, a narrower band (creating a "worse" PAC) creates more PACs and less (but more sensitive or "whippy") supports.

EXHIBIT 6.6 Graphic Representation of PAC/Support Structure for $400 Million 5.5% MBS

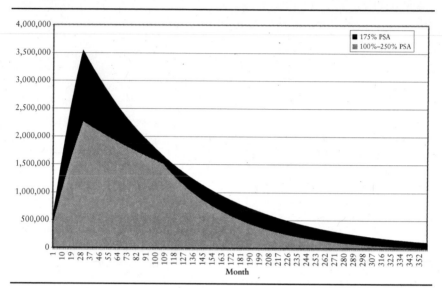

EXHIBIT 6.7 PAC Schedules for $400 Million 5.5% Deals with Different Bands

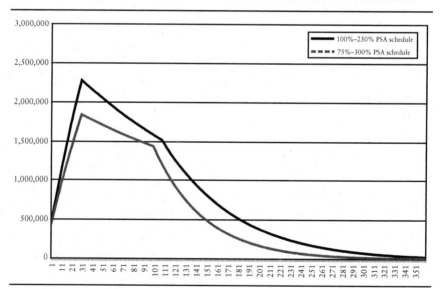

A simple deal (referenced as *Deal-02*) structured using the same collateral pool as in the prior section is shown in Exhibit 6.8 The average lives of the bonds created in Deal-02, as well as the MBS collateral, are shown at a variety of prepayment assumptions in Exhibit 6.9. The exhibit highlights the fact that, at the time of issuance the average life of the PAC is designed to remain stable within the PAC bands. The support bond, by contrast, has an average life which is much more volatile than either the PAC or the underlying collateral. This is a result of the prepayment "leveraging" effect of the schedule, as discussed previously in this section. The actual dollar amounts of the PAC schedule at different points in time are shown in Exhibit 6.10.

Like a balance sheet, a PAC/support structure is a snapshot of relative proportions at a point in time. After issuance, as time passes and the deal experiences actual prepayments, the relative proportions of

EXHIBIT 6.8   Deal-02: CMO Structure with One PAC and One Support Bond

Tranche	Par Amount	Coupon Rate
P (PAC)	$284,984,594	5.5
S (Support)	115,015,406	5.5
Total	$400,000,000	

Payment rules:
1. For *payment of periodic coupon interest.* Disburse periodic coupon interest to each tranche on the basis of the amount of principal outstanding at the beginning of the period.
2. For *disbursement of principal payments.* Disburse principal payments to tranche P based on its schedule of principal repayments. Tranche P has priority with respect to current and future principal payments to satisfy the schedule. Any excess principal payments in a month over the amount necessary to satisfy the schedule for tranche P are paid to tranche S. When tranche S is completely paid off, all principal payments are to be made to tranche P regardless of the schedule.

EXHIBIT 6.9   Average Lives of Collateral and Bonds Structured in Deal-02

	PSA (PAC band 100%–250%)								
	0	50	75	100	165	250	400	600	800
Collateral	19.2	14.4	12.7	11.2	8.6	6.4	4.5	3.2	2.6
P	15.8	10.2	8.6	7.7	7.7	7.7	5.5	4.0	3.2
S	27.7	24.9	22.7	20.0	10.7	3.3	1.9	1.4	1.1

EXHIBIT 6.10 Monthly Principal Payments and PAC Schedule for Deal-02 ($400 million 5.5% coupon pass-throughs with a 6.0% WAC and 358 WAM assuming a PAC band of 100% to 250% PSA)

	100% PSA	250% PSA	PAC Schedule
1	603,349	905,962	603,349
2	671,785	1,075,156	671,785
3	740,025	1,243,849	740,025
4	808,033	1,411,824	808,033
5	875,773	1,578,866	875,773
6	943,211	1,744,759	943,211
7	1,010,311	1,909,287	1,010,311
8	1,077,038	2,072,236	1,077,038
9	1,143,357	2,233,394	1,143,357
10	1,209,235	2,392,550	1,209,235
11	1,274,636	2,549,495	1,274,636
12	1,339,527	2,704,025	1,339,527
13	1,403,873	2,855,937	1,403,873
14	1,467,643	3,005,032	1,467,643
15	1,530,802	3,151,118	1,530,802
16	1,593,318	3,294,003	1,593,318
17	1,655,159	3,433,506	1,655,159
18	1,716,294	3,569,446	1,716,294
101	1,561,958	1,641,939	1,561,958
102	1,553,853	1,618,135	1,553,853
103	1,545,791	1,594,665	1,545,791
104	1,537,770	1,571,526	1,537,770
105	1,529,790	1,548,713	1,529,790
211	879,892	312,797	312,797
212	875,297	307,919	307,919
213	870,726	303,113	303,113
346	431,936	29,297	29,297
347	429,646	28,692	28,692
348	427,368	28,097	28,097
349	425,102	27,511	27,511
350	422,848	26,936	26,936
351	420,605	26,369	26,369
352	418,374	25,812	25,812
353	416,154	25,265	25,265
354	413,946	24,726	24,726
355	411,749	24,196	24,196
356	409,563	23,676	23,676
357	407,388	23,163	23,163
358	405,225	22,660	22,660

PACs and supports changes, leading to changes in the bands of the remaining PACs. To understand this concept, it is important to understand the actual process of allocating monthly cash flows. As an example, assume a simple deal with one PAC (P) and one support class (S). The monthly principal cash flows would be allocated as follows:

- Pay P to its balance schedule.
- Pay remaining cash flow to S.
- If S is paid off, pay remaining cash flow to P.

In the event of sustained faster prepayments, it is likely that S will be paid off. In that case, the payment rules would essentially be the same as for a sequential structure. Keep in mind that it is highly unlikely that realized prepayment speeds will be equivalent to those assumed in structuring the deal and creating the PAC schedule. Therefore, the face value of supports, and the proportion of supports relative to the PACs they are supporting, will change as the deal ages. This means that the protection offered by PAC structures is neither constant nor guaranteed, but can erode when prepayments deviate substantially from those established by the structuring band.

An eroding PAC band might change from 100% to 250% PSA at issuance to 115% to 235% nine months after the deal is closed. The 115% to 235% PSA band is referred to as an effective band. If the band deteriorates further, it may at some point be referred to as a "bruised" or "dented" PAC; when the band is entirely eliminated, the bond becomes a "broken" or "busted" PAC. Note also that a broken PAC can still have a schedule; the lack of an effective band means that that there are no prepayment speeds at which the schedule can be met.

In addition, fast and slow realized prepayment speeds impact the structure differently. Because the upper band dictates the schedule for the later cash flows, fast prepayment speeds disproportionately impact the longer PACs, and cause their upper band to deteriorate. The effect on the structure is illustrated in panel A of Exhibit 6.11. Conversely, as shown in panel B of Exhibit 6.11, slow speeds tend to cause the lower band on short PACs to increase, as there is not enough principal cash flow to meet the schedule. In this case, the band does not deteriorate, since the slow speeds pay off the support bonds more slowly and give the PACs more support. Rather, the band tends to shift upward, so that an initial band of 100% to 250% PSA might change to 175% to 325% over time.

As suggested by Exhibit 6.6, creating PACs from the entire pool of collateral means that the PAC cash flows run for the entire term of the collateral, that is, from month 1 through 360 (or shorter, if the WAM of the collateral is less than 360 months). However, in certain deals, only a portion of the PAC cash flows are structured as PAC tranches, which creates

EXHIBIT 6.11   Impact of Different Realized Prepayment Speeds on PAC Structure
Panel A: Prepayments Above Upper Band

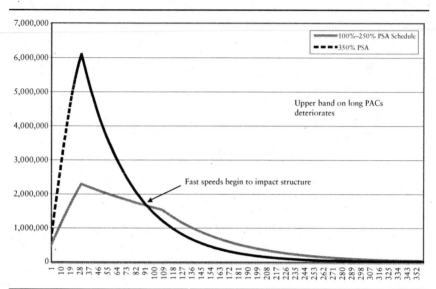

Panel B: Prepayments Below Lower Band

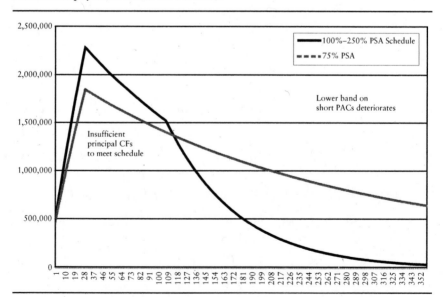

interesting structuring permutations. In the above example, suppose that the PACs in a deal begin paying principal cash flows after month 20 (called *locking out* the PACs). In that case, the short PAC cash flows are mixed with the support cash flows early in the life of the deal. Bonds structured from these cash flows are *barbelled* in nature, and often have attractive average life and duration profiles at issuance. However, the profile of the bonds changes over time as the bonds age. A major change occurs when the lockout expires and the structured PACs begin to receive principal. Since no more PAC cash flows are available to be directed to the barbell tranche, the bond then becomes a pure support bond.

Exhibit 6.12 shows an example, of this technique using the structure with the PAC schedule derived for the 100% to 250% PSA band shown previously. This structure locks out the PACs until month 20, that is, the PAC cash flows structured and sold as PAC tranches begin with the cash flows in month 20. As described above, the PAC cash flows from month 1 through 19 are mixed together with the support cash flows. After that, the PAC cash flows support PAC tranches that are sold to investors. The cash flows in the shaded area in Exhibit 6.12 are, therefore, an amalgamation of PAC and support cash flows with performance characteristics that change over time in an unpredictable fashion.

Note that a similar phenomenon occurs if the longer PAC cash flows are "cut off," meaning that the long PAC and support cash flows are

EXHIBIT 6.12 Graphic Representation of PAC/Support Structure with PACs Locked Out until Month 20

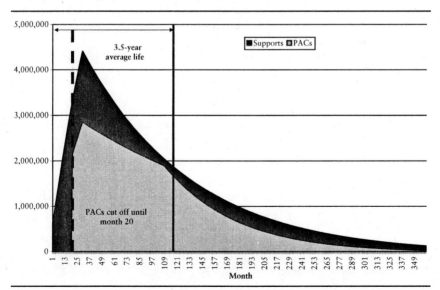

mixed together. This creates tranches with cash flows that are somewhat more volatile than long sequentials. However, demand for these cash flows is often strong because of the perception that the cash flows of very seasoned collateral (which will be collateralizing these tranches when they ultimately begin to pay principal) are inherently stable.

Creating a Series of PAC Bonds

Most CMO PAC structures have more than one class of PAC bonds. Exhibit 6.13 shows six PAC bonds created from the single PAC bond in Deal-07. We refer to this CMO structure as Deal-03. The total par value of the six PAC bonds is equal to $284.9 million, which is the amount of the single PAC bond in Deal-02.

Exhibit 6.14 shows the average life for the six PAC bonds and the support bond in Deal-03 at various prepayment speeds. From a PAC bond in Deal-02 with an average life of 7.7, we have created six PAC bonds with an average life as short as 1.0 years (P-A) and as long as 18.3 years (P-F) if prepayments stay within 100% and 250% PSA.

EXHIBIT 6.13 Deal-03: CMO Structure with Six PACs Bonds and One Support Bond

Tranche	Par Amount	Average Life
P-A	23,217,400	1.0
P-B	93,217,500	3.5
P-C	21,889,000	5.9
P-D	44,572,200	7.5
P-E	65,418,800	10.9
P-F	36,669,700	18.3
S	115,015,400	10.7

Payment rules:
1. *For payment of periodic coupon interest.* Disburse periodic coupon interest to each tranche on the basis of the amount of principal outstanding at the beginning of the period.
2. *For disbursement of principal payments.* Disburse principal payments to tranches P-A to P-F based on their respective schedules of principal repayments. Tranche P-A has priority with respect to current and future principal payments to satisfy the schedule. Any excess principal payments in a month over the amount necessary to satisfy the schedule for tranche P-A are paid to tranche S. Once tranche P-A is completely paid off, tranche P-B has priority, then tranche P-C, etc. When tranche S is completely paid off, all principal payments are to be made to the remaining PAC tranches in order of priority regardless of the schedule.

EXHIBIT 6.14   Average Lives of the PACs In Deal-03 Assuming Different
Prepayment Speeds

				PSA (PAC Band 100% to 250%)					
	0	50	75	100	165	250	400	600	800
P-A	2.3	1.3	1.1	1.0	1.0	1.0	1.0	1.0	1.0
P-B	10.2	5.1	4.1	3.5	3.5	3.5	3.1	2.5	2.1
P-C	15.9	8.8	7.1	5.9	5.9	5.9	4.3	3.2	2.6
P-D	18.4	11.1	9.0	7.5	7.5	7.5	5.2	3.7	3.0
P-E	21.8	15.1	12.5	10.9	10.9	10.9	7.3	5.1	3.9
P-F	24.6	19.9	18.5	18.3	18.3	18.3	12.5	8.5	6.3

As expected, the average lives are stable if the prepayment speed is between 100% and 250% PSA. Notice that even outside this range the average life is stable for several of the PAC bonds. For example, PAC P-A is stable even if prepayment speeds are as high as 800% PSA. For the PAC P-B, the average life does not vary when prepayments are between 100% and 250% PSA.

This demonstrates the earlier point, illustrated in Exhibit 6.11A, that fast prepayment speeds have less of an impact on the short end of the PAC cash flow than on the longer part of the schedule. Put differently, at least some of the support bond is available to protect the P-A tranche throughout its life. Even at 800% PSA, for example, the support bond is not fully paid off until month 21; at that prepayment speed, the P-A is paid off by month 20. (This also highlights the difference between the structuring band and the effective band, as mentioned previously.)

By contrast, the P-B bond does not pay off completely at 800% PSA until month 30, well after the support has been paid off. Thus, the longer the PAC bond's average life, the less chance it has that the support bond will remain outstanding at fast prepayment speeds. In turn, this reduces the effective upper band of the PACs.

A major implication of this discussion is that PAC deals have an implicit time element which is not readily apparent when examining the structure at issuance. One way to demonstrate this is to calculate the effective bands at a point in time in the future if prepayment speeds diverge from the structuring band. This is demonstrated in Exhibit 6.15. The table in the exhibit shows the effective bands for the different PACs in the deal if various prepayment speeds are run for a period of one year. From the table in the exhibit, we note the following:

EXHIBIT 6.15 Effective Bands for PACs in Deal-03 at Different Prepayment Speeds After 12 Months

		12-Month PSA					
		50	75	165	400	600	800
P-A	Lower	302	180	100	106	111	117
	Upper	896	896	639	639	639	639
P-B	Lower	116	107	102	108	114	121
	Upper	305	303	298	282	268	253
P-C	Lower	103	102	102	110	118	127
	Upper	278	277	272	260	249	237
P-D	Lower	103	102	103	114	125	146
	Upper	259	258	255	246	238	230
P-E	Lower	102	101	102	115	134	153
	Upper	255	255	253	239	215	188
P-F	Lower	84	83	85	94	103	113
	Upper	253	253	252	243	230	214

■ The effective bands are not identical to the structuring band even if the deal prepays at the pricing speed. As described previously, the effective upper band for the P-A tranche is significantly higher than the 250% PSA structuring band; the effective lower band for the P-F tranche, however, is lower than the structuring band of 100% PSA.

■ At slower early speeds, the effective upper bands of all tranches increase. This is because the slow prepayment speeds leave more support bonds available to support the PACs if speeds subsequently increase. However, the lower band of the short PACs also increases at slow speeds, since there is not enough principal being created to meet their schedule.

■ Fast early speeds result in the deterioration of the effective PAC bands of virtually all the tranches. For the short PAC, the erosion only impacts the lower band. However, both the lower and upper effective bands are impacted for the P-B through P-F tranches since the fast speeds paydown the support bonds faster than initially planned. This leaves less support for the PACs after the first 12 months.

Note that like the PAC cash flow, the supports can also be tranched sequentially, in order to create different average lives. This does not change the way the support bonds interact with the PACs. This type of time-tranching is done, as in other sectors, to create bonds that more closely match the investment needs of various clienteles. For example, a short support bond might be sold to an investor looking for prepayment speeds to remain fast or increase, while longer supports often appeal to retail investors looking for high current yields who are not particularly sensitive to changes in average lives and durations. In addition, all sectors of the support cash flow may be structured further into so-called MBS derivatives.[1]

Finally, note that multiple PAC groups with different cash flow priorities can be structured within a deal. After creating an initial PAC/support structure, the support cash flows may be used to structure second level PACs. This creates so-called PAC2s, meaning that they have secondary priority for cash flows behind the first tier of PACs (i.e., the PAC1s). PAC2s generally have narrower bands than the PAC1s, and the balance schedule is met only after that of the PAC1s. Designating the PAC1s as P1 and the PAC2s as P2, the payment rules for this type of deal might be:

- Pay P1 to its balance schedule.
- Pay P2 to its balance schedule.
- Pay remaining cash flow to S.
- If S is paid off, pay remaining cash flow to P2.
- If P2 is paid off, pay remaining cash flow to P1.

This suggests that if prepayments are fast enough to pay off the supports, the PAC2s become the supports for the PAC1s. Additional levels of PAC bonds (and deals can be structured with three and four levels of PACs) also create more leverage in the structure, making the average life and duration profile of the supports and lower-tier PACs increasingly unstable. The important concepts, however, are that multiple schedules can be created within a deal, with differing degrees of priority. This holds true for the PAC structure, as well as other structuring variations that utilize schedules, as we will subsequently discuss.

TARGETED AMORTIZATION CLASS BONDS

A *targeted amortization class*, or TAC, bond resembles a PAC bond in that both have a schedule of principal repayment. The difference between a PAC bond and a TAC bond is that the former has a relatively wide PSA range over which the schedule of principal repayment is pro-

---

[1] These typically consist of interest- and principal-only securities, as well as floater/inverse floater combinations. We discuss these structures in Chapter 7.

tected against contraction risk and extension risk. A TAC bond, in contrast, has a single prepayment speed from which the schedule of principal repayment is protected. As a result, the prepayment protection afforded the TAC bond is less than that for a PAC bond. As we shall explain, the creation of a bond with a schedule of principal repayments based on a single prepayment rate results in protection against contraction risk but not extension risk. Thus, while PAC bonds are said to have two-sided prepayment protection, TAC bonds have one-sided prepayment protection.

To understand why this is the case, take a simple deal with one TAC (T) and one support class (S). Monthly principal cash flows are allocated as follows:

- Pay T to its balance schedule;
- Pay remaining cash flow to S; then
- If S is paid off, pay remaining principal to T.

At prepayment speeds faster than the TAC schedule speed, the TAC has call protection as long as the support bond remains outstanding. At speeds slower than the TAC speed, by contrast, there is not enough monthly principal to meet the TAC's schedule, causing the average life of the TAC to extend.

There are a number of different structuring variations where TACs are used. In some cases, TACs are structured as an alternative to PACs, with the highest cash flow priority within the deal. In other cases, a support bond may be structured as a TAC by giving it a schedule. This gives it better protection from contraction risk than a standalone support. As with the PAC/support structure, deals with TACs can be viewed as utilizing a structuring technique where a schedule is generated and utilized to allocate principal payments. Both structures also create support bonds, which act to cushion the impact of varying prepayments on the bond having the schedule. As with all bonds with schedules, the difference is mainly in how the schedule is created and where it stands in priority within the structure.

Z-BONDS AND ACCRETION-DIRECTED TRANCHES

Z-bonds are tranches where the bond coupon is accrued by adding the interest to the face value of the bond. While the term "Z-bond" or "Z" is borrowed from zero-coupon bonds in the government strip market, it is a misnomer, since the bonds have a coupon that is only paid to the investor in cash at the point where the bonds begin paying principal (i.e., when the lockout expires). The interest that normally would be paid to the parent bond during the lockout period is deferred and added to the Z's principal value in a process called accretion. The interest, in turn, is "directed" to a different bond in the structure. This directed cash flow can either form the principal for an entirely new tranche or be combined with an existing tranche to smooth the cash flow profile.

The logic is illustrated in panels A and B of Exhibit 6.16. The timing of principal and interest cash flows on a locked-out tranche at different prepayment speeds is shown in panel A, while panel B shows the same cash flows converted into a Z-bond (which only pays interest after the lockout expires) and a separate principal cash flow comprised of the Z-bond's accreted interest. By splitting normal interest-paying bonds into accrual bonds (the Z) and an accretion-directed class, the overall deal execution can be improved by either creating very stable bonds (which trade at narrow spreads) or using the accreted interest to improve the profile of existing tranches to make them more marketable (and ultimately have them trade at tighter spreads). At the same time, the long duration of the Z-bond appeals to investors with longer-dated liability structures. In addition, reinvestment risk is ameliorated; since Zs accrete at the coupon rate, the reinvestment rate is locked in as long as the bond accrues.

EXHIBIT 6.16   Generation of Z-bond and Accretion-Directed Cash Flows
Panel A: Graphic Representation of Bond First and Last Principal Payments by Prepayment Speed

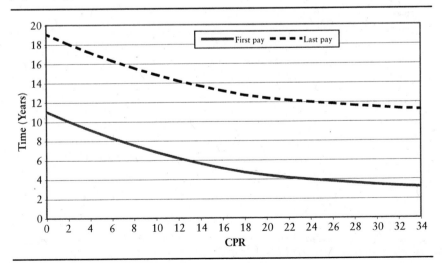

EXHIBIT 6.16 (Continued)

Panel B: Graphic Representation of Hypothetical Tranche Cash Flows

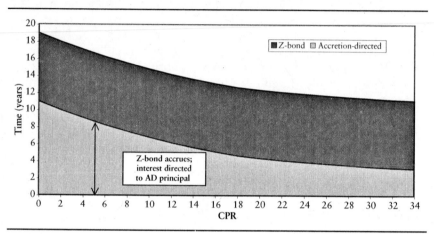

Bonds structured using the accreted interest of the Z-bond (known as *accretion-directed* (or AD *bonds*)) have very stable average life and duration profiles because of the characteristics of interest cash flows generated by the parent bond when it is locked out. Pure interest payments on a locked-out tranche cease once the lockout expires. Since the earliest principal payment is not normally delayed greatly even at slow speeds, the AD bond generally has greater stability than other bonds in the structure. Note that in such structures, the principal available is unchanged, as the combined face value of the Z-bond and any AD bonds equals that of the original parent tranche.

A subset of the accretion-directed universe is the VADM (an acronym for *Very Accurately Dated Maturity*). VADMs are standalone AD bonds structured to be free from extension risk even in the absence of prepayments (i.e., if prepayments are 0% CPR). The bonds also have relatively short "legal final maturities," which is the last possible date for principal to be paid in any scenario. In order to create these bonds, the amount of the Z-bond must be relatively large, resulting in large amounts of accretions. Such bonds appeal to investors with no tolerance for extension exposure, as well as depositories and other conservative investors seeking bonds with short legal final maturities (often for regulatory considerations).

Generally, the size of the Z-bond is a function of the coupon of the parent tranche and lockout and is calculated as follows:

$$\text{Z-bond face value} = \text{Parent tranche} \div [1 + (\text{Coupon}/12)]^{\text{Lockout (in months)}}$$

As an example, a $50 million face value tranche with a 6% locked out for 60 months can create $37 million Z-bonds, with the remaining $13 million being AD bonds. Note that the amount of Z-bonds that can be created increases either as the lockout period of the parent tranche decreases or the coupon is reduced.

To see this, consider Deal-04, a hypothetical CMO structure with the same collateral as Deal-01 and with four tranches, each with a coupon rate of 5.5%. The difference is in the last tranche, Z, which is an accrual tranche. The structure for Deal-04 is shown in Exhibit 6.17.

There are a number of noteworthy aspects to Exhibit 6.17. Note that while the average lives for tranches A, B, and C are unchanged from the original sequential deal, the principal balance of the tranches are all larger. Tranche Z, by contrast, is smaller than tranche D in Deal-01. Effectively, part of the balance of the parent sequential bond has been pushed forward to the shorter bonds in the deal. In addition, the average life profile of bonds A-C is "smoother" or less volatile than those of the

EXHIBIT 6.17   Deal-04: A Hypothetical Four-Tranche Sequential Pay Structure with an Accrual Bond Class

Tranche	Par Amount	Coupon Rate (%)	Average Life
A	206,514,000	5.5	3.4
B	46,302,000	5.5	7.3
C	111,726,000	5.5	10.9
Z	35,458,000	5.5	19.5
Collateral	400,000,000	5.5	8.6

Payment rules:
1. *For payment of periodic coupon interest.* Disburse periodic coupon interest to tranches A, B, and C on the basis of the amount of principal outstanding at the beginning of the period. For tranche Z, accrue the interest based on the principal plus accrued interest in the previous period. The interest for tranche Z is to be paid to the earlier tranches as a principal paydown.
2. *For disbursement of principal payments.* Disburse principal payments to tranche A until it is completely paid off. After tranche A is completely paid off, disburse principal payments to tranche B until it is completely paid off. After tranche B is completely paid off, disburse principal payments to tranche C until it is completely paid off. After tranche C is completely paid off, disburse principal payments to tranche Z until the original principal balance plus accrued interest is completely paid off.

EXHIBIT 6.18 Average Life of Sequential Bonds in Deals with and without Z-bonds (Deal-01 and Deal-04)

		100	125	165	250	400	500	600	700
Tranche A	No Z-bond	4.7	4.1	3.4	2.7	2.0	1.8	1.6	1.5
	With Z-bond	4.5	4.0	3.4	2.7	2.0	1.8	1.6	1.5
Tranche B	No Z-bond	10.4	8.9	7.3	5.3	3.8	3.2	2.8	2.6
	With Z-bond	9.9	8.7	7.3	5.5	3.9	3.4	3.0	2.7
Tranche C	No Z-bond	15.1	13.2	10.9	7.9	5.3	4.4	3.8	3.4
	With Z-bond	14.1	12.7	10.9	8.3	5.9	4.9	4.3	3.8

bonds in the original structure, as shown in Exhibit 6.18. This represents the effects of the accreted interest from the Z-bond that is now being directed to the shorter bonds in the structure.

Z-bonds can be structured from sequential, PAC, or support cash flows. Support Z-bonds often have very complex structures and trade at substantial discounts to parity, appealing to investors looking to make highly leveraged bets on fast prepayments. From the structurer's perspective, the creation of a support Z-bond has a similar purpose to those created in a sequential deal. The accretions created by the support Z (especially at slower speeds) can be directed to a shorter support tranche, serving to smooth the short support's average life and duration profile in order to make it more marketable. We explore this in more depth later in this chapter.

Exhibit 6.19 shows a simple sequential structure (Deal-05) where the Z-bond's accretions are used to create a VADM. The balances of tranches A-C are the same as those of Deal-01, the original sequential deal. In this case, an extra VADM tranche is created that utilizes the accretions to create one bond that has virtually no extension risk. The average life profile of the bonds in Deal-05 is shown in Exhibit 6.20. The table shows that even in the absence of prepayments (i.e., 0% PSA), the average life of tranche V does not extend beyond 8.1 years, the same as at the 165% PSA pricing speed.

A SIMPLE STRUCTURING EXAMPLE

To illustrate how the different structuring techniques can be utilized, the following section shows a simple problem often encountered by structurers: what is the most efficient way to smooth the profile of a short support to make it marketable to relatively conservative investors such as banks

EXHIBIT 6.19 Deal-05 CMO Sequential Pay Structure with a VADM Tranche

Tranche	Par Amount	Coupon Rate (%)	Average Life
A	194,500,000	5.5	3.4
B	36,000,000	5.5	7.3
C	96,500,000	5.5	10.9
V	39,602,000	5.5	8.1
Z	33,398,000	5.5	19.8
Collateral	400,000,000	5.5	8.6

Payment rules:
1. *For payment of periodic coupon interest.* Disburse periodic coupon interest to tranches V, A, B, and C based on the amount of principal outstanding at the beginning of the period. The interest earned by tranche Z is to be paid to tranche V as a paydown of principal and accrued as interest to tranche Z.
2. *For disbursement of principal payments.* Disburse interest accrued by tranche Z as principal to tranche V until it is completely paid off. Concurrently, disburse principal to tranche A until it is completely paid off. After tranche A is completely paid off, disburse principal to tranche B until it is completely paid off. After tranche B is completely paid off, disburse principal to tranche C until it is completely paid off. After tranche C is completely paid off, disburse principal payments to tranche V until it is completely paid off. After tranche V is completely paid off, disburse principal payments to tranche Z until the original mortgage balance plus accrued interest is completely paid off.

EXHIBIT 6.20 Average Lives for Tranches in Deal-05

	0	100	165	200	400	500	600
A	12.4	4.7	3.4	3.1	2.0	1.8	1.6
B	21.6	10.4	7.3	6.3	3.8	3.2	2.8
C	25.0	15.1	10.9	9.4	5.3	4.4	3.8
V	8.1	8.1	8.1	8.0	6.1	5.3	4.6
Z	28.6	24.0	19.8	18.1	11.4	9.4	8.0

and depositories? For background, the bank regulatory agencies (collectively known as the Federal Financial Institution Examination Council or FFIEC) released a set of rules in 1992 governing investments in MBS. Known as the FFIEC rules, they stated that structured MBS should meet the following criteria at the time of purchase:

■ Their base-case average life should not exceed 10.0 years.

■ Their projected average life should not shorten by more than six years, or extend by more than four years, in interest rate scenarios where the yield curve shifts plus or minus 300 basis points in a parallel fashion.
■ Their projected price should not decline by more than 17.0% in the event of a 300 basis point rate shift.

Securities that did not meet these standards were classified as "high-risk investments." In theory, depositories could buy high-risk investments if they could demonstrate that such purchases would reduce the interest rate exposure of the institution. In practice, it meant that bonds purchased by regulated institutions almost always met these standards. (While the rules were rescinded in 1998, some investors continue to utilize the criteria as standards for judging the appropriateness of MBS investments.)

Therefore, a challenge for structurers is to take short support bonds and modify them to the extent that they can comply with the FFIEC rules. In the following hypothetical examples, we use a number of different structuring techniques to transform a short support bond into a FFIEC-eligible or "bank bond" with a 3.5-year average life. The profile of a short support bond created by time-tranching the support created by Deal-02 is shown in Exhibit 6.21. Note that its average life at 115% PSA (which is the assumed prepayment speed in a rates-up 300 basis points scenario) extends to 11.5 years; the 8.0-year extension of the average life from the base case does not meet the FFIEC test's standards.

One approach would be to take the supports off the base-case PAC/support deal (using 30-year 5.5s with a 100% to 250% PSA structuring band) and give them a schedule, making them PAC2s or lower-priority PACs. To accomplish this, the PAC2 is given a PAC band of 132% to 175% PSA, and targeted to have a 3.5-year average life at 165% PSA. This is shown as Option 1 in Exhibit 6.22, which shows the basic details of the structure, as well as the profile of the bank bond.

As with most structuring options, there are trade-offs that accompany this potential solution. One is that the band of the PAC2 may deteriorate in the fashion discussed previously. This would mean that the

EXHIBIT 6.21   Average Life and Duration Profile of 3.5-Year Support Bond

PSA	100	115	125	165	200	300	500
Ave. Life	15.4	11.5	9.2	3.5	2.4	1.5	1.0
Duration	10.1	7.9	6.6	3.0	2.2	1.4	1.0

Goal: Creating 3.5-year bond in base case that extends to 7.5-year average life at 115% PSA.

EXHIBIT 6.22 Options for Creating a Bank Bond
Option 1: Create bank bond as a PAC2
PAC1: 100% to 250% PSA band, no lockout
Bank Bond: PAC2, 132% to 175% PSA band

Bond	Percent of Deal
PACs	71.3%
Bank bond	7.3%
Support	21.5%

PSA	100	115	125	165	200	300	500
Avg. Life	13.1	7.5	4.8	3.5	3.5	3.1	2.1
Duration	9.1	5.7	3.9	3.0	3.0	2.8	1.9

Option 2: Create bank bond as PAC2 with wider PAC1 bands
PAC1: 90% to 300% PSA band, no lockout
Bank Bond: PAC2, 145% to 175% PSA band

Bond	Percent of Deal
PACs	62.6%
Bank bond	12.5%
Support	25.0%

PSA	100	115	125	165	200	300	500
Avg. Life	10.7	7.5	5.8	3.5	3.5	3.5	2.4
Duration	7.7	5.7	4.6	3.0	3.0	3.0	2.2

Option 3: Create bank bond as PAC2 while locking out the PAC1s
PAC1: 100% to 250% PSA band, 20-month lockout
PAC2: Schedule @ 145% PSA

Bond	Percent of Deal
PACs	65.5%
Bank bond	18.1%
Support	16.4%

PSA	100	115	125	165	200	300	500
Avg. Life	10.5	7.5	5.9	3.5	3.6	2.5	1.7
Duration	7.0	5.4	4.5	2.9	3.0	2.2	1.6

EXHIBIT 6.22 (Continued)
Option 4: Create bank bond by using accretions from support Z
PAC: 95% to 250% PSA band, no lockout
Bank Bond: No band, receives accretions from support Z

Bond	Percent of Deal
PACs	69.9%
Bank bond	19.9%
Support Z	10.2%

PSA	100	115	125	165	200	300	500
Avg. Life	9.4	7.4	6.3	3.5	2.6	1.7	1.2
Duration	6.9	5.6	4.9	3.0	2.3	1.6	1.1

bond's profile might become more volatile over time, particularly if interest rates and prepayment speeds "whipsaw." (This highlights the point made earlier in this chapter that a PAC structure is like a balance sheet, in that it is a snapshot at the point of issuance.) The other downside of this option is that the bank bond is relatively small, comprising only about 7% of the deal.

A second approach, also creating the bank bond as a PAC2, would be to change the PAC1 structure such that the structuring band is wider, making less volatile support bonds. This approach is shown in Option 2 in Exhibit 6.22. This alternative uses a structuring band for the PAC1s of 90% to 300% PSA. This means that the lower band of the PAC2 can be at a faster PSA speed.

The benefits of this approach vis-à-vis Option 1 are (1) the bank bond is larger and (2) it has less average life extension at prepayment speeds slower than 115% PSA. The downside of this structure, however, is that the wider bands create fewer PACs to sell. Since the PACs trade at a the lowest yields, creating fewer of them means that the same execution would require that they trade to significantly tighter spreads than those PACs structured at 100%–250% PSA. This execution is not always attainable in the market. In addition, the bank bond itself must receive stronger execution relative to that created in the earlier deal, since it comprises a larger portion of the structure.

Option 3 shown in Exhibit 6.22 involves structuring bands of 100%–250% PSA for the PAC1s, but locks out the PAC1s for the first 20 months. The bank bond is still structured as a PAC2 with 145%–175% PSA bands, but the cash flows of the short PACs now flow into the bank bond, smoothing its profile and making it an even larger percentage of the deal. Note that the bank bond in this structure has, in the base case, even less extension at 100% PSA than the bond structured using the wider band (i.e., Option 2).

The major problem with the structure under Option 2 is that the cash flows of the bank bond are heavily front-loaded, since it is partially comprised of the short PACs. This is illustrated in Exhibit 6.23. This exhibit shows the monthly principal cash flows as a percentage of the face value of the bank bonds in Options 1 and 3. Since both bonds have the same average life, the principal cash flows for the Option 3 bond run for a much longer period of time (i.e., the bond has a longer window), making its principal cash flows "barbelled" in nature. As the PAC cash flows embedded in the bank bond amortize, its profile changes. Exhibit 6.24 shows the average life of the bond created in Option 3 at the deal's settlement, and in month 20. Note that the average life profile of the bond is more volatile in

EXHIBIT 6.23 Percentage of Total Face Value Paid as Monthly Principal for Different Structuring Options

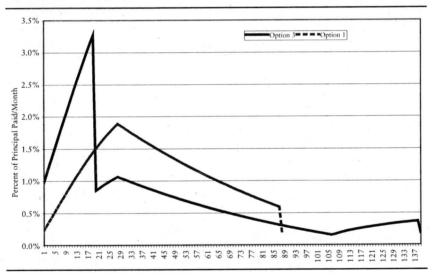

EXHIBIT 6.24 Average Life Profile of Bank Bond Created in Option 3 at Settlement and at Month 20

PSA	100	115	125	165	200	300	400	500
Settlement	10.4	7.5	5.9	3.5	3.5	2.4	1.9	1.7
Month 20	13.1	9.4	7.2	3.6	3.7	1.8	0.9	0.5

month 20, particularly at slower prepayment speeds. In addition, the bond's base-case average life is slightly longer, even though the bond has been outstanding for almost two years. This phenomenon is a manifestation of the structuring method illustrated in Exhibit 6.12. While it creates bonds that have an ostensibly stable profile, the technique introduces a time dimension to MBS analysis that is not widely understood.

The final structuring option, Option 4, using Z-bond accretions to smooth the short support's profile, is shown in Exhibit 6.22. In this example, there is no PAC2 created. The PACs are structured with a 95%–250% PSA structuring band. The supports are created by tranching the support bond into a short-support and a long-support Z, and the deal is structured such that the accretions from the Z are directed to the support.

Structured in this manner, the bank bond's face amount is large, and its profile is fairly robust, in that it does not change a great deal either with small changes in prepayments or as time elapses. The main difficulty with Option 4 is the marketability of the support Z. Such bonds tend to trade at very wide spreads and high yields, and the market for them is not as broad and deep as it is for other segments of the CMO market. Thus, demand for support Zs can be sporadic; unless the demand for this type of bond is unusually high, execution for this structure will not be as strong as for other options. Therefore, this option is only feasible when demand for long support Zs is high.

CHAPTER 7

Fundamental MBS Structuring Techniques: Divisions of Interest

As with the division and structuring of principal cash flows, interest cash flows can also be altered and redirected within a structure. The factors driving the structuring of interest are identical to those in principal structuring discussed in the preceding chapter. The goal is to create bonds that, by appealing to different segments of the fixed income investment community, maximize the proceeds generated by creating and selling the deal. By redistributing interest within the deal, bonds can be created with different degrees of exposure to interest rates and/or prepayment speeds. As examples, the following bonds can all be structured off either a pool of collateral or a parent tranche:

- *Floaters.* A bond where the interest adjusts (or "floats") with a benchmark index have minimal exposure to changes in interest rates (i.e., its duration is very short).
- *Principal-only (PO) tranches.* Bonds that pay no coupon interest to the holder. Sold at a deep discount to investors, its returns are based on the rate at which principal is returned to the investor. These bonds typically have very long and volatile durations, since their prices are affected not only from the impact of a different discount rate on the cash flow's present value, but by changing prepayment speeds.
- *Interest-only (IO) tranches.* Bonds that pay only interest to the investor, based on the remaining balance of a notional principal amount. These bonds can be viewed as a form of an annuity, since their value increases the longer they remain outstanding. Since prepayment speeds and interest rates are negatively correlated, this means that the duration of an IO is, in most cases, negative.

There are some fundamental differences in structuring mortgage-related principal and interest. As mentioned previously, there is a fixed amount of principal associated with a deal, and the principal available to be distributed is invariable. Interest, however, is a function of the outstanding principal balance. The total amount of interest available in a deal, therefore, depends on the prepayment speed experienced by the collateral pool. However, the amount of interest available to be paid to the tranches in a deal is constant at any particular point in time. Therefore, changing the coupon of a bond is a process of reallocating interest within the structure.

The simplest structure in which interest and principal is redistributed is an IO/PO trust. In this form, a pool of collateral is divided into IO and PO tranches. The PO receives only the principal paid by the obligors on the underlying loans, including both scheduled principal payments and prepayments. The IO class receives only the interest cash flows generated by the collateral. While the IO tranches have a quoted principal face value, it is notional; it represents the outstanding principal balance from which the interest cash flows are generated.[1] Note that an IO/PO trust is actually not a structured security, but is created by using a trust structure. Therefore, cash flows are not reallocated or tranched within the structure, nor is there any residual interest.

Often, however, a structured transaction can be optimized by redistributing interest within the structure. In some cases, the coupon of a bond must be reduced in order to drop its dollar price. This is particularly true for tranches targeted to banks and other depository institutions; securities offered at a significant premium over par often are not attractive to this market segment. Another common technique is to convert some of the existing tranches from fixed rate into floating rate securities. There are a number of clienteles for floating rate securities, depending on their average life, cap structure, and liquidity, which include:

- Banks and corporate treasurers that will use highly liquid floaters as a higher-yielding alternative to cash.
- More aggressive depository institutions that buy the longer-floating rate securities (that typically carry higher margins) as part of their core investment portfolio; these institutions can earn a relative high return on assets and equity with less interest rate risk.
- Investors that take and manage credit risk rather than interest rate risk.

---

[1] The first IO/PO trusts were structured in the late 1980s, after the Federal Reserve changed the delivery system to accept notional securities (i.e., bonds with no principal component).

This chapter addresses the techniques commonly utilized to redistribute coupon interest within a structured transaction. Note that the different methodologies are not mutually exclusive, as some techniques will serve multiple purposes (i.e., a variation on a floater structure is often used to reduce or "strip" the coupons of bonds in the structure, as we will discuss). Finally, decisions on how to redistribute interest cannot be made without considering the division of principal. For example, a steep yield curve typically means that tranches with short average lives trade above par if their coupons are the same as the underlying collateral. Therefore, the ability to create short-average-life bonds (typically targeted to banks in this type of regime) is often contingent on being able to strip the short tranche's coupon to one that creates a bond with a price at or below par.

COUPON STRIPPING AND BOOSTING

One of the common structuring techniques is reducing or "stripping" the coupon of a bond or series of bonds to make such securities more appealing to investors that seek par or discount-priced securities. As noted in the discussion on time tranching on floater/inverse structuring, fixed rate collateral pools and parent bonds in the mortgage-backed securities (MBS) universe have fixed dollar amounts of interest associated with them. Changing the coupon of a bond within a prime MBS structure, therefore, is a process of reallocating interest within the structure. As such, stripping the bond coupon creates interest cash flows that must be either directed elsewhere in the structure or sold as IO securities or tranches.[2]

The simplest form of coupon stripping is to split the parent bond into two tranches. Interest taken from one bond (the "discount," in this case) is allocated to the other bond (the "premium"), creating a "parallel split." As a simple example, a $10 million face value tranche with a 5.5% coupon can be split into $5 million of bonds with a 5.0% coupon and $5 million of a 6.0% coupon bond. This split suggests that there is greater demand for both the 5.0% and 6.0% coupon bonds (the "children") than the original 5.5% parent tranche.

IOs can be created at a number of different levels within the deal. The entire collateral pool can be stripped. For example, Fannie Mae 6.0s can be stripped into 5.5s by creating an IO tranche, which will be identical in form to a trust IO. This technique is shown in Exhibit 7.1. The notional face value of the IO to be sold is calculated as follows:

---

[2] In some cases, the coupon of a bond or cash flow has to be increased to appeal to certain types of investors focused on current yield.

EXHIBIT 7.1 Stripping a Collateral Pool by Creating an IO Tranche

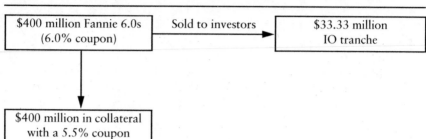

IO face value

$$= \text{Collateral face value} - \left(\left[\frac{\text{Target coupon}}{\text{Collateral coupon}} \right] \times \text{Collateral face value} \right) \quad (7.1)$$

In the example, $400 million face value of 6.0% collateral can be stripped by selling $33.33 million of an IO tranche, creating $400 million of collateral with a 5.5% coupon. However, what is important to understand is that while the coupon of the collateral is now 5.5%, it will continue to exhibit the prepayment characteristics of Fannie 6.0s.

Interestingly, one variation on this technique is to split the collateral into equal face values of POs and IOs, and then partially recombine them, leaving some trust IO to be sold separately. In this case, a trust is actually created; the deal's collateral therefore is a mismatched amount of the IO and PO off the same trust. Exhibit 7.2 illustrates how this technique works for the same $400 million face value of Fannie Mae 6.0s. In this case, $400 million in collateral with a 5.5% coupon is created, leaving $33,333,333 in trust IO to be sold. It should be noted that this methodology is not commonly used, since the trust IO created will typically be small and quite illiquid.

Another variation is to create an *IO tranche*. Such securities receive only interest cash flows, and do not receive any principal payments. Rather, their face value is notional and is used solely to calculate the dollar value of the interest cash flows received by the IO holder in any month. For example, holders of a $10 million notional face value of an IO with a 5.5% coupon receive $45,833 in interest cash flows per month. The notional value of the IO factors down as the parent bond receives principal payments. The IO holder is disproportionately affected by prepayments, since the asset generating interest cash flows declines in size.

As an example, a structurer might attempt to improve the execution on a PAC/support structure by stripping the PACs in a deal. This can either be done by stripping the coupon of the entire PAC group (i.e.,

EXHIBIT 7.2 Stripping a Collateral Pool by Creating and (partially) Recombining Trust IO and PO (created as a hypothetical trust X)

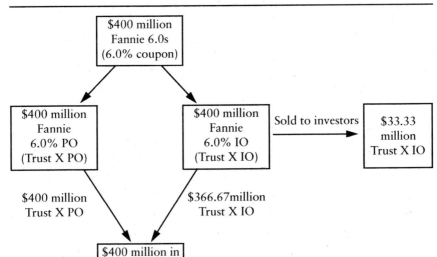

before time-tranching it), or by stripping only some of the PACs. The latter is commonly seen in regimes of a steep yield curve and low short interest rates; the PACs may be more attractive at par or near-par prices, while the longer PACs might be more easily marketed with fuller coupons. IOs created off PACs are, logically enough, called *PAC IOs*.

The notional sizing of IO tranches is somewhat arbitrary, and based on the coupon associated with the tranche. Using the example above, a $10 million face value of a 5.5% coupon can be split into a $10 million tranche with a 5.25% coupon, and $10 million notional bonds with a 0.25% coupon. For the sake of appearance, the coupon on such securities will be adjusted upward, often so that it is consistent with the parent bond original coupon (i.e., 5.5%). This means that the notional value of the IO must be adjusted downward in order for the IO holder to receive the same cash flows. Sizing the IO tranche is done as follows:

$$\text{Notional value of IO with new coupon}$$
$$= \frac{\text{Old coupon}}{\text{New coupon}} \times \text{Original notional value} \qquad (7.2)$$

In the above example, $10 million of an IO tranche with a 0.25% coupon can be converted to a tranche with a 5.5% coupon and a notional face value of $454,545.

As in the previous chapter, it is often helpful to see the structuring technique in the context of a deal. Exhibit 7.3 shows Deal-04 (a sequential 5.5% structure with a last-cash-flow Z-bond) with 25 basis points stripped off the first tranche (or, as it is sometimes referenced, the *front bond*). The front bond in the resulting Deal-05 has the same face value as in the earlier deal described in the previous chapter; however, an IO with a notional face value of roughly $9.3 million is also created. Note that because the IO is notional, the overall deal still has a principal value of $400 million.

Other common structures involve stripping the 5.5% parent tranche to a 5.0% child tranche and a tranche with a super-premium coupon such as 8%. The super-premium tranche can either be sold as a "cushion bond" to investors that expect prepayments to slow, or used as the parent tranche for a floater/inverse IO combination, a technique discussed later in this chapter.

EXHIBIT 7.3   Deal 05: Deal 04 Restructured to Reduce the Coupon Rate of Tranche A to 5.25% by Creating an IO

Tranche	Par Amount	Coupon Rate (%)	Average Life
A	206,514,000	5.25	3.4
IO	9,387,000	5.50	3.4
B	46,302,000	5.50	7.3
C	111,726,000	5.50	10.9
Z	35,458,000	5.50	19.5
Collateral	400,000,000	5.50	8.6

Payment rules:
1. For *payment of periodic coupon interest*. Disburse periodic coupon interest to tranches A, B, and C on the basis of the amount of principal outstanding at the beginning of the period. For tranche IO, disperse periodic interest based on notional principal value of tranche at the beginning of the period. For tranche Z, accrue the interest based on the principal plus accrued interest in the previous period. The interest for tranche Z is to be paid to the earlier tranches as a principal paydown.
2. For *disbursement of principal payments*. Disburse principal payments to tranche A until it is completely paid off. After tranche A is completely paid off, disburse principal payments to tranche B until it is completely paid off. After tranche B is completely paid off, disburse principal payments to tranche C until it is completely paid off. The notional balance of tranche IO is reduced proportionately with the decline in the balance of tranche A. After tranche C is completely paid off, disburse principal payments to tranche Z until the original principal balance plus accrued interest is completely paid off.

The formula for sizing the tranches in a discount/premium split is as

Discount tranche size

$$= \left[\frac{\text{Premium coupon} - \text{Parent coupon}}{\text{Premium coupon} - \text{Discount coupon}} \right] \times \text{Parent balance} \qquad (7.3)$$

$$\text{Premium tranche size} = \text{Parent tranche size} - \text{Discount tranche size} \quad (7.4)$$

For example, a $10 million face value tranche with a 5.5% coupon can be split into 5.25% and 8% coupon bonds as

$$\text{Size of 5.25\% tranche} = \left[\frac{8\% - 5.5\%}{8\% - 5.25\%} \right] \times 10,000,000$$

$$= \$9,090,909$$

$$8\% \text{ tranche size} = \$10,000,000 - \$9,090,909 = \$909,091$$

FLOATER/INVERSE FLOATER COMBINATIONS

As with many structuring techniques, floater/inverse floater (or "inverse") combinations can be structured from a variety of cash flows, including the entire collateral pool. The objective in creating floater/inverse combinations is to improve deal execution by taking advantage of the very low yields associated with floating rate bonds, especially when the yield curve is steep. Creating floating rate bonds (i.e., bonds where the coupon changes periodically based on an index) from fixed rate underlying cash flows also implies the creation of a bond where the coupon changes inversely with the floater coupon (and thus the index), known as the *inverse floater*. In agency and private label deals, the inverse floater is structured as a separate tranche that mimics the principal cash flow profile of the underlying bond. The coupon, however, changes inversely with the change in the index and thus the floater coupon, since interest available to be paid to the inverse is limited by the interest paid to the floater.

There are several noteworthy aspects to structures that include floating rate bonds:

■ Early in the inception of such deals, floater deals did not incorporate inverse floaters as tranches. Rather, the inverse floating rate coupon was sold as part of the residual interest.

- Once structured, both floaters and inverses can be treated as parent bonds and retranched, creating highly complex structures.
- Floating rate mortgage ABS structures created from fixed rate, subprime collateral generally do not utilize inverse floaters. As discussed in Chapter 9, the so-called excess spread (i.e., the spread between the monthly note rate of the loan and the rate paid to the floating rate bonds) is used to enhance the credit of the senior tranches through a variety of mechanisms.

Floaters are structured such that their coupon adjusts periodically (typically monthly) and is derived as the index level plus a fixed margin. A floater quoted as "LIBOR plus 50," for example, means that the floater coupon adjusts monthly to be 50 basis points over the index (which typically is one-month LIBOR), at some point around the record date of the floater. The creation of a floating rate tranche from a fixed rate collateral pool or parent tranche prime sector necessitates the simultaneous creation of an inverse floater (or, simply, an inverse). As we demonstrate, the inverse floater coupon is based on a formula that pays the remaining interest of the fixed rate parent bond after the floater's coupon is calculated.

The fundamentals of structuring floaters off fixed rate collateral are quite straightforward. The fixed rate coupon of the collateral (either a collateral pool or a parent tranche) generates the total interest available to be paid. In its most simple form, the floater's maximum coupon rate (or cap rate) is the fixed rate coupon. If the floater's coupon (i.e., the index plus the margin) is less than the cap rate, the remaining interest is available to be paid to another tranche. Thus, an inverse floater, or a tranche where the coupon adjusts inversely with the level of the index, is simultaneously created. An illustration of this technique is shown in Exhibit 7.4.

Note that in the above example, the floater receives all principal from the underlying collateral. Therefore, the inverse floater receives only interest, and can be described as an *inverse IO* or IIO. The inverse is sometimes sold in this form. However, inverses are often structured with some principal amount; alternatively, the inverse IO can also be utilized as an alternative means of stripping coupon and selling an IO to investors.

The previous example is somewhat oversimplified. As described, the floater cap is the same as the collateral coupon rate. This is typically much lower than the cap level desired by floating rate investors. While it is possible to augment the floater's cap with derivative contracts bought in the capital markets (as we discuss in the section on corridor floaters in Chapter 8), investors typically prefer all the floater's coupon income to be generated by the collateral, eliminating both counterparty exposure and the possibility of a balance mismatch. It is possible to create floaters with cap rates higher than the collateral, with two structural implications:

EXHIBIT 7.4   Allocation of Fixed Rate Interest to a Floating Rate Tranche and the Remaining Coupon

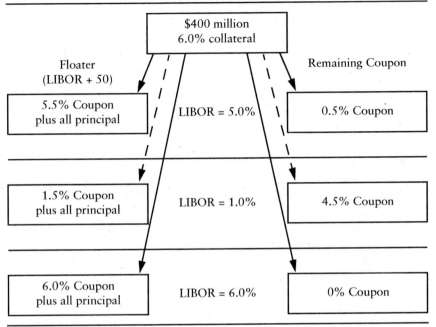

1. Not all the collateral or parent tranche's principal can be allotted to the floater, creating a somewhat smaller floater tranche.
2. Depending on the proportions, the inverse floater's coupon will no longer change pro rata with changes in the index. Typically, it will change more rapidly than the index, which means that the inverse's coupon is leveraged with respect to the index.

The leverage or *multiple* is defined as part of the inverse's structure. The inverse's multiple is a function of both the chosen floater cap and the collateral coupon (which dictates how much interest is available to pay the two bonds). The inverse's leverage is also inversely proportional to its face value, i.e., a smaller inverse would typically have the largest multiple. Similar to the coupon on the floater, the inverse's coupon resets on a monthly basis, defined by a predetermined formula.[3]

---

[3] Note that the multiple on an inverse IO is typically 1.0 (i.e., the IIO coupon changes on a one-to-one basis with the index). This is because coupon leveraging is a function of the proportion of floater and inverse principal; an IIO has no principal (with the exception of the notional balance).

As shown later in this section, the inverse's leverage increases either as the floater's cap is lowered, or as the collateral coupon is raised. Most floater/inverse combinations are structured to create the smallest possible inverse floater in size. As inverses trade to relatively high yields, minimizing the size of the inverse floater maximizes the proceeds of the structure. Additionally, inverse buyers typically like the highest possible multiple, since it maximizes the leverage of the position and, by implication, the yield to which it will trade. (This is often called creating a maxleverage inverse.) By implication, this suggests that dealers always have an incentive to market floaters with the lowest possible cap. (Theoretically, floaters with double-digit caps can be created; however, it would create a large, low-leverage inverse floater, which would be uneconomical to the structure.)

The generation of a floater/inverse floater combination using the maximum leverage is a fairly straightforward process of dividing the available interest from the parent bond for the floater and inverse under different scenarios. The minimum coupon of the floater (if LIBOR declines to 0%) is the floater's margin. In a simple numerical example, assume that the structurer creates a floater with an 8.0% cap and a 50 basis point margin off a $100 million parent tranche with a 6.0% coupon. This generates the following calculations:

- Total annual interest available = $100,000,000 × 0.06 = $6,000,000 (which is also the maximum interest available to the floaters)
- Maximum amount of floaters that can be created = $6,000,000 ÷ 0.08 = $75,000,000 face value
- Inverse floater face value = $100,000,000 − $75,000,000 = $25,000,000
- Ratio of floaters to inverses = 3:1 = Coupon leverage of inverse (for every 100 basis point change in the index, the floater's coupon changes 100 basis points, while the inverse's coupon changes 300 basis points)
- Minimum floater coupon = 0.5% (assuming LIBOR drops to 0%)
- Minimum floater coupon interest at 0.5% = $75,000,000 × 0.005 = $375,000
- Maximum interest available to inverse = $6,000,000 − $375,000 = $5,625,000
- Maximum inverse coupon = $5,625,000 ÷ $25,000,000 = 22.5%

Quoted as formulae, the coupons of the two bonds are expressed as

$$\text{Floater coupon} = 0.5\% + (1 \times \text{LIBOR})$$

$$\text{Inverse floater coupon} = 22.5\% - (3 \times \text{LIBOR})$$

Assuming an initial LIBOR rate of 3.0%, the floater will have a coupon of 3.5%; the inverse floater's initial coupon will therefore be 13.5%. If LIBOR moves to 5%, the coupons and total interest for the floater and inverse, respectively, are:

- Floater coupon = 5.0% LIBOR plus 50 basis point margin = 5.5%
  Total annual floater interest = $75,000,000 × 5.5% = $4,125,000
- Inverse coupon = 22.5% − (3 × 5%) = 22.5% − 15% = 7.5%
  Total annual inverse interest = $25,000,000 × 7.5% = $1,875,000
- Total annual floater and inverse interest = $4,125,000 + $1,875,000 = $6,000,000 (which equals the total interest available from the parent tranche)

The dynamics of the above example are illustrated in Exhibit 7.5, while Exhibit 7.6 shows how available interest is divided between the floater and inverse at different levels of the index. The slope of the line dividing the floater and inverse interest, given a level of the index, is negative 3. The intercept (i.e., the amount of interest when the index is 0%) is $5,625,000, reflecting the 50 basis points of interest that would be paid to the floater solely from the margin.

Note that the floater formula also contains a coupon multiple. This is typically 1, implying that the floater will change at the same absolute rate as the index. However, floaters are occasionally created that have a multiple that is not equal to 1, creating so-called *super floaters*. Like regular floaters, super floaters in the prime universe are structured to have an inverse floater, with the leverage calculated in the same way as described above.

As a general formula, the inverse multiple (or leverage) is calculated as

$$\text{Inverse floater multiple} = \frac{\text{Parent coupon}}{\text{Floater cap} - \text{Parent coupon}} \quad (7.5)$$

In the example used above, the inverse floater multiple would be 3.0×, or

$$\frac{0.06}{0.08 - 0.06} = 3.0$$

The formula indicates that the inverse floater multiple (or, more accurately, the inverse's maximum possible leverage) is a function of both the floater cap and the parent coupon. The multiple on an inverse

EXHIBIT 7.5   Mechanics of Floater/Inverse Combination (Initial 1-mo. LIBOR = 3.0%)

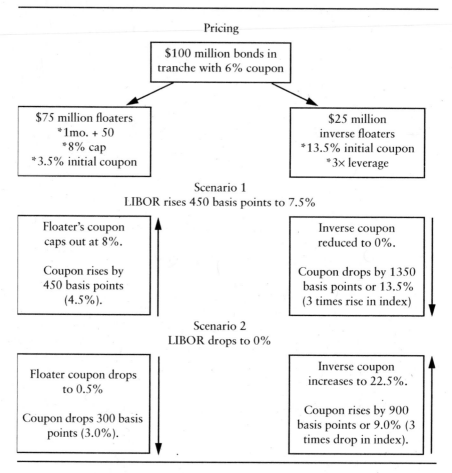

Pricing

$100 million bonds in tranche with 6% coupon

$75 million floaters
*1mo. + 50
*8% cap
*3.5% initial coupon

$25 million inverse floaters
*13.5% initial coupon
*3× leverage

Scenario 1
LIBOR rises 450 basis points to 7.5%

Floater's coupon caps out at 8%.

Coupon rises by 450 basis points (4.5%).

Inverse coupon reduced to 0%.

Coupon drops by 1350 basis points or 13.5% (3 times rise in index)

Scenario 2
LIBOR drops to 0%

Floater coupon drops to 0.5%

Coupon drops 300 basis points (3.0%).

Inverse coupon increases to 22.5%.

Coupon rises by 900 basis points or 9.0% (3 times drop in index).

increases as the parent tranche coupon increases or as the floater cap is reduced. More simply, the inverse multiple is the ratio of the face values of the floater and inverse floater. In the example, there are $75,000,000 floaters and $25,000,000 inverse floaters, for a ratio of 3:1. As we see in a subsequent section, this is the easiest way to calculate the leverage for more complex combinations.

A sample deal where the front bond is divided into a floater/inverse floater combination is shown in Exhibit 7.7. This deal, labeled Deal-06, takes Deal-04 and restructures the A class into a floater (using an 8% cap floater and a 50 basis point margin) and a maximum-leverage inverse with a 2.2× coupon multiple.

EXHIBIT 7.6   Annual Division of Interest Payments between Floater and Inverse Floater at Different Index Levels

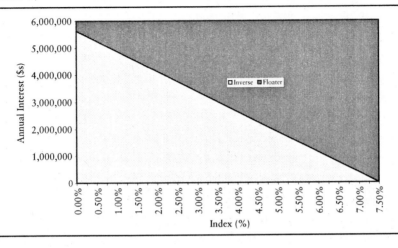

EXHIBIT 7.7   Deal-06: Deal-04 Restructured to Make Tranche A into a Floater/ Inverse Floater Combination

Tranche	Par Amount ($)	Coupon Rate (%)	Average Life	Reset Formula
FL	141,978,375	3.5	3.4	0.50 + (LIBOR × 1)
INV	64,535,625	9.9	3.4	16.5 − (LIBOR × 2.2)
B	46,302,000	5.5	7.3	Fixed
C	111,726,000	5.5	10.9	Fixed
Z	35,458,000	5.5	19.5	Fixed
Collateral	400,000,000	5.5	8.6	

Payment rules:

1. *For payment of periodic coupon interest.* Disburse periodic coupon interest to tranches FL, INV, B, and C on the basis of the amount of principal outstanding at the beginning of the period. For tranche Z, accrue the interest based on the principal plus accrued interest in the previous period. The interest for tranche Z is to be paid to the earlier tranches as a principal paydown. The maximum coupon rate for FL is 8%; the minimum coupon rate for INV is 0%.

2. *For disbursement of principal payments.* Disburse principal payments to tranches FL and INV until they are completely paid off. The principal payments between tranches FL and INV should be made in the following way: 68.75% to tranche FL and 31.25% to tranche INV. After tranches FL and INV are completely paid off, disburse principal payments to tranche B until it is completely paid off. After tranche B is completely paid off, disburse principal payments to tranche C unil it is completely paid off. After tranche C is completely paid off, disburse principal payments to tranche Z until the original principal balance plus accrued interest is completely paid off.

Coupon Stripping Using Inverse IOs

As noted previously, inverse IOs or IIOs are frequently used as a means of stripping coupons and selling IO cash flows to investors. This technique uses a combination of structuring techniques. As an example, assume that a structurer wanted to strip a 5.5% coupon parent bond to have a 5.25% coupon (i.e., strip 25 basis points off the bond). In a floater/IIO combination, the structurer would follow the following steps:

- Create a variation on a discount/premium split, where the premium tranche has a very high coupon (typically equal to the current level of floater caps either in the market or targeted to an investor). In this case, assume that the dealer wishes to create a floater with an 8.0% cap. Using equations 7.3a and 7.3b, $100 million of a parent bond with a 5.5% coupon would be structured into $90,909,091 of a tranche with a 5.25% coupon, creating $9,090,909 of a bond with an 8% coupon.
- Create a floater/inverse IO combination from the 8.0% coupon premium bond, as described previously.

Assuming that one-month LIBOR is 3.0% at the time the deal is priced, and the floater has a margin of 50 basis points, the coupon of the floater would initially be 3.5%. As in the example in Exhibit 7.4, the inverse IO receives all coupon interest remaining after the floater is paid LIBOR + 50 basis points, until the coupon of the floater reaches 8.0% (i.e., it is paid all the interest from the parent tranche). The inverse IO would initially have a coupon of 4.5%.

Because the IIO has no principal component, both the floater and IIO have coupon leverage of 1.0×; the multiple on the floater would be positive 1.0, while the IIO multiple would be negative 1.0. However, even though the coupon leverage is 1.0×, the yield of the bond is highly sensitive to the level of the index, as well as assumed and realized prepayment speeds (as are all IOs and IO-like tranches).

The target market for inverse IOs consists of investors looking to make highly leveraged bets on the level of short interest rates and/or prepayment speeds. For example, investors that look for a steeper yield curve might buy inverse IOs. The coupons on IIOs rise commensurately with a drop in short rates, while the steeper yield curve imputes higher long interest rates, which typically drive expected and realized prepayment speeds. An illustration of this technique is shown in Exhibit 7.8.

To illustrate how this technique works in the context of a deal, Exhibit 7.9 shows Deal 07. This deal uses the same sample deal (i.e., Deal 04, the sequential deal with the last-cash-flow Z) and strips the front tranche to a 5.25% coupon by creating a floater/inverse IO combination.

EXHIBIT 7.8 Example of Stripping 5.5% Collateral Using a Floater/Inverse IO Combination (initial 1-month LIBOR = 3.0%)

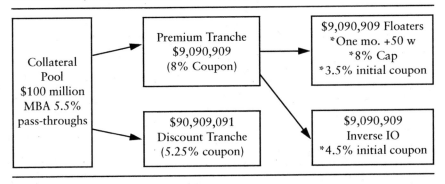

EXHIBIT 7.9 Deal-07: Deal-04 Restructured to Reduce the Coupon Rate of Tranche A to 5.25% by Creating a Floater and Inverse IO

Tranche	Par Amount ($)	Coupon Rate (%)	Average Life	Reset Formula
A	187,740,000	5.25	3.4	Fixed
FL	18,774,000	3.50	3.4	0.50 + (LIBOR × 1)
IIO	18,774,000	4.50	3.4	8.0 − (LIBOR × 1)
B	46,302,000	5.50	7.3	Fixed
C	111,726,000	5.50	10.9	Fixed
Z	35,458,000	5.50	19.5	Fixed
Collateral	400,000,000	5.50	8.6	

Payment rules:
1. *For payment of periodic coupon interest.* Disburse periodic coupon interest to tranches A, B, and FL based on the basis of the amount of principal outstanding at the beginning of the period. For tranche IIO, disperse periodic interest based on notional principal value of tranche at the beginning of the period. For tranche Z, accrue the interest based on the principal plus accrued interest in the previous period. The interest for tranche Z is to be paid to the earlier tranches as a principal paydown. The maximum coupon rate for FL is 8%; the minimum coupon rate for IIO is 0%.
2. *For disbursement of principal payments.* Disburse principal payments to tranche A and FL proportionately until they are completely paid off. After tranche A and FL are completely paid off, disburse principal payments to tranche B until it is completely paid off. The notional balance of tranche IIO is reduced pro rata with the decline in the balance of tranche FL. After tranche B is completely paid off, disburse principal payments to tranche C until it is completely paid off. After tranche C is completely paid off, disburse principal payments to tranche Z until the original principal balance plus accrued interest is completely paid off.

It is interesting and useful to note that the floater/inverse IO structuring technique was used almost exclusively as a method of coupon stripping until 2005. Its advantage to the deal execution is twofold. First, the normal positively sloped yield curve allows the floater to be sold at relatively low yields, maximizing the proceeds garnered from this structure (as opposed to either selling a premium coupon tranche or a straight IO). In addition, the demand for floating rate bonds is consistently strong, making that part of the structure relatively easy to sell.

However, the size of the floater created by this mechanism is generally small. In the example in Exhibit 7.8, stripping $100 million in 5.5s to have a 5.25% coupon would create just over $9 million of floaters with an 8.0% cap, and just over $14 million of 7.0% cap floaters. The relatively small size of the floater is a disadvantage to the floater/inverse IO technique since floater investors are typically institutions seeking to make large leveraged investments.

In 2005, structurers began creating floaters where the coupon cap was the same as the parent bond's coupon, creating much larger floating rate tranches and IIOs with very high-yield leverage. (This structuring derivation is very similar to the example in Exhibit 7.4, where passthroughs with a 6.0% coupon are structured to create LIBOR floaters with a 6.0% cap.) To structure floaters with a cap high enough to entice investors, the cap is augmented by a cap corridor purchased in the derivative markets. This type of structure is only being done in the private label market, as the GSEs do not allow derivative contracts to be included in their structures. We explore these bonds, called *corridor-cap floaters*, in Chapter 8 where we discuss private label CMO structures.

TWO-TIERED INDEX BONDS (TTIBs)

A *two-tiered index bond* or TTIB is a bond, created as part of a floater/inverse floater combination, which combines elements of both fixed rate tranches and inverse floaters. The bonds are designed to have a fixed coupon rate as long as the reference index is below a certain threshold level. If the index breaches that level, the TTIB's coupon floats inversely with the index, causing it to drop precipitously from its initial level. This makes an investment in a TTIB similar in concept to being short cap contracts, giving the investor large interest cash flows so long as the index remains below the threshold (or strike) level. The term "two-tiered index bond" derives from the creation of two levels of the index that drive the combination's coupon rate. The TTIB's strike rate is the rate where the inverse floater coupon reaches 0%, and the TTIB begins to float inversely to the index. (The strike on a regular inverse is the same as the effective cap of the floater; for a LIBOR floater with an 8.0% cap and a .50 basis point margin, that level is 7.5%.)

In addition to meeting the demand for MBS that have the attributes of a short position in caps, the creation of TTIBs increases the possible leverage on the resulting inverse floater. This results from diverting a fixed portion of the coupon interest available to the inverse to the TTIB, making its coupon more sensitive to changes in the index. The structuring of a hypothetical floater/TTIB/inverse floater combination is illustrated in Exhibit 7.10. The diagram takes the floater/inverse floater

EXHIBIT 7.10   Mechanics of Floater/Inverse Floater/TTIB Combination (Initial 1-mo. LIBOR = 3.0%)

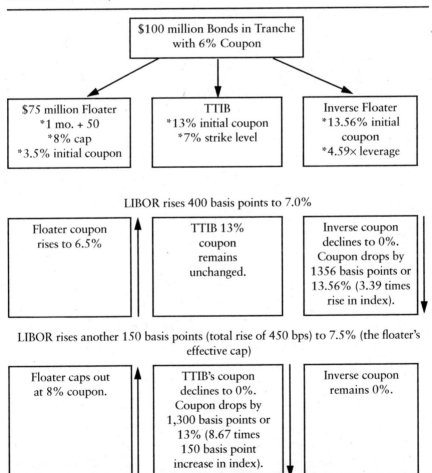

combination shown in Exhibit 7.5 and inserts a TTIB into the combination, increasing the coupon multiplier of the inverse. The exhibit also indicates what would happen to the combination's coupons if LIBOR rose to different levels, illustrating the "two-tiered" character of the bond described above.

The size of the TTIB (as well as the inverse floater) is dictated by the TTIB's coupon and strike level, and is similar to the calculation for the floater/inverse floater combination (i.e., without the TTIB). Referring to the earlier example (i.e., LIBOR + 50 basis points, 8.0% cap), we have the following values:

- Total interest available = $6,000,000
- Maximum amount of floaters = $75,000,000
- Combined face value of inverse floaters and TTIB = $25,000,000
- Maximum interest available to inverse floater and TTIB = $5,625,000
- Interest paid to floater at 3.0% LIBOR = $2,625,000

In order to calculate the sizes of the inverse and TTIB, the coupon and strike level of the TTIB must be determined. In the example, we assume that the strike rate and coupon are 7.0% and 13%, respectively, as shown in Exhibit 7.10. (Note that the strike must be less than the effective cap, that is, the floater's cap less the margin.) In this case, the calculations are as follows:

- Minimum interest available to floater = $6,000,000 − $5,625,000 = $375,000
- Face value of TTIB = $375,000 ÷ 13% = $2,884,615
- Face value of inverse = $25,000,000 − $2,884,615 = $22,115,385
- Inverse floater leverage = $75,000,000 ÷ $22,115,385 = 3.391×
- Inverse floater initial coupon = ($2,625,000 + $375,000) ÷ $22,115,385 = 13.56%

It is useful to observe how changes in the coupon and strike level of the TTIB impact the sizing of the inverse and TTIB. If the TTIB's coupon is reduced, all other factors unchanged, the TTIB becomes larger in size, and the inverse becomes both smaller and more leveraged. Assuming an 8.0% coupon and 7.0% strike for the TTIB, the calculations are:

- Face value of TTIB = $375,000 ÷ 8% = $4,687,500
- Face value of inverse = $25,000,000 − $4,687,500 = $20,312,500
- Inverse floater leverage = $75,000,000 ÷ $22,115,385 = 3.692×
- Inverse floater initial coupon = ($2,625,000 + $375,000) ÷ $20,312,500 = 14.77%

Now, assume that the strike rate is reduced to 6.0%, effectively reducing the cap of the floater and thus increasing the leverage of the nonfloater portion of the combination. (As shown earlier, the inverse multiple is inversely related to the cap of the floater.) If we hold the TTIB coupon at 13.0%, the calculation is as follows:

- Amount of interest available to floater at strike (i.e., 6.5% coupon rate) = $4,875,000
- Interest available to inverse and TTIB at strike level = $6,000,000 − $4,875,000 = $1,125,000
- TTIB face value = $1,125,000 ÷ 13% = $8,653,846
- Inverse face value = $25,000,000 − $8,653,846 = $16,346,153
- Inverse leverage = $16,346,153 ÷ $75,000,000 = 4.588×
- Inverse initial coupon = [$6,000,000 − ($2,625,000 + $1,125,000)] ÷ 16,346,153 = 13.76%

Holding the strike rate at 6.0% while dropping the coupon to 8.0% gives the following calculation:

- TTIB face value = $1,125,000 ÷ 8% = $14,062,500
- Inverse face value = $25,000,000 − $8,653,846 = $10,937,500
- Inverse leverage = $10,937,500 ÷ $75,000,000 = 6.857×
- Inverse initial coupon = [$6,000,000 − ($2,625,000 + $1,125,000)] ÷ 10,937,500 = 20.57%

These examples indicate that the inverse floater's multiple or leverage is inversely related to both the strike level and coupon of the TTIB. Put differently, reducing the TTIBs strike and/or coupon rate has the effect of increasing the leverage of the inverse floater in the combination.

It is important to remember that in this framework, the TTIB is still an inverse floater. If LIBOR exceeds the strike rate, the TTIB no longer has a fixed coupon; at that point, its coupon will adjust based on its reset formula, in the same fashion as a regular inverse.

A variation on a TTIB called a *digital TTIB* allows for the creation of bonds where the interest rate is either a fixed rate (as in all TTIBs) or 0%, without the creation of a true floating rate tranche. In this case, a TTIB and another bond (sometimes called a *digital PO* or an *anti-TTIB*, which has an initial coupon rate of 0%) are created. The TTIB has a fixed coupon; it receives all the interest allocated to the parent bond until the benchmark index reaches a certain level. Once the threshold is reached, all interest is directed to the anti-TTIB, and the coupon of the TTIB drops immediately to 0%. A simple example of this variation is shown in Exhibit 7.11. Note that the face value of the digital TTIB is

EXHIBIT 7.11   Example of "Digitial TTIB" and "Digital PO"

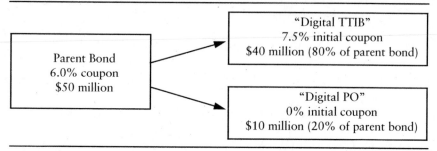

Note: Coupon of TTIB is 7.5% until LIBOR > 7.0%, then TTIB coupon is 0%. Coupon of PO is 0% until LIBOR > 7.0%, then PO coupon is 30%.

calculated as a variation on equation (7.2), as the two children effectively have fixed coupons. The size of the TTIB is the ratio of the parent coupon to the child coupon times the face value of the parent. The remainder is the face value of the digital PO.

EXCESS SERVICING IOs

The *excess servicing IO trust* is an offshoot of the IO market discussed earlier in this chapter. The logic behind the creation of these deals is unlike the other techniques mentioned previously, since it is not based on taking loans and redistributing their cash flows to improve execution. Rather, it is a means of distributing interest cash flows to investors that are created as part of the pooling process. Instead of holding excess servicing, originator/servicers use the excess servicing IO trust as a means of liquefying their balance sheets and free up capital by efficiently distributing the excess servicing asset to investors.

In Chapter 2, we discussed the process of pooling loans. Excess servicing is the cash flow strip off individual loans securitized in agency pools, as part of the process of pooling loans. This portion of the mortgage servicing right (or MSR) is a result of the process of creating fixed-coupon pools from loans with a variety of note rates. Excess servicing is analogous to IO cash flows in that it represents part of the stream of interest generated by each loan. (By contrast, the holder of base servicing typically accrues additional benefits, such as the names and addresses of borrowers for cross-marketing purposes, as well as interest earned from holding payments such as property tax impoundments.)

There have been markets for unsecuritized servicing for many years. Like the market for raw loans, trading excess servicing assets can be a cumbersome process, with a significant amount of paperwork accompanying each trade. In addition, a pool of servicing assets has a weighted average or WAC coupon. WAC coupons are common in some products, such as ARM pools, but they are associated with a degree of uncertainty. For example, imagine three loans with a face value of $100,000 that have note rates of 6.125%, 6.25%, and 6.375%. The WAC of a pool holding these loans would initially be 6.25%. However, if the 6.125% loan is paid off, the WAC of the pool increases to 6.3125% (not accounting for the effects of amortization). The same phenomenon occurs with unsecuritized excess servicing, where the coupons are weighted by the face value of the associated loans. The uncertainty caused by the WAC coupon, as well as the difficulties in accounting for and trading servicing, made it difficult for hedge funds and other investors that buy IOs to invest in servicing.

The concept of excess servicing IO was designed to overcome the difficulties associated with servicing as an asset. These deals are a means of converting excess servicing held by servicers into tradeable securities. By creating a structured security transaction, a pool of excess servicing is converted into a liquid trust where the bulk of the deal has fixed coupons. The process creates securities that are indistinguishable from trust IOs that are created as part of IO/PO deals.

Excess servicing IO structures produce a series of fixed rate IO tranches, along with a small WAC tranche, from pools of excess servicing stripped from fixed rate loans, typically with conforming loan balances. The pools represent excess servicing strips from an issuer's production over a period of time. The initial step involves grouping the excess servicing cash flows into narrow note rate buckets (typically in 50 basis point increments), based on the WAC of the underlying loans. Group A may be comprised of all loans with note rates between 6.5% and 6.99%, Group B might have all loans with note rates between 7.0% and 7.49%, etc. Each group is then structured independently, as described below, in order to produce fixed and WAC coupon tranches. The initial process of creating the different groups from a population of excess servicing is illustrated in Exhibit 7.12.

Note that the grouping of loans in narrow note rate buckets has the additional benefit of limiting the dispersion of note rates within a group. Agency pools, for example, can have significant dispersion in the note rates of the loans within pools. While normal execution economics typically cause pool WACs to be within roughly 45 to 65 basis points of their coupon rates, there are often small amounts of loans that have note rates significantly higher than the pool WAC. This dispersion can cause prepayment speeds to be faster than anticipated, adversely impacting the value of securities, such as IOs, that are highly sensitive to prepayment speeds. However, the practice of grouping servicing into

EXHIBIT 7.12   A Hypothetical Example of Structuring Excess Servicing into an
Excess Servicing IO Deal

---

1. Excess Servicing Portfolio
Representing 95,000 loans issued in Q2 2005
*$15,000,000,000 face value of loans
*15 basis points weighted average strip
*Note rates ranging from 5.5% to 8.0%

---

2. Portfolio Divided into Five Groups
A—Note rates 5.5–5.99%, 1,000 loans, $100 million face value
B—Note rates 6.0–6.49%, 22,000 loans, $4.2 billion face value
C—Note rates 6.5–6.99%, 55,000 loans, $8.2 billion face value
D—Note rates 7.0–7.49%, 14,000 loans, $2.0 billion face value
E—Note rates 7.5–8.00%, 3,000 loans, $500 million face value

---

3. Groups Are Structured into Fixed Coupon and WAC Tranches
A—1 fixed coupon tranche, 1 WAC tranche
B—3 fixed coupon tranches, 1 WAC tranche
C—4 fixed coupon tranches, 1 WAC tranche
D—1 fixed coupon tranche, 1 WAC tranche
E—1 fixed coupon tranche, 1 WAC tranche

---

groups defined by a small range of WACs causes the dispersion of note
rates within the group to be limited, improving the performance of IOs
structured from the group.

Once the groups are created, fixed rate portions of the servicing are
sliced from each loan in the group, based on how much excess servicing
is attached to the loan. As an example, imagine that Group A was comprised of four loans with face values and excess servicing as follows:

- Loan 1—$100,000 face value, 23 basis points
- Loan 2—$250,000 face value, 19 basis points
- Loan 3—$175,000 face value, 17 basis points
- Loan 4—$225,000 face value, 12 basis points

The structuring process involves iteratively stripping a constant
amount of servicing off as many loans in the group as possible. The first
iteration might create a tranche with a face value of $750,000, and a
coupon rate of 12 basis points. This would leave the following:

- Loan 1—$100,000 face value, 11 basis points (23 less 12)
- Loan 2—$250,000 face value, 7 basis points
- Loan 3—$175,000 face value, 5 basis points
- Loan 4—$225,000 face value, 0 basis points

The second iteration would strip 5 basis points from loans 1 to 3, creating a tranche with a face value of $525,000 and a 5 basis point coupon rate. This would leave:

- Loan 1—$100,000 face value, 6 basis points (11 less 5)
- Loan 2—$250,000 face value, 2 basis points
- Loan 3—$175,000 face value, 0 basis points
- Loan 4—$225,000 face value, 0 basis points

The next iteration would strip 2 basis points off loans 1 and 2, creating a tranche with a 2 basis point coupon and a face value of $350,000. Loan 1 would be left with 4 basis points of servicing. This would create the following structure:

Tranche 1: $750,000 face value, 12 basis points coupon rate
Tranche 2: $525,000 face value, 5 basis points coupon rate
Tranche 3: $350,000 face value, 2 basis points coupon rate
Tranche 4: $100,000 face value, 4 basis point coupon rate

Tranche 4 in this example represents the WAC tranche, or more accurately is the tranche from the group that has a WAC coupon. It is the residual of the structuring process, in that it is comprised of the cash flows left over after the iterative stripping process is completed. The process is illustrated in Exhibit 7.13. Note that once the note rates of the groups are defined, as shown in Exhibit 7.12, each group is structured independently.

In actuality, the loan groups are comprised of many thousands of loans. Therefore, the process of creating each group's structure is complex, and is often treated as a constrained optimization process. The following are some constraints used by issuers to generate a structure:

- Create fixed rate tranches with a minimum face value and/or proceeds. (Typical minimum sizes are $10 million notional face value or $2 million in proceeds; anything smaller is considered an odd lot by the market, and will trade to a concession.)
- Create as small a WAC tranche as possible. (WAC tranches also trade at a concession, since they are less liquid and more difficult to value.)

EXHIBIT 7.13 Schematic Representation of the Process of Structuring One Group into Excess Servicing IO Tranches

Initial Collateral

Loan 1—$100,000 face value, 23 basis points
Loan 2—$250,000 face value, 19 basis points
Loan 3—$175,000 face value, 17 basis points
Loan 4—$225,000 face value, 12 basis points

Process	Resulting Structure	Remaining Collateral
Iteration 1		
Strip the loan with the least excess servicing (12 bps) to 0 and then remove the same strip from the other loans.	Tranche 1—$750,000 face value, 12 basis point coupon	Loan 1—$100,000 face value, 11 basis points Loan 2—$250,000 face value, 7 basis points Loan 3—$175,000 face value, 5 basis points Loan 4—$225,000 face value, 0 basis points
Iteration 2		
Strip the loan with the least excess servicing (5 bps) to 0 and then remove the same strip from the other loans.	Tranche 2—$525,000 face value, 5 basis point coupon	Loan 1—$100,000 face value, 6 basis points Loan 2—$250,000 face value, 2 basis points Loan 3—$175,000 face value, 0 basis points Loan 4—$225,000 face value, 0 basis points
Iteration 3		
Strip the loan with the least excess servicing (2 bps) to 0 and then remove the same strip from the other loans.	Tranche 3—$350,000 face value, 2 basis point coupon	Loan 1—$100,000 face value, 4 basis points Loan 2—$250,000 face value, 0 basis points Loan 3—$175,000 face value, 0 basis points Loan 4—$225,000 face value, 0 basis points
Iteration 4		
When no more excess servicing can be stripped, remainder is pooled into WAC tranche	Tranche 4 (WAC)—$100,000 face value, 4 basis point coupon	

■ Keep the WACs of the tranches similar to that of benchmarks used in the IO market. (Excess servicing IOs are typically valued at a percentage of a liquid benchmark IO trust. If the WAC of a tranche diverges significantly from that of the benchmark, it will be difficult to value, and will trade poorly.)

However the deal is structured, the goal of the process is to maximize the proceeds generated from converting a large pool of WAC servicing into a structure comprised largely of fixed rate IO tranches.

To convert the coupons into normal, 50 basis point increment coupons, the nominal coupon is divided by the desired coupon and then multiplied by the face amount of the loans. The process of calculating the notional value of each tranche is identical to the method used in calculating notional face values for tranched IOs discussed earlier in this chapter, using equation (7.2). For example, if a tranche has a coupon rate of 14 basis points and a face value of $2.6 billion, it could be converted into a tranche with a 5.5% coupon and a notional value of $66.1 million as follows:

$$\text{Notional value} = \left[\frac{0.14}{5.5}\right] \times 2,600,000,000 = \$66,181,818$$

Note that the face value of tranches is typically large, as it includes the amount of every loan contributing cash flow to the tranche. In addition, the "desired coupon" for the excess servicing trust does not have to be the same as the coupon into which the loans were pooled. For example, a loan with a 6.375% note rate can be securitized into a Fannie 5.5% pool. However, the excess servicing from that loan could be placed in a group to be structured into 6.0% fixed rate IO (as well as the WAC tranche). This decision is made at the point where the servicing is segregated into note rate buckets, using the process shown in Exhibit 7.12.

CHAPTER 8

Structuring Private Label CMOs

The private label CMO market encompasses a variety of product and structuring variations. Technically, any deal that is not securitized under an agency or GSE shelf (i.e., Ginnie Mae, Freddie Mac, or Fannie Mae) can be considered *private label* as the issuing entity has no connection to the U.S. government (either explicit or implicit). Such deals must have some form of credit enhancement in order to create large amounts of investment-grade bonds. The convention in the markets, however, is to limit the private label sector to the securitization of prime, first-lien fixed and adjustable rate loans. Other products, such as deals backed by subprime and second-lien loans, are classified as *mortgage-related asset-backed securities*, a subset of the ABS category.

In some sense, this classification scheme has become fairly arbitrary. Mortgage credit has evolved over time from discrete sectors to a continuum. As the dividing line between the alt-A and subprime sectors blur, the structuring form has become the primary factor distinguishing the two sectors. For example, if one type of structure offers superior execution for a loan, chances are good that it will be securitized using such a structure, irrespective of the classification of the loan. Thus, the two sectors are distinguishable as much by their structural forms as their collateral classification. For the purposes of this book, *private label deals* will be those using the fairly straightforward form of credit enhancement called *senior/subordination* or *shifting interest* structures (described in Chapter 5). *Mortgage ABS* utilizes more complex credit enhancement schemes, combining subordination with other mechanisms to create the largest possible amounts of investment-grade tranches. This mechanism, called the *overcollateralization* or *OC structure*, is examined in Chapter 9.

Conventional loans with nonconforming loan balances (called *jumbo loans*) have long been securitized in private label deals. Conforming balance, alt-A loans have also been securitized in private label structures, but the dynamics of the securitization have evolved over time, due largely to the involvement of the GSEs in the sector. A brief discussion of the changing involvement of the GSEs in this sector, in fact, gives some useful perspective on its evolution during the period after 1998.

For example, most conforming alt-A production in the late 1990s was securitized in private label structures and comingled with jumbo-balance loans. As research indicated that conforming balance, alt-A loans had favorable prepayment performance over similar loans with larger balances, issuers increasingly segregated their conforming alt-A production into separate private label deals.

The GSEs then began to actively include alt-A loans in their MBS pools. In addition to their desire to increase their share of a growing market, they became increasingly comfortable with their ability to accurately predict the product's credit performance and price the guaranty fees. By 2004, issuers increasingly sought to maximize loan proceeds by comparing agency pooling versus private label execution. As we subsequently discuss, optimal execution is not constant over time, but can differ depending on both market conditions and different dollar costs of credit enhancement.

Aside from the presence of credit enhancement, private label deals share many features and structuring techniques with agency CMOs. There are some important differences, however, due to the nature of the loans collateralizing the deal as well as legal and regulatory issues associated with the different shelves. These include the following issues:

- Private label deals can be structured such that derivatives, such as caps and cap corridors, can be inserted into the structures as risk mitigators. The GSEs, by contrast, do not allow for their inclusion in deals.
- The loans collateralizing private label deals are generally assumed to prepay faster than those in agency pools. The convention in the agency market is to structure deals using a base-case prepayment speed consistent with median prepayment speeds reported by Bloomberg. Private label deals, by contrast, are structured either to a market convention (i.e., PSA speeds ranging from 250% to 300%) or a predefined ramp (i.e., 6% to 18% CPR ramping over 12 months). The ramp is defined in the prospectus and, as described in Chapter 3, it is typically called the *prospectus prepayment curve*, or PPC (100% PPC is simply the base ramp defined at the time of pricing).
- Private label deals typically have cleanup calls. These are inserted into deals to relieve the trustees from the burden of having to oversee deals with very small remaining balances. The calls are triggered when the current face of the deal and/or collateral group declines below a prede-

termined level; the percentages triggering the call can vary, but are typically either 5% or 10% of the remaining balance. (As we discuss in Chapter 9, OC structures typically are structured to insure that the call is exercised, using a stepup provision.)

This chapter first details the mechanisms involved in creating the internal credit enhancement typically utilized in private label deals. It also details some of the factors involved in gauging optimal execution (i.e., private label versus agency pooling) for conforming balance loans. It will then discuss a number of structuring variations unique to the sector. Some structures such as NAS bonds have been utilized in agency structures from time to time; other variations, such as the inclusion of cap contracts necessary to create corridor-cap floaters, can for a variety of reasons only be utilized within the framework of a private label structure.

Note that while the focus of the chapter is on the structuring of fixed rate loans, hybrid ARMs can be structured in a similar fashion. Deals typically divide the collateral into groups based on their product type (i.e., 3/1s, 5/1s, etc.); the senior bonds are then either sold as passthroughs or time-tranched.

PRIVATE LABEL CREDIT ENHANCEMENT

The first step in structuring the credit enhancement for a private label deal is to split the face value of the loans into senior and subordinated interests. The senior bonds have higher priority with respect to both the receipt of interest and principal and the allocation of realized losses, and are generally created with enough subordination to be rated AAA by the credit rating agencies. In most cases, the subordinate interests are subdivided (or tranched) into a series of bonds that decline sequentially in priority. The subordinate classes normally range from AA in rating to an unrated first-loss piece. These securities are often referenced as the *six-pack*, since there are six broad rating grades generally issued by the rating agencies. In the investment-grade category, bonds range from AA to BBB; noninvestment grade ratings decline from BB to the unrated first-loss piece. The structure (or "splits") of a hypothetical deal is shown in panels A and B of Exhibit 8.1, while a schematic detailing how and losses are allocated within the structure is contained in Exhibit 8.2.

Internal credit enhancement requires two complimentary mechanisms. The cash flows for deals are allocated through the mechanism of a *waterfall*, which dictates the allocation of principal and interest payments to tranches with different degrees of seniority. At the same time,

EXHIBIT 8.1   Measuring Subordination by Percentage of Deal Size and Credit
Support for a Hypothetical $400 Million Deal with 3.5% Initial Subordination
Panel A. Tranche Size as a Percentage of the Total Deal

	Face Value ($)	Percent of Deal
AAA	$386,000,000	96.50%
AA	6,000,000	1.50%
A	2,600,000	0.65%
BBB	1,800,000	0.45%
BB	1,200,000	0.30%
B	1,200,000	0.30%
First Loss (Nonrated)	1,200,000	0.30%
Total Subordination	14,000,000	3.50%

Panel B. Tranche Size Measured by Percentage of Subordination for Each Rating
Level (i.e., credit support)

	Face Value ($)	Credit Support (%)[a]
AAA	$386,000,000	3.50%
AA	6,000,000	2.00%
A	2,600,000	1.35%
BBB	1,800,000	0.90%
BB	1,200,000	0.60%
B	1,200,000	0.30%
First Loss (Nonrated)	1,200,000	0.00%

[a] Calculated by summing the deal percentages of all tranches junior in priority. As
an example, if cumulative losses on the deal were 0.40%, the First Loss and B-rated
tranche would be fully exhausted, but the BBs and above would not be affected.

the allocation of realized losses is also governed by a separate prioritiza-
tion schedule, with the subordinates typically being impacted in reverse
order of priority.

While the original subordination levels are set at the time of issuance (or, more precisely, at the time the attributes of the deal's collateral
are finalized), deals with internal credit enhancement are designed such
that the amount of credit enhancement grows over time. Private label
structures generally use a so-called *shifting interest mechanism*, in
which the subordinate classes (or subs) do not receive principal prepay-

EXHIBIT 8.2   Schematic of Hypothetical Structure with Cash Flow and Loss
Allocations

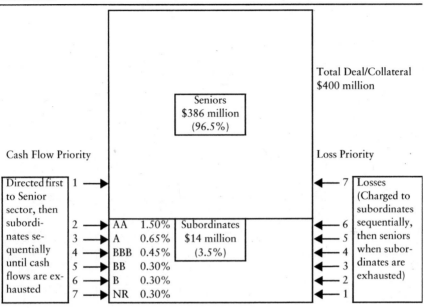

ments for a period of time after issuance, generally five years for fixed
rate deals. (This is the origin of the shifting interest term by which the
structuring form is often referenced.) After the lockout period expires,
the subs begin to receive prepayments on an escalating basis. It is only
after 10 years that the subs receive a pro rata allocation of prepayments.
Locking out the subs means that as the collateral experiences prepayments, the face value of the subs grows in proportion relative to the
senior classes; the senior classes receive all the collateral prepayments
during the lockout period and hence decline proportionately over time.
A typical shifting interest schedule, along with notes on the effect of the
principal reallocation, is shown in Exhibit 8.3.

The shifting interest mechanism in private label ARM deals is similar but not identical to that utilized in fixed rate structures. In order to
determine when the subordinated tranches can begin to receive prepaid
principal, ARM deals combine a longer initial lockout schedule with a
credit enhancement test. The subordinate tranches are scheduled to be
locked out from receiving prepayments for 120 months, after which prepayments are allocated to the subordinates based on a schedule that
scales in over five years. The proportions (30% in year 11, 40% in year
12, 60% in year 13, 80% in year 14, and 100% thereafter) are the same

EXHIBIT 8.3   Shifting Interest Example for Subordinates on a Fixed Rate Prime Deal

Months 1–60	Subs completely locked out from prepayments (receive amortization only)
Months 61–72	Subs receive 30% of pro rata share of prepayments
Months 73–84	Subs receive 40% of pro rata share of prepayments
Months 85–96	Subs receive 60% of pro rata share of prepayments
Months 97–108	Subs receive 80% of pro rata share of prepayments
Month 109+	Subs receive 100% of pro rata share of prepayments

Effects of Shifting Interest Structure:
1. Senior bonds paydown faster than subs.
2. Seniors make up proportionately less of the deal.
3. Subordination grows, providing senior bonds more protection.
4. Subordinate bonds have to protect fewer senior bonds (deleveraging).
5. Subordinate bonds have excellent call protection.

as those of fixed rate structures. However, once the ARM deal's total subordination percentage doubles, the subordinate tranches can begin to receive prepayments. Once the *doubling test* has been satisfied, the subordinates receive 50% of their pro rata share of prepayments up to the 36th month after issuance; after that point, they receive their full pro rata share of prepaid principal.

The shifting interest mechanism (and its equivalent in OC structures) have become a standard feature in structured deals for a number of reasons. The most obvious reason stems from the need to insure that the senior securities retain their triple-A rating. At any prepayment speed greater than zero, the effective amount of subordination grows as the loan collateral prepays. The prepayment lockout also augments the deal credit enhancement to compensate for the effects of unexpectedly fast prepayments. The assumption in the mortgage world has traditionally been that prepayments are faster for better-quality borrowers who have the means and sophistication to refinance and thus decrease their payments. However, as the higher credit loans prepay over time, the loans remaining in the pool are presumed to be weaker in credit, a situation that is generically referred to as *adverse selection*. Due to the existence of the shifting interest mechanism, the proportional amount of subordination grows faster at higher prepayment speeds, causing the deal to deleverage faster. Exhibit 8.4 shows how the sizes of the senior and subordinate classes of the previously described hypothetical structure change over time at the pricing speed, and also shows the resulting growth of the subordination percentage.

EXHIBIT 8.4   Collateral and Subordinate Balances Over Time for a Hypothetical Deal at 300% PSA, Initial Subordination 3.5%

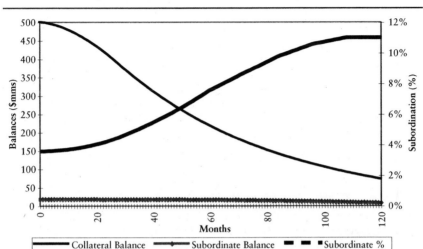

Deals often have more than one collateral group securitized in the same transaction to minimize costs. Typically, the collateral groups will have different characteristics that make them difficult to commingle. For example, a deal may have separate collateral groups comprised of 30- and 15-year loans. Depending on the collateral in question, the two groups can have separate subordination groups. Alternatively, one set of subs serves as credit support for both groups, in a so-called "Y structure." This creates larger subordinate classes, which generally are more liquid and subsequently trade to tighter spreads.

Agency Pooling Versus Private Label Deal Execution

As with all execution decisions, the calculation of optimal execution for conforming balance loans is a question of maximizing the loan's proceeds, taking into account all revenues and costs associated with the competing securitization vehicles. This is particularly true for loans with "alty" characteristics that increase the costs associated with credit enhancement. There are a number of trade-offs that must be taken into account when evaluating relative execution, including:

1. *The proceeds realized from the sale of the security created.* The proceeds from the agency pass-through are derived from the TBA price for the coupon created, adjusted for the settlement month; the proceeds for

the private label deal are those received for the triple-A senior tranche, and are typically quoted as a spread behind same-coupon Fannie Mae TBAs.

2. *The cost associated with credit enhancement.* For an agency pool, the cost is the guaranty fee (or g-fee) paid to the agency which, as described previously, is akin to a credit wrap on the individual loan. Credit enhancement in a private label deal is the cost of the subordination, resulting from selling some of the loan's principal at a concession to the price of the senior tranches.

The impact of the first item is fairly clear: the smaller the concession between agency and the senior private label securities, the better the execution for the private label option. With respect to the second point, however, the dynamics of the credit enhancement trade-off can be impacted by the level of interest rates and expected prepayment speeds, as well as the number of basis points of guaranty fee associated with a particular loan. We noted in Chapter 2 that the guaranty fee is quoted in terms of basis points from the loan's interest cash flow. This means that the monetized value of the guaranty fee (i.e., the actual dollar cost of GSE credit enhancement) is a function of either intercoupon swaps or guaranty fee buydown multiples. Since these are essentially interest-only cash flows, their value is strongly influenced by prepayment speeds and the level of mortgage rates. By contrast, subordination is a direct dollar cost to the securitization, and is independent of prepayment speed expectations. This means that optimal execution on alt-A loans in a rising rate environment can often swing to private label transactions because the dollar cost of credit enhancement for the agency pooling option is rising relative to the private label alternative, even if both subordination levels and guaranty fees remain constant. In turn, this often diverts production from agency pools to conforming private label securitizations when interest rates rise and expected prepayment speeds decline.

As an example, we will compare execution alternatives for a 5.75% loan under the following assumptions:

- Best coupon execution for both options is a 5.5% coupon.
- Both options require the retention of 25 basis points of base servicing.
- The senior portion of the private label deal trades 23/32s behind Fannie Mae 5.5% TBAs.
- The guaranty fee paid to the GSE in question would be 20 basis points.
- The private label deal has 5% subordination.
- The guaranty fee buydown multiple quoted by the GSE is 6.0×.
- The subordinates collectively trade 12 points behind Fannie 5.5% TBAs.

■ Total costs for the deal are 1/8 of a point (i.e., 0.125% of the deal's face value).

The results of the analysis are shown in Exhibit 8.5. In the example, the best execution would be as an agency pool because the dollar cost of credit enhancement (1.2% of the loans's face value) would be lower than that associated with private label execution (1.475%). However, Exhibit 8.5 also indicates that the breakeven cost of subordination is a guaranty fee of 24.6 basis points. Therefore, a more impaired or "alty" loan, which would require a guaranty fee of 25 basis points or more, would offer optimal execution in a private label transaction.

One other implication of this methodology is that the execution dynamics are not static in the face of changing interest rates and prepayment speeds, even if guaranty fees and private label pricing are left unchanged. Since guaranty fees are part of the interest cash flow generated by the loan, their value (like any interest or IO-heavy cash flow) is sensitive to prepayment expectations. Therefore, changes in interest rates and prepayment expectations will also cause buydown multiples to change. Using the example shown in Exhibit 8.5, a decline in the guaranty fee buydown multiple from 6.0× to 4.0× would increase the breakeven guaranty fee for an impaired loan (i.e., the level of the guaranty fee where the issuer would be indifferent between execution options) to almost 37 basis points. This reflects the declining dollar value of the g-fee buydown, cheapening agency execution relative to private label securitization.

EXHIBIT 8.5   Comparison of Execution for Conforming Balance 5.75% Loan as a 5.5% Agency Pool and a Private Label Security

Agency Pool		Private Label Deal	
1. Guaranty fee (g-fee) assumed (basis points)	20	1. Senior tranches (95% of deal trading 23/32s behind Fannie 5.5s)	0.75
2. G-fee multiple	6.0	2. Subordinates (5% of deal trades 12 points behind Fannies)	0.6
		3. Deal costs	0.125
Dollar Cost of Guaranty Fee		*Dollar cost of private label credit enhancement*	
G-fee multiple × G-fee (1 × 2)	1.20	Total cost of subordination (1 + 2 + 3)	1.475
Breakeven level of g-fee (in basis points) to private label execution (1.475/6.0)			24.6

This suggests that there is an element of rate directionality to execution dynamics. All things equal, private label execution becomes more economical when rates rise and prepayment expectations are reduced, even if subordination levels, subordinate pricing, and guaranty fees remain unchanged.

PRIVATE LABEL SENIOR STRUCTURING VARIATIONS

Nonaccelerated Senior Bonds

Nonaccelerated senior bonds or *NAS bonds* have their origins in the profile of prime subordinate tranches. The lockout and prepayment protection inherent in the shifting interest structure creates long-duration bonds that have stable average life and duration profiles. However, many investors that have a need for these types of tranches cannot invest in subordinate securities, often because of regulatory prohibitions (such as ERISA for pension funds). The NAS bond mimics the cash flow structure of subordinates while creating bonds that are senior in loss priority. While the initial concept was introduced in the prime market, mortgage ABS deals also are structured with NAS tranches, although the bonds are created in a slightly different fashion.

Similar to subordinate tranches, NAS bonds do not receive principal payments for the first five years. After year 5, the proportional amount of principal received generally scales up on a yearly basis, in the same fashion as the shifting interest, lockout schedule shown in Exhibit 8.3. One difference between NAS and subordinate bonds is that subs receive amortized principal during the first five years, while NAS bonds typically have a complete lockout of both amortized and prepaid principal. After the lockout schedule expires (generally after year 10), the NAS tranches receive their full pro rata share of principal cash flows from the collateral. The resulting cash flow pattern is serrated in appearance, as shown in Exhibit 8.6, reflecting the stepped nature of the principal cash flows and the impact of the schedule on their timing.

NAS tranches typically comprise 10% of original face value of a deal, although some structuring derivations will have original NAS percentages of 20% or higher. Allocation of cash flows is very similar in concept to the shifting interest mechanism utilized in the senior/sub structure. The principal allocation is accomplished by taking the NAS bonds as a percentage of the outstanding balance of the collateral—the "NAS Percentage" in the prospectus—and multiplying it by the proportion of principal it is scheduled to receive, denoted in the prospectus as

EXHIBIT 8.6   Cash Flows for Representative NAS Bond at 300% PSA

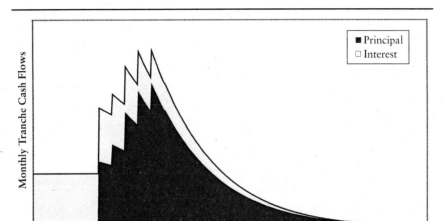

the "NAS Distribution Percentage" or "Shift Percentage." The schedule is generally the same as that used to define the shifting interest mechanism (as illustrated in Exhibit 8.3), although the NAS schedule is referenced in the prospectus separately. As an example, assume that the NAS Distribution Percentage in month 65 is 30% (meaning it receives 30% of its pro rata share of principal). At that point, the rest of the senior bonds will have partially paid down such that the NAS bond at that point comprises 20% of the deal (growing from the original 10% at origination). Multiplying the 30% Distribution Percentage by the 20% prevailing NAS percentage suggests that in month 65 the NAS bond receives 6% of the principal generated by the collateral pool.

There are some structuring derivations designed to improve the profile of the NAS bonds by creating *Super-NAS bonds*. One method is to time-tranche the NAS bond into two bonds. The cash flows (and thus the profile) of the front bond are dictated by the schedule, while the longer tranche is essentially a sequential cash flow. A more recent technique is to accelerate the NAS bond slightly by changing the way the NAS percentage is calculated. Instead of the traditional calculation described earlier (i.e., the NAS bond balance divided by the outstanding collateral balance), a constant amount is added to the NAS balance. This constant is sometimes referenced as the *catalyst*. By changing the numerator of the fraction, more cash flow is directed to the NAS bonds than by using the standard proportional calculation, which subsequently causes the average life and duration of the NAS to extend less at slower prepayment speeds.

The presence of NAS bonds (along with the shifting interest subordinates) in a deal changes the profile of the remaining (i.e., senior non-NAS) bonds. These bonds (which are also categorized as *accelerated seniors*) have more volatile average life and duration profiles than those of pure sequentials created through simple time-tranching. This is because the subordinates and NAS bonds (or shifting interest bonds) have schedules; the accelerated seniors only receive principal after the schedule is met, in the same fashion as supports in a PAC/Support deal.

The impact of the shifting interest bonds on the profile of the accelerated seniors is, however, less pronounced than that of PACs on the support bonds in a structure. This is because the combined proportion of the subordinates and NAS bonds is much smaller than the 50%–70% PACs typically comprising a PAC/Support deal. The impact of the shifting interest schedule on the accelerated seniors is also somewhat different due to the nature of the schedule. As discussed previously, the schedule typically begins after month 60, and scales in over the following 60 months. The cash flows of the senior non-NAS bonds are "accelerated" for the first 60 months by the fact that they receive more than their pro rata portion of principal; after that point, they only receive principal once the schedule for the shifting interest bonds is met.

This pattern is illustrated in Exhibit 8.7. The area under the curve is the total principal cash flow at the pricing speed of 300% PSA. For the first 60 months, the senior non-NAS bonds receive almost all the princi-

EXHIBIT 8.7   Monthly Principal Cash Flow Allocations in a Private Label Deal: $500 Million Face Value, 6.0% Net Coupon Rate, 300% PSA Pricing Speed

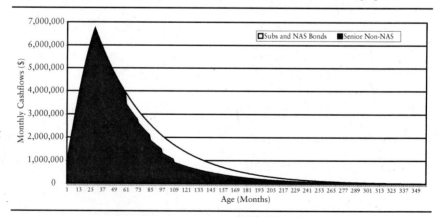

pal generated by the collateral. (As noted previously, the subordinates typically receive a pro rata allocation of scheduled principal payments.) After month 60, the shifting interest bonds receive an increasing share of principal, and by month 120 the two groups receive roughly the same amount of principal cash flow.

There are a number of implications to this cash flow structure. As noted, the presence of a schedule causes the bonds to have more volatile profiles than pure sequentials. The delay of the allocation of principal until month 60 means that the leveraging effect of the NAS only impacts the bonds that receive cash flows at the time the schedule takes effect. The effect is analogous to the performance of bonds with barbelled cash flows discussed in Chapter 6 in that the profile of the cash flows changes over time. This is illustrated in Exhibits 8.8 and 8.9. Both exhibits take the cash flows generated by straight sequential and shifting interest structures and carve them up into a series of 12-month sequential cash flows based on the final payment date of the tranche at the pricing speed of 250% PSA. Put differently, tranche A captures the cash flows from issuance through month 12, tranche B uses the cash flows from month 13 through month 24, and so on. (For the purposes of this discussion, we reference sequentials from shifting interest structures as *leveraged sequentials*; the bonds from the straight sequential structure will be called *unleveraged sequentials*.)

EXHIBIT 8.8   Average Lives of Different Cash Flows in Leveraged and Unleveraged Sequential Structures, Cash Flows Time-Tranched Yearly

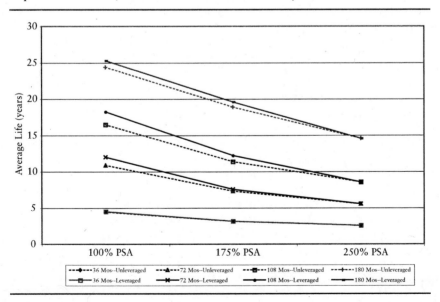

EXHIBIT 8.9 Percentage Increase in Average Life from 250% PSA to 125% PSA for Leveraged and Unleveraged Sequential Structures, Pass-Through Cash Flows Tranched Yearly

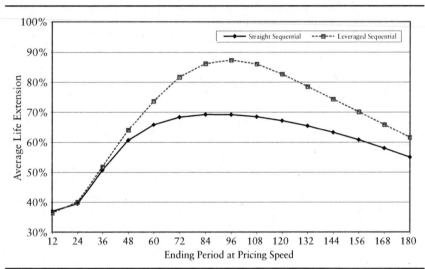

Exhibit 8.8 shows the average life of a few of the leveraged and unleveraged sequential tranches at prepayment speeds of 175% and 100% PSA. The exhibit indicates that the very short bonds in the structures (i.e., bonds with cash flows from month 25 through 36 at the pricing speed) have virtually identical extension profiles. The intermediate cash flows in the leverage structure exhibit significantly more average life extension, however, reflecting the diversion of principal from the accelerated seniors to the subordinates and NAS bonds. This effect is further illustrated in Exhibit 8.9, which shows the extension in percentage terms for all "tranches" in both structures when speeds are slowed from 250% to 125% PSA. It is clear from this exhibit that the greatest incremental extension is concentrated in the middle of the shifting interest or leveraged sequential structure.

This attribute of private label deals complicates some structuring decisions. As an example, time-tranching a *wide-window front sequential*, which would typically have an average life of roughly 3.5 years, creates a very stable short bond, but a volatile intermediate class, with around a 6.0-year average life. In order to create the tranched structure, the structurer would typically need to have expressions of interest for the 6.0-year, as there is a limited constituency for volatile intermediate tranches.

In light of these considerations, an important attribute of private label deals is the front-loaded nature of the principal cash flows. Put differently, the short cash flows in the structure comprise a large proportion of the face value of the deal compared to agency deals. This reflects both the acceleration of the principal resulting from the shifting interest structure, as discussed above, along with the faster prepayment assumptions used in structuring private label deals, particularly those collateralized by jumbo loans. One implication of this phenomenon is that deal execution is highly dependent on the level at which the short cash flows are sold.

Localized PACs and Super-Stable Bonds

Both the structure and collateral characteristics of private label deals make it difficult to structure PACs in the fashion discussed in Chapter 6. In agency CMO deals, the PACs and supports are typically comprised of principal cash flows generated over the full term of the collateral. This is very difficult to do in most private label structures, due to a number of issues, which include:

- The front-loading of principal cash flows due to the faster prepayment assumption, as mentioned in the previous section.
- The limited amount of longer senior non-NAS principal cash flows.
- The leveraging created by the shifting interest bonds.

Together, these factors make it difficult to create PAC schedules that are effective for intermediate and long bonds. This means that somewhat different structuring techniques must be utilized in order to optimize deal execution and meet the demand from different investors for a variety of profiles.

As the private label PAC market is less standardized than in the agency sector, there is more flexibility with respect to the PAC bands utilized. While bands based on the PSA model are often utilized, it is not uncommon to see PAC bands generated as a multiple of the pricing ramp or even in CPR terms. The lack of standardization, however, reflects the difficulties inherent in creating traditional PACs within private label structures.

One structuring variation is the creation of localized PACs. In Chapter 6, we noted that in its basic form PAC schedules are typically created for the life of the deal; the resulting PAC and support bonds are then time-tranched. In a localized support, the process is reversed. The accelerated sequentials are first time-tranched; at that point, a PAC schedule is generated for one of the sequential tranches (normally the front sequential for reasons described already) and the parent tranche is divided into PAC and support tranches.

Another variation used to structure the front sequential cash flows is to create *super-stable tranches* (SST). The SST is conceptually similar to that of the localized PACs in that the front sequential is used as the parent bond. Once the sequential structure is created, the SST bond is then created using the following steps:

1. Tranche the front sequential into a short-current, pay-sequential bond and a longer, locked-out tranche.
2. Assign a fixed dollar amount of monthly principal cash flow to the locked-out sequential bond. This bond then becomes the SST bond, and the fixed principal payment acts as the SST bond's schedule. The short sequential now has a much more volatile average life profile, and acts as support for the SST.

The presence of the schedule has a number of effects on the SST bond. In addition to stabilizing its profile, it acts to both shorten the average life of the SST bond and makes it a current payer (i.e., it pays principal concurrently with the support bond). The schedule is similar to sinking funds seen in corporate bond structures; for this reason, the bonds are sometimes referenced as *sinkers*. An illustration of this process is shown in Exhibit 8.10.

The primary difference between structuring PACs and SSTs is in how the schedule is created. In PACs, the schedule is generated as a function of principal cash flows calculated at the prepayment speeds dictated by the PAC bands. The monthly scheduled principal payment for the SST is typically generated as a percentage of the original face value of the tranche, and is stable in dollar terms. This is illustrated by the example in Exhibit 8.11, which shows cash flows for hypothetical SST and localized PAC bonds created from the same 3.0-year average life parent bond. The SST comprises 48% of the parent bond's face value, and receives $550,000 per month (roughly 1.4% of the bond's face value). The PAC is structured with a 6%–20% CPR band.

One implication of Exhibit 8.11 is that the SST bond receives more principal from its schedule than does the PAC. All things equal, this gives the SST better extension protection than the PAC, as long as enough principal is generated to meet the schedule. Note also that the scheduled principal payments to the SST drop below the $550,000 level at month 60, when the shifting interest bonds (i.e., the subordinates and NAS bonds) begin to receive principal.

EXHIBIT 8.10 Example of Creating a Structure with a Super-Stable Bond where All Average Lives Run at 100% PPC Pricing Speed (8%–20% CPR Over 12 Months)

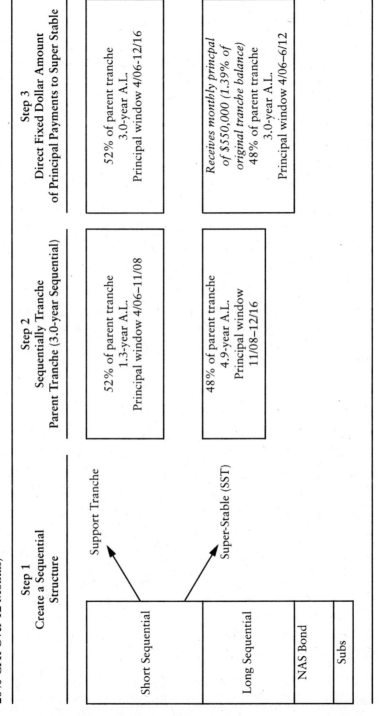

Step 1 Create a Sequential Structure	Step 2 Sequentially Tranche Parent Tranche (3.0-year Sequential)	Step 3 Direct Fixed Dollar Amount of Principal Payments to Super Stable

Support Tranche

Super-Stable (SST)

Short Sequential

Long Sequential

NAS Bond

Subs.

52% of parent tranche
1.3-year A.L.
Principal window 4/06–11/08

48% of parent tranche
4.9-year A.L.
Principal window
11/08–12/16

52% of parent tranche
3.0-year A.L.
Principal window 4/06-12/16

*Receives monthly princpal
of $550,000 (1.39% of
original tranche balance)*
48% of parent tranche
3.0-year A.L.
Principal window 4/06–6/12

EXHIBIT 8.11 Payment Schedules for Localized PAC and Super-Stable Bonds

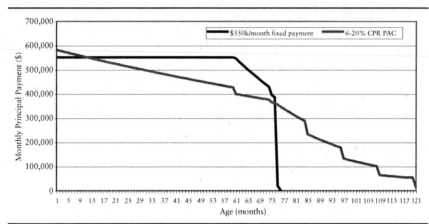

To create SST bonds with the desired average life and profile, structuring is an iterative process of both sizing the SST (i.e., the different sizes of the two bonds created in step #1 above) and allocating different fixed monthly payments to the schedule. While the process can be somewhat cumbersome, the ability to specify both the proportions of the two bonds and the amount of cash directed to the super-stable tranche gives the structurer more flexibility in creating bonds and tweaking their average life and profile. By contrast, the attributes of localized PACs are a function of the assigned PAC bands. (The average lives of localized PACs also typically falls out based on the structuring bands, as well as the average life of the parent bond. While it is possible to specify average lives, the highly front-loaded cash flows of private label sequentials make it difficult to target an average life for the PAC without skewing the relative proportions.)

Variations of the structuring technique have evolved over time, reflecting the desire to have more flexibility in tweaking the profile of both the SST and support bonds. For example, one method generates the schedule as a function of the declining balance of the SST bond, instead of as a fixed dollar amount. This typically creates stable sinker bonds that nonetheless have more average life variability than a true SST bond, while the profile of the support bond is improved.

Corridor-Cap Floaters

As noted in the previous section, the relative size of the front-end, senior non-NAS cash flows makes their execution highly important to the execution of the entire deal. One structuring variation used in all MBS sectors (both agency and private label) is to split cash flows into floater/

inverse floater combinations. This acts both to improve the deal execution and meet the strong and persistent demand for floating rate assets.

The basic techniques for structuring floating rate bonds were discussed in Chapter 7. Exhibit 8.12 uses an exhibit from that earlier chapter to demonstrate how a simple floater/inverse IO (IIO) combination can be structured from collateral or a parent tranche with a 6.0% coupon. As we noted previously, however, there are trade-offs associated with this technique. If the whole tranche is to be utilized, the cap of the floater equals the coupon of the collateral; this level is typically lower than that desire by investors in floating rate bonds. If the floater cap is to be raised to a higher level, a premium/discount split must be used to create parent bonds with a high enough cap, limiting the proportion of the parent that can be structured into the floater/IIO combination.

A solution to this conundrum in private label deals is the inclusion of amortizing cap corridors. In general terms, corridors are offsetting long and short positions in caps with the same expiration but different strike rates. An investor seeking to raise the cap on a floating rate asset would buy the lower strike cap and sell the one with the higher strike. Since the premium on a lower strike cap is greater than on the one with a higher strike, the resulting corridor has a positive cost.

EXHIBIT 8.12 Allocation of Fixed Rate Interest to Floating Rate and Inverse IO Tranches

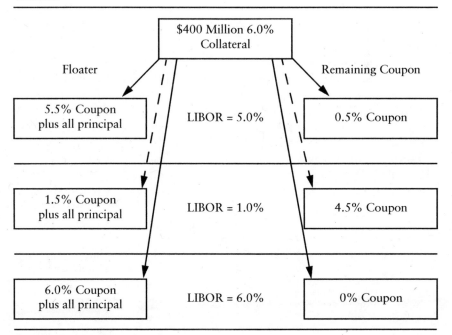

Utilizing cap corridors allows dealers to structure entire tranches into floater/inverse IO combinations. This creates large floater tranches with a cap (referred to as the *hard cap*) equal to the parent tranche's coupon. The cap corridor us used to raise the cap on the floater to a level acceptable to investors. The revised cap level is referenced as the *effective cap*, and is the strike level of the higher cap in the corridor. Cap corridors are typically used in deals with floater/inverse IO combination where the parent's coupon rate (and thus the floater's structuring cap) is lower than that desired by investors. The corridor is purchased from derivative dealers and embedded in the structure, with the effect of increasing the effective cap of the floater to the higher cap's strike rate. The cost associated with the corridor is effectively deducted from the floater's margin. As we discuss in the remainder of this chapter, this means that both the strike levels and longevity of the corridor have a direct impact on the return and risk profile of the corridor-cap floater.

While this concept is quite simple, the behavior of corridor-cap floaters is not straightforward. Because of the way the corridors are structured, the effective cap is not necessarily constant, and can deteriorate over the life of the floater under certain conditions. The value and riskiness of different corridor-cap floaters are a function of both how the corridors are structured and the level of the hard cap associated with the floater. (Unlike the effective cap, the hard cap cannot change.)

Since mortgage cash flows are impacted by both scheduled and unscheduled principal payments, the corridors must be written with an amortization schedule. This schedule is defined at the time of issuance, and can be quoted as either a percentage of the pricing ramp or at a static CPR. Since the corridor is structured at a constant speed but the floaters receive principal cash flows based on the underlying prepayment rate of the collateral, the potential exists for a mismatch between the balances of the floater and the cap corridor. When the deal's prepayment speeds exceed the ramp, the floater tranche pays down faster than the corridor, leaving more corridors than bonds. In theory, this should raise the effective cap to a level higher than the strike level of the higher cap. However, the effective cap of the floater normally never rises above the higher strike, since the corridor is typically quoted as the lesser of the preset amortizing balance or the balance of the floater. (For accounting reasons, some investors will not invest in floaters where the effective cap is greater than the level of the higher cap's strike.)

The effective cap is, however, impacted when realized prepayment speeds are slower than the speed at which the corridor is structured (or *struck*). At slow prepayment speeds, the balance of the floater will exceed that of the corridor, causing the effective cap of the floater to decline. Persistently slow prepayment speeds will eventually cause the effective cap to decline to the level of the floater's hard cap. This is shown in Exhibit 8.13, which shows the effective cap at prepayment speeds slower than the 11% CPR strike speed of a hypothetical corridor-cap floater. At 11% CPR and faster, the effective cap is unchanged; however, at even slightly slower constant speeds, the effective cap eventually declines to 6.5%, the floater's hard cap.

This suggests that the cap corridor's pricing speed is a critical driver of value for the corridor floaters. Floaters with a corridor struck at a faster prepayment speed have a greater risk that the effective cap will deteriorate. However, the corridor is effectively a shorter derivative (since its average life is reduced at faster speeds). This means that the cost of the cap corridor is reduced, thereby increasing the amount of margin that can be paid to the floater. The opposite is the case if the corridor is struck at a slow speed. The risk that the effective cap will erode over time is reduced, at the cost of a lower floating rate margin. (Note that the speed at which the corridor is struck has no impact on the cash flows directed to the inverse IO.)

The type of loan collateral backing the deal also has an impact on the corridor floater's attributes. Because of the risks associated with slow prepayment speeds, the ideal collateral consists of loans that have relatively fast base-case prepayment speeds. As a result, most deals containing corridor floaters are backed by alt-A and other impaired loans

EXHIBIT 8.13   Effective Cap for Corridor Floater at Different Prepayment Speeds: 6.5% Hard Cap, Corridor Struck at 11% CPR

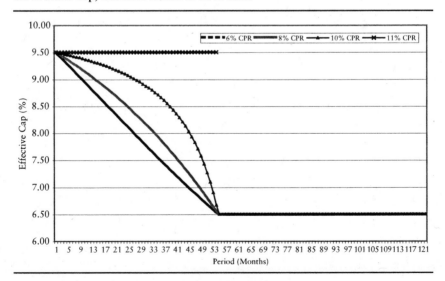

(such as reperforming loans) that consistently exhibit rapid prepayments, as discussed in Chapter 4, due largely to high levels of credit curing and involuntary prepayments.

Finally, the floater's hard cap also impacts its value. As mentioned above, the level of the hard cap cannot change over the life of the floater. Thus, a higher hard cap provides increased protection to the floater's coupon in the event that the corridor deteriorates. As an example, a floater with a 5.5% hard cap that resets at LIBOR plus 30 basis points would "cap out" when LIBOR reaches 5.20% without the benefit of the corridor. The same bond with a 6.5% hard cap would not cap out until LIBOR reaches 6.20%. The value of the higher hard cap is especially important when more aggressive (i.e., faster) pricing speeds are used to structure the corridor.

CHAPTER 9

The Structuring of Mortgage ABS Deals

In the prior chapter, we noted that the emphasis in structures in the mortgage ABS sectors is different from that in structures involving prime first-lien residential loans. Loans that fall into the general category of mortgage ABS are riskier than those in prime deals, either because the loans are granted to borrowers with impaired credit (which greatly increases their expected defaults and losses) or are in an inferior lien position (which creates high-loss severities). As such, these loans are characterized by higher note rates than those in the prime first-lien sector, reflecting risk-based pricing on the part of lenders.

The challenge in structuring mortgage ABS deals is to create cash flow protection and credit enhancement for the senior securities in the most efficient possible way. The optimal form of credit enhancement for deals backed by risky loans with high note rates is the overcollateralization (OC) structure, introduced in Chapter 5. This structure allows the higher note rates associated with these riskier loans to be converted into credit enhancement. In addition to the utilization of excess spread as credit enhancement, deals securitizing these types of risky loans must have higher levels of subordination than shifting interest structures in the prime sector. While this chapter primarily addresses mortgage ABS deals, our objective is to explore the mechanisms associated with the OC structure, as they are more complex than the traditional shifting interest structures utilized in the prime sector.

For the purposes of this chapter, mortgage ABS deals are collectively referred to as *ABS structures*. As such, these deals should not be confused with ABS deals securitizing assets such as auto loans and credit cards, which have many different features. Additionally, the term *residential deal* is also used interchangeably with *prime deal* in this chapter, utilizing the admittedly oversimplified terminology used in the market. The following discussion focuses on structures using subprime loans as collateral. As noted in Chapter 5, however, deals backed by other asset classes in the prime sector (such as alt-A ARMs) have also utilized the OC structure. This form of credit enhancement has increasingly become cost-efficient vis-a-vis the shifting interest structuring form; in addition, it creates large amounts of floating rate senior bonds, meeting the demand for LIBOR-based assets.

FUNDAMENTALS OF ABS STRUCTURES

ABS deals have various forms of credit enhancement, which is higher than that associated with residential deals. In the residential sector, credit enhancement levels (i.e., the credit support for the senior, AAA-rated tranches) vary depending on the type of loan securitized, but typically do not exceed 10% for the most risky loan categories. In contrast, ABS deals generally have initial enhancement levels in excess of 20%. A challenge with ABS deals is also to efficiently utilize the incrementally higher note rate of the underlying loans in providing credit support, effectively converting interest cash flows into principal. Understanding this requires the introduction of two concepts. One is excess spread, which (as noted previously) is the difference between interest received from borrowers on the loans and paid to the securities. While all deals technically have excess spread, it is not large enough in residential deals to supplement credit enhancement. However, due to the high note rates associated with risky loans, the amount of excess spread in a typical ABS deal is relatively high. A diagram of a hypothetical deal's cash flows and excess spread is shown in Exhibit 9.1. (Note that the exhibit was constructed for expository purposes; the rates chosen do not necessarily represent real-world examples.)

The other concept is overcollateralization, or OC, which refers to the fact that the face value of loans collateralizing the deal is greater than the amount of bonds. OC is created through two mechanisms. One way is to structure a smaller number of bonds at issuance, which is referenced as *initial* OC. The other mechanism is to utilize some or all of the excess spread to pay down bonds faster than simply through the return of principal. This is called acceleration or *turboing*. A depiction of the allocation of cash flows with and without turboing is shown in Exhibit 9.2. These two techniques are utilized (either independently or in conjunction with each other) to augment the subordination of ABS deals.

EXHIBIT 9.1   Gross and Net Interest and Excess Spread for a Hypothetical $100 Million Subprime Collateral Pool (8% GWAC, 3.75% net coupon)

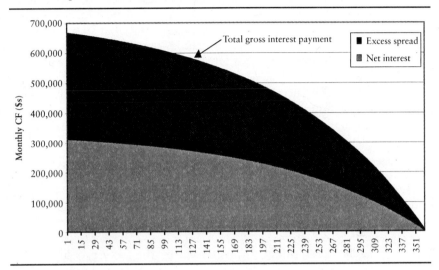

EXHIBIT 9.2   Normal Cash Flow Allocation and Allocation with Turboing to Create Overcollateralization

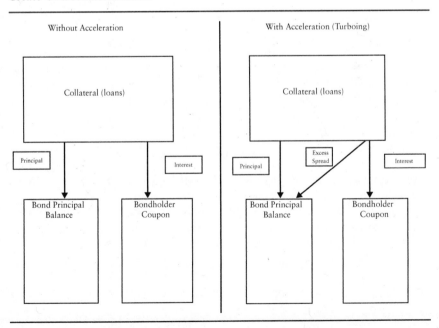

The credit support mechanisms utilized in ABS deals have a number of implications. Quoting the percentage of credit enhancement in an ABS deal (as is routinely done in residential deals) can be misleading. In part, this is because the excess spread is available to make up losses. Additionally, the credit enhancement includes the amount of OC. Therefore, deals that do not have initial OC but rather achieve the target level through turboing will not have the OC show up in initial enhancement levels. Another difference is that OC by definition is equity in a deal. Therefore, the residual (which represents the deal's equity interest) in an ABS structure has much more importance than that in residential deals. In the latter, the residual usually does not receive any cash flows, since the amount of collateral and bonds is the same. The residual has value only as an entity for tax purposes and, as noted earlier, is referred to as *noneconomic residual*. As such, tax effects generally cause the non-economic residuals to have a negative value at issuance. In an ABS structure, by contrast, the residual has economic value, meaning that it is expected to receive cash flows when other, more senior interests are satisfied. As such, the residual is positioned at the lowest point of the waterfall with respect to cash flow priority.[1] Exhibit 9.3 shows a graphical depiction of a simple waterfall in an ABS structure.

However, what is commonly referred to as *the residual* is really a combination of two entities: the excess cash flows (securitized either as the C or XS tranches) and the noneconomic residual (created as an R or NER tranche). While the face value of the R bond is typically small, the C tranche's face value in notional terms can be significant, depending on how much OC is created, either as up-front OC or through the turboing mechanism. In addition, the residual sometimes receives the proceeds from prepayment penalties paid by borrowers.[2] As we will discuss later in this chapter, some structuring techniques attempt to further enhance execution by effectively tranching the residuals.

Mortgage ABS deals are typically structured such that the senior and subordinate bonds are largely comprised of LIBOR-based floaters. Depending on the composition of the collateral and the level of short interest rates, this type of structure often creates large amounts of excess spread. The excess spread allows for the creation of floaters, since it is sufficient enough to obviate the need for inverse floaters (as in prime deals described in previous chapters). However, there are often mismatches between the timing of rate adjustments on the collateral and

---

[1] As described in Chapter 8, a deal's waterfall describes how principal and interest cash flows are allocated within the structure.

[2] Prepayment penalty proceeds are frequently dedicated to separate tranches. We discuss these P tranches later in this chapter.

EXHIBIT 9.3   Schematic Representation of Cash Flow Waterfall for Mortgage ABS Deal (with economic residual)

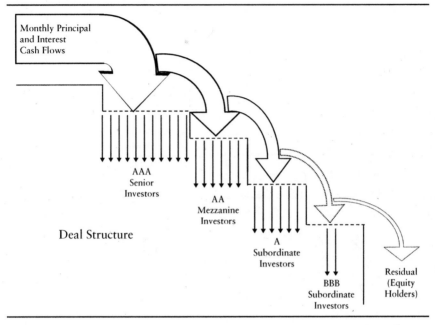

the underlying bonds. Most floaters are structured to reset monthly, while the loan collateral may be comprised of hybrid ARMs (which typically have a fixed coupon for two or three years after funding) and fixed rate loans. This potential mismatch creates what is known as an *available funds cap*. This means that in certain extreme rate scenarios, there might not be enough interest to fully pay the coupon of the floating rate bond. Structures typically have the greatest amount of available funds cap risk immediately after issuance, since the hybrid ARM loans in the collateral do not begin to reset for two or three years. Exhibit 9.4 shows the available funds exposure for a representative deal over time given different instantaneous rate shocks.

Note that the basis risk implicit in ABS structures also has implications for the credit protection of the senior bonds in the structure. In a scenario when rates increase sharply immediately after issuance, the structure's excess spread is reduced; the bond coupons reset higher immediately, while the loan collateral continues to pay a fixed coupon rate until the reset date. In addition to creating available funds cap risk, a sharp spike in short rates would also reduce the amount of excess spread available for either direct credit support (i.e., to be paid to the bonds in the structure if they experience losses) as well as to turbo the bonds and build OC.

EXHIBIT 9.4   Example of Available Funds in Different Instantaneous Rate Shift Scenarios

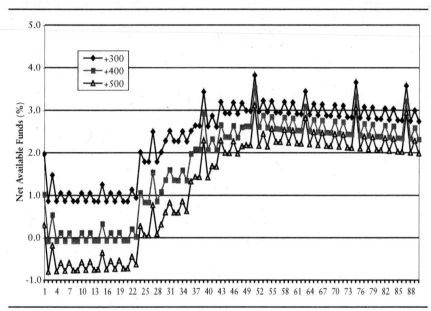

The available funds cap exposure and basis risk is often mitigated by the utilization of derivative contracts in the structure. For example, a series of cap contracts or corridors can be purchased and placed within the structure, with the cap premiums paid for at issuance and treated as a cost to the deal. Alternatively, a swap can be utilized; in this case, the cost of the swap would be paid out of the deal's excess spread. The contracts are often structured to be based on amortizing balances at a designated prepayment speed or vector to create a declining balance schedule. (Some deals utilize swaps written to a lesser-of schedule. This means that the contract is priced at a predetermined amortization schedule. The contract is then written such that cash flows are exchanged based on the lesser of the actual amortized balance or the balance run at the pricing speed.) The purpose of the cap contracts is generally to smooth out the available funds schedule; eliminating available funds cap risk entirely would typically be prohibitively expensive, as the option premium would absorb too much of the excess spread necessary for credit enhancement.

Swap contracts are also used to minimize a deal's basis risk. Embedded swaps serve the dual role of augmenting the deal's credit support, while reducing the bonds' available funds cap exposure. Similar to the cap contracts discussed previously, the swaps are sometimes structured as so-called *lesser-of contracts*, to minimize the possibility of a mismatch between the balance of the bonds and the swap contract.)

CREDIT ENHANCEMENT FOR MORTGAGE ABS DEALS

As noted above, mortgage ABS credit enhancement utilizes a combination of subordination, excess spread, OC, and derivatives. The structure ultimately utilized for any particular deal is a function of (1) the attributes of the collateral; and (2) the amount of enhancement necessary to secure the desired ratings on different bonds from the rating agencies. In addition to the utilization of excess spread and OC, there are a few differences between subordination in the prime and ABS sectors. The mechanism for growing ABS subordinates as a portion of the deal and allocating principal to the subordinates differs somewhat from the shifting interest mechanism in residential structures. In addition, ABS subordinates are typically not structured to create as many low-rated subordinates as residential deals. As described in the previous chapter, prime deals have a "six-pack" of subordinates, with the lowest tranche in the credit spectrum being an unrated first-loss piece. ABS deals are generally structured down to the triple-B-minus level, although some deals are structured with subs rated as low as double B. In these deals, the excess spread and the residual serve as the first-loss components.

As previously noted, OC can be created at issuance (by structuring initial OC) or generated over time by utilizing excess spread to turbo the deal. In either case, the deal will have a target OC amount, which is the OC (as a percentage of the face value of the deal's loan collateral) scheduled to be generated by a certain point in time. This stepdown date is the point in time at which principal and interest cash flows can be released to the residual, depending on how the deal's waterfall is specified. It is either a calendar date (e.g., 36 months after issuance) or the month where the deal's total subordination reaches a certain point (typically twice the original subordination percentage). Prior to the stepdown date, excess spread is directed to the bonds in the deal (beginning with the senior bonds) until the OC target is met. (Typically, the OC target is defined as a percentage of the original collateral balance prior to the stepdown date; after the stepdown, the target is typically twice the stated percentage of the current balance of the collateral.) In addition to creating OC, the mechanism insures that the principal of the senior bonds is reduced before any principal is released to the subordinates. In addition, the subordinates are locked out from receiving principal payments, typically for 36 months (as long as the balance of the seniors remains above zero.) This is a similar process to the shifting interest allocation of principal in the prime sector. Both these mechanisms act to deleverage the senior classes and increase their credit protection after the deal is settled. (One difference is that while the shifting interest structure locks out unscheduled principal, the subs are locked out from receiving all principal in OC structures prior to the stepdown.)

Credit enhancement on mortgage ABS deals can be characterized as a series of decision trees that control the distribution of monthly principal and interest. Cash flows are allocated within a structure based on specific factors designed to protect the integrity of the bonds. The factors driving the allocation of cash flow (or, put differently, the nodes of the decision trees) are:

- Whether stepdown date has been reached.
- Whether a trigger event has occurred.
- Whether the OC target is met.
- Whether the deal has absorbed any principal losses.

A flow chart showing how a typical deal works is shown in Exhibit 9.5.

Prior to the stepdown date, interest available after paying the coupon of the senior and subordinated bonds is used to turbo the bonds and create OC until the target OC is met. Principal is allocated in priority order to the senior and subordinate classes, respectively, until they are paid off. After the deal steps down, and assuming the deal's triggers are passed, interest remaining after the bond coupons are paid can be passed to the residual holder, provided that the bonds have not absorbed principal losses. (If losses have been taken by the bonds, the excess interest is directed to recoup such losses, again in order of their priority. Interest shortfalls are also paid to the bonds before the residual can receive cash.) Principal is paid to the senior and subordinate bonds, subject to limits on principal distribution described in the prospectus. (This amount, called the *optimal distribution percentage*, dictates how large the subordinate classes must be relative to the outstanding principal balance of the senior bonds.)

The deal's triggers are tests embedded in the structure to protect the senior bondholders in the event the underlying collateral exhibits abnormally high levels of delinquencies and losses at any point in time. The tests are specified to be met on a monthly basis; however, they are often specified as trailing average levels of delinquencies, as well as the cumulative level of losses, relative to the remaining balances of either the deal or the subordinates. (Triggers are highly deal- and issuer-specific, depending on expectations for how the collateral ultimately performs.)

EXHIBIT 9.5   Decision Tree and Flows of Principal and Interest in a Typical Subprime ABS Structure

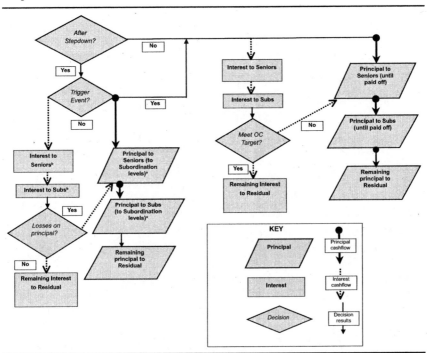

---

[a] Subject to limits on how much is paid to each tranche described in the prospectus.
[b] Subject to the availability of funds.

If a trigger event occurs (i.e., the trigger is failed) after the step-down date, cash flows are distributed as if the stepdown had not occurred. In this case, excess spread is used to reduce the balance of the seniors (and the subordinates, if the seniors are fully amortized), and the subordinates are locked out from receiving principal until the senior tranches are paid off.

FACTORS INFLUENCING THE CREDIT STRUCTURE OF DEALS

As with residential deals, rating agencies play a key role in determining the credit enhancement required for a deal. In prime deals, the rating agencies decide the levels of subordination needed to allow the bonds in the structure to attain the desired rating, based on the attributes of the collateral pool. In addition to the subordination levels, the rating agencies also consider other factors in rating the components of an ABS deal. These include:

- The correct level of target OC needed to adequately protect the bonds in the deal.
- Whether the OC target can be met through excess spread based on realistic assumptions.

The structuring decisions required to garner desired ratings are based on a number of interacting considerations. Under normal circumstances, losses are not expected to begin accumulating until the collateral has seasoned by 12 to 24 months, mitigating the need for initial OC. However, the rating agencies may require initial OC for a specific deal based on either collateral- or bond-specific factors. Some examples might include the following:

- If the rating agencies believe that the excess spread on risky loans is not sufficient enough to build OC in time to meet the target OC level, initial OC may be required in the deal.
- A larger proportion of longer hybrids (e.g., 3/27s instead of 2/28s) results in higher available funds cap risk. In turn, the amount of excess spread available to turbo the bonds is potentially limited, necessitating the inclusion of initial OC.
- A pool of collateral perceived as being particularly risky might have a higher target OC level which could create the need for initial OC in spite of high-excess spread levels.

ADDITIONAL STRUCTURING ISSUES AND DEVELOPMENTS

Deals are also commonly structured with embedded derivatives as part of the credit support mechanism. The presence of the swap within a structure acts to augment its credit support by reducing the basis risks embedded in the deal. As discussed in the section on available funds risks, there is often a fundamental mismatch in many deals between the bonds within a deal and the collateral backing it. In a scenario of sharply rising rates, the amount of excess spread is reduced, particularly soon after the deal is issued; the collateral continues to pay a fixed note rate, while the coupons on the bonds within the deal (which reset on a monthly basis) rise. In addition to mitigating potential available funds shortfalls, embedded swaps act to augment the excess spread in scenarios where interest rates spike. This allows the rating agencies to reduce the amount of required credit enhancement at each rating level, and typically reduces both the target OC percentage and the amount of initial OC.

The notional value of the swap is calculated in a number of different ways; the methods used vary across issuers and underwriters depending on economic and accounting considerations. The term of the swap and the swap's declining balance are based on the composition of collateral backing the deal, along with the speed assumption utilized. The swap is typically structured as declining balance derivative contracts, with the speed determined at the time of issuance. The swaps are sometimes structured to have a lesser-of balance guarantee; as noted previously, this means that the swap balance cannot exceed the balance of the bonds and create a mismatch if prepayment speeds for the collateral are fast. (This feature, along with many others, can vary across issuers.)

The swap obligates the structure (or some entity within the structure) to pay fixed cash flows in exchange for floating rate payments, based on an amortizing notional balance. Since the rate on the fixed rate component or "leg" is typically higher than that of the floating rate leg, the swap initially has a net cash outflow. The net outflow initially reduces the deal's excess spread by the difference in rate between the fixed and floating legs. From the perspective of credit enhancement, the utilization of swaps involves trading off slightly lower initial excess spread under unchanged rate scenarios versus enhanced excess spread levels if rates were to spike. This is particularly true early in the life of the deal (i.e., before the collateral begins to reset), when the basis exposure is greatest.

To illustrate this trade-off, panels A and B of Exhibit 9.6 show comparisons of excess spread levels under different interest rate scenarios for hypothetical ABS deals with and without embedded swaps. The deals were representative of transactions structured in mid-2006 using adjustable and fixed rate subprime loans (although roughly 93% of the loans backing the structures were ARMs). The deal without the swap was structured to have initial OC of 3.8%, with a target OC percentage of 4.7%; the deal with the swap had initial and target OC of 3.65%. Comparing the two structures, panel A of Exhibit 9.6 indicates that the deal containing an embedded swap had slightly lower levels of excess spread in unchanged LIBOR scenarios vis-à-vis the deal structured without a swap. (The average difference between the excess spread of the two deals was 22 basis points over the deal's first 40 months.) This difference is attributable to the net initial cash outflow associated with the swap. However, the excess spread when the swap is present is much greater when forward LIBOR is projected to rise by 300 basis points immediately after issuance, as illustrated by panel B of Exhibit 9.6. The average difference between the excess spread for the two deals is 168 basis points

EXHIBIT 9.6 Excess Spread for Representative ABS Structures with and without Embedded Swaps

Panel A: Forward LIBOR Unchanged

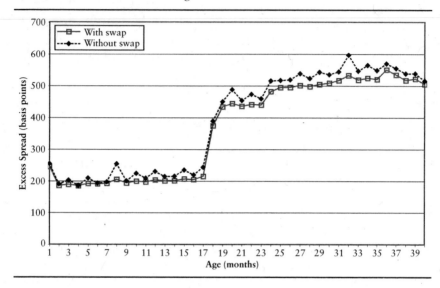

Panel B: Forward LIBOR +300 Basis Points

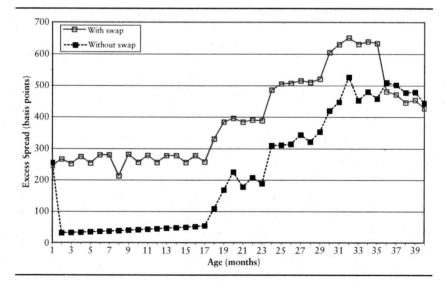

over the first 40 months; the difference is 210 basis points for the first 18 months, when the structure is most vulnerable to a spike in LIBOR.

As noted, the residual is the equity interest in the deal, and is entitled to receive cash at certain points in the life of the deal, assuming the underlying collateral exhibits adequate performance. Some subprime originators seek to maximize the amount of cash received at securitization rather than receiving cash over time through the residual. In this case, a *net-interest margin bond* or NIM is created through a separate transaction.

The NIM is, in part, comprised of the portion of the residual that receives cash in excess of that needed to fund OC, referenced earlier in this chapter as either the C or XS tranches. In addition, the NIM often is entitled to the proceeds from the payment of prepayment penalties. Prepayment penalties are costs associated with prepaying the loan that serve as a refinancing disincentive. When loans having prepayment penalties are prepaid, the proceeds of the penalties traditionally have gone to the loan servicer. Generally, the penalties are not part of the cash flow waterfall and, therefore, are not utilized to cover losses. A commonly seen alternative is to create separate tranches, called *P bonds*, which receive the proceeds of prepayment penalty payments. In many cases, the P bond is repurchased by the servicer, providing the same cash flows in certificated form. P bonds can also be either sold to investors as a hedge against prepayments. However, in transactions with NIMs, the P bond serves in combination with the C bond to collateralize the NIM.

NIMs are generally created as a separate securitization, taking the C and P bonds from deals and using them as collateral to back the NIM. NIMs are typically fixed rate securities with short average lives that are entitled to substantial amounts of the cash flows from the C and P bonds. Note that in order to structure the NIM with the desired rating (typically triple-B), the rating agencies require the NIMs to be funded up front, that is, through initial OC.

A deal innovation that has been used periodically is so-called *deep mortgage insurance* or deep MI. In the prime market, loans with loan-to-value (LTV) ratios greater than 80% typically require private mortgage insurance to guarantee the loan principal value in excess of 80%. As an example, if all the loans in a deal had an 85% LTV, mortgage insurance covering 5% of the loan's face value would be required at loan funding. Mortgage insurance is typically not utilized in subprime lending; however, mortgage insurance can be purchased on a package of subprime loans as part of the securitization process. In subprime structures utilizing deep MI, the underwriter buys a policy from an mortgage insurance company that would cover the loans to a lower LTV (typically to 60% or below). In a deep MI structure covered to 60%, a fee would be paid out of the excess spread to a mortgage insurance provider in exchange for insuring the difference between the LTV of each loan in the structure and a 60% LTV ratio. Due to the incremental protection of the deep MI policy, this type of structure typically required significantly lower subordination levels. However, deal execution becomes contingent on the cost of the mortgage insurance policy. In periods of perceived increased defaults, when such policies become more expensive, the usage of deep MI becomes less attractive as a structuring option. Additionally, investors generally prefer credit enhancement based on the built-in support mechanism of the typical senior/sub structure, as opposed to that provided by a mixture of internal credit enhancement and the MI insurer's ability and willingness to pay claims. For example, the MI provider may waive claims that they perceive are due to fraud, which ultimately requires a workout between the servicer and MI insurer. Therefore, quantifying the true level of incremental credit protection offered by deep MI is difficult.

In both the residential and ABS markets, deals are often issued using different pools of collateral, each of which collateralizes a separate group of bonds. With respect to credit enhancement for multiple collateral groups, the deal structure might be based upon one set of subordinates supporting both groups of senior bonds, in a so-called Y *structure*. However, when the collateral groups are materially different, execution may be enhanced if each group is supported by its own subordination and credit enhancement mechanism. A related mechanism is cross-collateralization. Typically, cross-collateralization is structured where excess spread from different collateral groups supports one another under some circumstances. An example would be a deal with two fairly similar collateral groups, 1 and 2. If collateral group 1 steps down before group 2, the excess from group 1 can be used to rebuild the OC of group 2. However, deals usually contain some restrictions on crossing. Using the above example, they typically allow OC from group 1 to be replenished, in the event that it has absorbed losses, by the excess spread from group 2. However, excess from one group generally cannot be used to build OC in the other under normal circumstances.

While the primary focus of ABS deal structuring relates to credit enhancement issues, there are some noteworthy developments in the structuring of the senior tranches of these deals. Both fixed and floating rate senior cash flows can be time-tranched. Fixed rate senior tranches can also be structured with NAS bonds, to meet investor demand for very stable intermediate assets. As noted earlier in the section on prime NAS bonds, however, ABS NAS bonds are created using different structuring conventions. Typically, the NAS bonds are structured to have first priority on senior cash flows, subject to a lockout percentage that dictates the portion of pro rata cash flows received. A typical lockout schedule might be as follows:

Months 1–36: 0%
Months 37–60: 45%
Months 61–72: 80%
Months 73–84: 100%
Month 85 and thereafter: 300%

The resulting NAS bond is structured such that cash flows are fully locked out for three years. The principal cash flows are scaled up in years four through six, and the bond receives its pro rata share of principal in the seventh year after issuance. At the conclusion of the seventh year, the bond receives three times its pro rata share of principal in order to incur rapid amortization and eliminate a long principal "tail." However, the viability of the schedule is contingent on the existence of other tranches that can absorb cash flow volatility, as with any bond that has a schedule. For instance, if prepayments are fast enough to pay the non-NAS tranches off very quickly, the lockout schedule can no longer be met.

Finally, ABS structures typically contain cleanup calls. Similar to those in the prime private label market, the calls eliminate the need for the master servicer to monitor and service large numbers of deals with small unpaid balances. To ensure that the call is exercised, most mortgage ABS deals have step-up provisions for coupons on the bonds potentially impacted by the call. Senior floating rate bonds typically have their margins double after the call becomes effective, while the margin on floating rate subordinate tranches typically increases by 50%. In fixed rate deals, the coupon of the longest sequential bond normally increases by 50 basis points after the optional redemption date.

Valuation and Analysis

Techniques for Valuing MBS

In this chapter and the next, we describe various models and methodologies for valuing and comparing mortgage-backed securities (MBS). This chapter discusses various measures used to measure potential returns. Chapter 11 is dedicated to explaining the various methods for estimating the interest rate risk of MBS. Because many approaches to measuring the interest rate risk of MBS require as an input the value of a security at different interest rate levels, we begin with the topic of valuation before introducing these measures. Valuation is also critical in applying other analytical tools such as total return analysis because the value of an MBS at the end of some investment horizon must be estimated.

We begin the current chapter by reviewing static cash flow yield analysis and the limitations of the *nominal spread* that results from this simple form of analysis. We then look at a better spread measure called the *zero-volatility spread*, but point out its limitation as a measure of relative value. The most commonly used and robust methodology used for valuing MBS, Monte Carlo simulation, is then described. A byproduct of this model is a spread measure called the *option-adjusted spread*. This measure is superior to the nominal spread and the zero-volatility spread because it takes into account how cash flows may change when interest rates change. Put differently, it explicitly values changes in cash flow patterns that result from the homeowners' prepayment option when interest rates change. While the option-adjusted spread is far superior to the two other spread measures, it is based on assumptions that must be understood by an investor; the sensitivity of the value of an MBS and option-adjusted spread to changes in those assumptions must also be taken into account.

STATIC CASH FLOW YIELD ANALYSIS

The yield on any financial instrument is the interest rate that makes the present value of the expected cash flow equal to its market price plus accrued interest. For MBS, the yield calculated is called a *cash flow yield*. The problem in calculating the cash flow yield of an MBS is that the security's cash flows are unknown, due to the effects of prepayments. Consequently, to determine a cash flow yield some assumption about the prepayment rate must be made.

The cash flows of an MBS typically occur monthly. The convention is to compare the yield on a mortgage-backed security to that of a Treasury coupon security by first calculating the MBS's *bond-equivalent yield*. The bond-equivalent yield for a Treasury coupon security is found by doubling the semiannual yield. However, it is incorrect to do this for an MBS because the investor has the opportunity to generate greater interest by reinvesting the more frequent cash flows. The market practice is to calculate a yield so as to make it comparable to the yield to maturity on a bond-equivalent yield basis. The formula for annualizing the monthly cash flow yield (or the *mortgage yield*) for an MBS is as follows:

$$\text{Bond-equivalent yield} = 2[(1 + i_M)^6 - 1]$$

where i_M is the mortgage yield; that is, the monthly interest rate that will equate the present value of the projected monthly cash flow equal to the market price (plus accrued interest) of the MBS.

All yield measures suffer from problems that limit their use in assessing a security's potential return. The yield to maturity has two major shortcomings as a measure of a bond's potential return. To realize the stated yield to maturity, the investor is assumed to: (1) reinvest the coupon payments at a rate equal to the yield to maturity; and (2) hold the bond to maturity. The reinvestment of the coupon payments is critical, and for long-term bonds can comprise as much as 80% of the bond's return. The risk of having to reinvest the interest payments at less than the computed yield is called *reinvestment risk*.

These shortcomings are equally applicable to the cash flow yield measure since (1) the projected cash flows are assumed to be reinvested at the cash flow yield and (2) the MBS is assumed to be held until the final payout based on some prepayment assumption. The impact of reinvestment risk, that is, the risk that the cash flow will have to be reinvested at a rate less than the cash flow yield, is particularly important for many MBS, because payments are monthly and both interest and principal must be reinvested. In particular, returns for high-yielding bonds are overstated; the yield to maturity method assumes that the proceeds will be invested in similar bonds that offer the same yield. Moreover, an additional assumption is that the projected cash flow is actually realized. If the prepayment experience is different from the prepayment rate assumed, the cash flow yield will not be realized.

Given the computed cash flow yield and the average life for an MBS based on some prepayment assumption, the next step is to compare the yield to the yield for a comparable Treasury security. "Comparable" is typically defined as a Treasury security with the same maturity as the average life of the MBS. Alternatively, it is defined as the interpolated yield of Treasury securities, using the average life of the MBS as the "maturity" for the Treasuries. The difference between the cash flow yield and the yield on a comparable Treasury security is called the *nominal spread*.

The nominal spread is the most commonly quoted measure of incremental returns. However, this spread masks the fact that a portion of the nominal spread is compensation for accepting prepayment risk. For instance, support tranches in a CMO structure are typically offered at large nominal spreads. However, the nominal spread incorporates the substantial prepayment risk associated with support tranches. Investors who evaluate MBS solely on the basis of nominal spread fail to determine whether that nominal spread offers adequate compensation given the substantial prepayment risk faced by the holder of a support tranche.

Instead of nominal spread, investors need a measure that indicates the potential compensation after adjusting for prepayment risk. This measure is called the *option-adjusted spread*. Before discussing this measure, we describe another spread measure often used for MBS called the *zero-volatility spread*.

ZERO-VOLATILITY SPREAD

The nominal spread has an additional weakness in that it compares the yield on assets with various patterns of monthly principal and interest cash flows (i.e., MBS) to the yields on a Treasury security (or securities, if the interpolated yield is used) paying semiannual interest with a bullet payment at maturity. A more accurate measure of spread is to compare an MBS to a portfolio of Treasury securities having the same cash flows. This spread is called the *zero-volatility spread*. While it does not take prepayment risk into account, it does account for the various patterns that principal payments on an MBS or CMO can take at a given prepayment speed.

The zero-volatility spread or *Z-spread* is a measure of the spread that the investor would realize over the entire Treasury spot rate curve if the mortgage security is held to maturity. It is not a spread off one point on the Treasury yield curve, as is the nominal spread. Rather, it is the spread that will make the present value of the cash flows from the MBS equal to the price of the MBS when discounted at the Treasury spot rate plus the spread. An iterative process is used to determine the zero-volatility spread.

In general, the shorter the average life of the MBS, the less the zero-volatility spread will differ from the nominal spread. The magnitude of the difference between the nominal spread and the zero-volatility spread also depends on the shape of the yield curve; the steeper the yield curve, the greater the difference.

VALUATION USING MONTE CARLO SIMULATION AND OAS ANALYSIS

While the Z-spread is a more realistic measure of relative value than the nominal spread measure, it also does not account for the impact of prepayments, and changing prepayment rates, on the value of the MBS. While the borrowers' ability to prepay is an option, it cannot be valued directly using traditional option valuation techniques. Rather, the value of this option, and the value of securities containing this type of embedded option, must be derived using complex alternative methodologies. This section is not intended as an in-depth technical description of the processes. It should rather serve as an introduction to the techniques, allowing the user to understand and interpret the output of the models, as well as the assumptions underlying the methodologies.

In fixed income valuation modeling, there are two methodologies commonly used to value securities with embedded options—the binomial model and the Monte Carlo model. The latter model involves simulating a sufficiently large number of potential interest rate paths in order to assess the value of a security along these different paths. This model is the most flexible of the two valuation methodologies for valuing interest rate sensitive instruments where the history of interest rates is important. MBS are commonly valued using this model. As explained below, a byproduct of a valuation model is the OAS.

The binomial model is used to value callable agency debentures and corporate bonds. This valuation model accommodates securities in which the decision to exercise a call option is not dependent on how interest rates evolved over time. That is, the decision of an issuer to call a bond will depend on the level of the rate at which the issue can be refunded relative to the issue's coupon rate, and not the path interest rates took to get to that rate. In contrast, there are fixed income securities and derivative instruments for which the periodic cash flows are interest rate path-dependent. This means that the cash flow received in one period is determined not only by the current interest rate level, but also by the path that interest rates took to get to the current level.

In the case of mortgage pass-through securities, prepayments are interest rate path-dependent because this month's prepayment rate depends on whether there have been prior opportunities to refinance since the underlying mortgages were originated. This phenomenon, referred to as *prepayment burnout*, implies that borrowers who have eschewed previous refinancing opportunities are either unable to refinance, or unaware of such opportunities. In addition to burnout effects, the nature of structured securities such as CMOs gives them an additional form of path-dependency. The cash flows to be received by a CMO tranche in any particular month often depend on the outstanding balances of other tranches in the deal, which were reduced (to a greater or lesser extent) by earlier principal payments. Thus, the history of prepayments is an important component to value, making the binomial model inappropriate for valuing MBS.

Conceptually, the valuation of pass-throughs using the Monte Carlo model is simple. In practice, however, it is very complex. The simulation involves generating a set of cash flows based on simulated future mortgage rates, which in turn imply simulated prepayment rates.

Valuation modeling for agency and senior private label CMOs is similar to valuation modeling for pass-throughs. However, the difficulties in valuing structured bonds are amplified because the issuer has carved up both the prepayment risk and the interest rate risk into tranches. The sensitivity of the pass-throughs comprising the collateral to these two risks is not transmitted equally to every tranche. Some of the tranches wind up more sensitive to prepayment risk and interest rate risk than the collateral, while some of them are much less sensitive. The objective is to find out where the value goes and where the risk goes so that one can identify the tranches with low risk and high value.

Overview of Monte Carlo Simulation

The valuation of MBS depends on the outcome of many variables. These variables include future interest rates, the shape of the yield curve, future interest rate volatility, prepayment rates, default rates and their timing, and recovery rates. Suppose that for each of these six variables, there are nine possible values that can be realized by each. Then the value of a mortgage security would depend on the six variables and the nine potential outcomes for each. One way to get a feel for the possible value is to calculate all possible outcomes. There would then be 10,077,696 (6^9) possible values for the mortgage security representing all possible combinations of the six variables. Furthermore, each of the 10,077,696 values for the mortgage security will not have the same probability of occurrence.

At the other extreme, an investor can take the "best guess" for the value of each variable and determine an estimated value for the mortgage security. The best-guess value of each variable is usually the expected value of the variable. However, there are serious problems with this shortcut approach. To understand the shortcomings, suppose the probability associated with the best guess for each variable is 75%. If the probability distribution for each variable is independently distributed, then the probability of occurrence for the best-guess value for the mortgage security would be only 18% (0.75^6). Consequently, an investor should not place a great deal of confidence in this best-guess estimate of the value of the mortgage security.

Between the extremes of enumerating and evaluating all possible combinations and the best-guess approach is the simulation approach. Simulation is more of a procedure than a model. It provides information about the range of outcomes, or more specifically, an estimated probability distribution of the outcomes. When used to value MBS, it provides a probability distribution for the value of a mortgage security. While the purpose is to describe the entire range of outcomes, only one parameter from the distribution generated is used in valuing mortgage-backed securities: the mean or average value. It is typically this value that is taken as the value of the mortgage security. While the rest of the information that is available from the probability distribution for the value of the mortgage security is generally ignored, it possesses information that can be useful in gauging the value of a security.

Steps in the Monte Carlo Methodology for Valuing a Mortgage Security

Monte Carlo simulations involve a series of interrelated steps. As noted previously, it is critical to understand the assumptions at each step. Not only do these assumptions having varying degrees of influence on the value of a mortgage security, but they will affect the measures of some of the interest rate risk measures described in the next chapter.

The steps in the methodology

Step 1: Simulate short-term interest rate and refinancing rate paths.
Step 2: Project the cash flow on each interest rate path.
Step 3: Determine the present value of the cash flows on each interest rate path.
Step 4: Compute the theoretical value of the mortgage security.

We will discuss each step next.

Step 1: Simulate Short-Term Interest Rate and Refinancing Rate Paths

An interest rate path is simulated for interest rates over the life of the mortgage security. If, for example, the mortgage security has a remaining life of 29 years, then interest rates will be simulated for 248 months. The number of months on an interest path will be denoted by T. The simulation requires the generation of multiple interest rate paths. The number of paths utilized depends on the model; at this time, assume that there are N paths. In the terminology of the Monte Carlo model, each interest rate path is called a "trial." Ultimately, the monthly interest rates are used to discount the projected cash flows that are obtained at Step 3.

The typical model uses the term structure of interest rates, as well as a volatility assumption, to generate a series of random interest rate paths. The term structure of interest rates is the theoretical spot rate (or zero coupon) curve for the market on the pricing date. The simulations should be calibrated so that the average simulated price of a zero-coupon Treasury bond equals today's actual price. Some dealers and vendors of analytical systems use the LIBOR curve instead of the Treasury curve, or give the user a choice of using the LIBOR curve. This choice may be due to either the investor's performance objectives, or the functionality of the investor's prepayment model. Some investors, for example, are interested in the spreads that they can earn relative to their funding costs, and LIBOR is a better proxy for that than the Treasury curve. (This measure is referenced as a LIBOR OAS or LOAS.) In addition, some prepayment models use LIBOR or swap rates as the refinancing rate, rather than outstanding Treasury rates.

Each model has its own method for projecting the evolution of future interest rates and its own volatility assumptions. Typically, there are few significant differences in the interest rate models of dealer firms and vendors, although their volatility assumptions, and how volatility is incorporated in the model, can differ greatly. The volatility assumption determines the dispersion of future interest rates in the simulation. Today, many vendors do not use one volatility number to generate the yield curve simulations. Instead, they use either a short/long yield volatility or a term structure of yield volatility. A short/long yield volatility means that volatility is specified for maturities up to a certain number of years (short yield volatility) and a different yield volatility for greater maturities (long yield volatility). The short yield volatility is assumed to be greater than the long yield volatility. A term structure of yield volatilities means that a yield volatility is assumed for each maturity.

The random paths of interest rates should be generated from an arbitrage-free model of the future term structure of interest rates, using values obtained from the derivatives markets. By arbitrage-free it is meant that the model replicates today's term structure of interest rates, an input of the model, and that for all future dates there is no possible arbitrage within the model.

While the short-term interest rate paths are eventually used to discount the mortgage security's cash flows, they are also used to generate the prepayment path or "vector," and thus the cash flows, for each interest rate path. What determines the prepayment vector is the refinancing rate available at each point in time, relative to the note rate of the mortgages in question. The refinancing rate represents the opportunity cost the mortgagor is facing each month. If the refinancing rates are high relative to the mortgagor's original coupon rate (i.e., the rate on the mortgagor's loan), the mortgagor will have less incentive to refinance, or even a positive disincentive (i.e., the homeowner will avoid moving in order to avoid refinancing). If the refinancing rate is low relative to the mortgagor's original coupon rate, the mortgagor has an incentive to refinance.

An assumption must be made about the relationship between refinancing rates and short-term interest rates. This is an important assumption and how it is handles varies from model to model.

Step 2: Project the Cash Flow on Each Interest Rate Path

The cash flow for any given month on any given interest rate path is equal to the scheduled principal for the mortgage pool, the net interest, and prepayments. Calculation of the scheduled principal is straightforward, based on the projected mortgage balance in the prior month. A prepayment model determines the unscheduled principal (i.e., prepayments) to be assumed for that month. Thus critical to the valuation process is the prepayment model employed. Note that a prepayment model is used, not a predetermined prepayment rate. One often hears about the valuation of MBS using Monte Carlo simulation based on a prepayment rate such as a single PSA speed. That is incorrect. There is a prepayment rate for each month on a given interest rate path and the rate for a given month across all interest rate paths is not necessarily the same. In theory, there can be $T \times N$ prepayment rates.

Since CMO deal structures have rules dictating how principal and interest is to be paid, calculating the cash flows for a senior CMO requires the deal to be "reverse engineered." In practice, there are vendors such as Intex Solutions that have reverse engineered virtually all agency and private label CMO deals. The process of calculating the cash flow for a given month on an interest rate path begins with calculating the scheduled principal, net interest, and prepayments for the collateral (i.e., the pool of agency pass-throughs). Given the total principal and interest paid to the tranche, based on the interaction of the cash flow rules and the prepayment model, the tranche's cash flows for each rate path is then determined.

Step 3: Determine the Present Value of the Cash Flows on Each Interest Rate Path

Given the cash flows on an interest rate path, the path's present value can be calculated. The discount rate for determining the present value is the simulated spot rate for each month on the interest rate path plus an appropriate spread. The spot rate on a path can be determined from the simulated future monthly rates. The relationship that holds between the simulated spot rate for month T on path n and the simulated future 1-month rates is:

$$z_T(n) = \{[1 + f_1(n)][1 + f_2(n)]...[1 + f_T(n)]\}^{1/T} - 1$$

where

$z_T(n)$ = simulated spot rate for month T on path n
$f_j(n)$ = simulated future 1-month rate for month j on path n

Consequently, the interest rate path for the simulated future 1-month rates can be converted to the interest rate path for the simulated monthly spot rates. Therefore, the present value of the cash flows for month T on interest rate path n discounted at the simulated spot rate for month T plus some spread is:

$$PV[C_T(n)] = \frac{C_T(n)}{[1 + z_T(n) + K]^T}$$

where

$PV[C_T(n)]$ = present value of cash flows for month T on path n
$C_T(n)$ = cash flow for month T on path n
$z_T(n)$ = spot rate for month T on path n
K = spread

The present value for path n is the sum of the present value of the cash flows for each month on path n. That is,

$$PV[\text{Path}(n)] = PV[C_1(n)] + PV[C_2(n)] +... + PV[C_{360}(n)]$$

where PV[Path(n)] is the present value of interest rate path n.

Step 4: Compute the Theoretical Value of the Mortgage Security

The present value of a given interest rate path can be thought of as the theoretical value of a pass-through if that path was actually realized. The theoretical value of the pass-through can be determined by calculating the average of the theoretical values of all the interest rate paths. That is, the theoretical value is equal to

$$\text{Theoretical value} = \frac{PV[Path(1)] + PV[Path(2)] + \ldots + PV[Path(N)]}{N}$$

where N is the number of interest rate paths.

Distribution of Path Present Values

The Monte Carlo model is a commonly used management science tool in business. It is employed when the outcome of a business decision depends on the outcome of several random variables. The product of the simulation is the average value and the probability distribution of the possible outcomes.

Unfortunately, the use of Monte Carlo simulation to value MBS has been limited to just the reporting of the average value, which is referred to as the theoretical value of the security. This means that the information about the distribution of the path present values is typically ignored. Yet this information is quite valuable.

For example, consider a well protected PAC bond. The distribution of the present value for the paths should be concentrated around the theoretical value. That is, the standard deviation should be small. In contrast, for a support tranche, the distribution of the present value for the paths could be wide or, equivalently, the standard deviation could be large.

Therefore, information about the distribution of the path present values should be obtained, and used in conjunction with either the bond's theoretical value or its option-adjusted spread.

Panels A through D of Exhibit 10.1 show schematic representations of these processes. The exhibits have no economic accuracy. They are simply attempts to illustrate how the simulation process works and the interrelationship between the different steps. Panel D of Exhibit 10.1 also shows the distribution of the present values which, as we noted, often contains information useful in valuing and analyzing different securities.

EXHIBIT 10.1   Schematic of Hypothetical Monte Carlo Process:
Panel A: Generation of Rate Paths by Interest Rate Model[a]

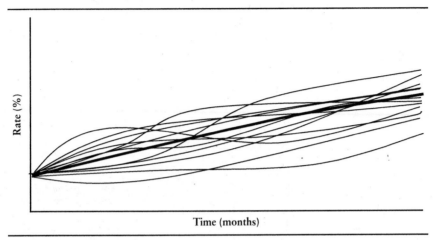

[a] The bold line represents the base-case interest rate path.

Panel B: Prepayment Vectors (in SMM) for Each Rate Path (from panel A) Generated by Prepayment Model

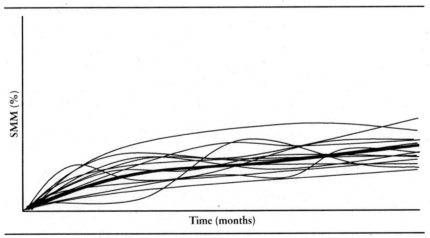

Option-Adjusted Spread

In the Monte Carlo model, the *option-adjusted spread* (OAS) is the spread K that, when added to all the spot rates of all interest rate paths, will make the average present value of the paths equal to the observed market price

EXHIBIT 10.1 (Continued)

Panel C: Monthly Cash Flows of Security Generated by Cash Flow Calculator and Prepayment Model (from panel B) for Each Rate Path

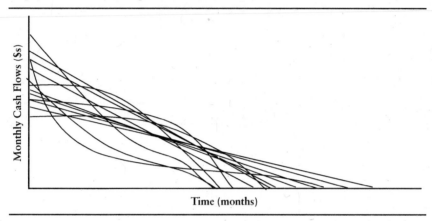

Panel D: Discounting Monthly Cash Flows (from panel C) Using Rate Paths (from panel A) Plus Spread

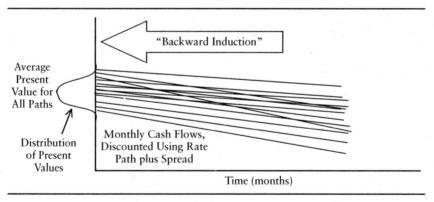

(plus accrued interest). Mathematically, OAS is the spread that will satisfy the following condition:

$$\text{Market price} = \frac{PV[Path(1)] + PV[Path(2)] + \dots + PV[Path(N)]}{N}$$

where N is the number of interest rate paths.

The procedure for determining the OAS is straightforward, although time consuming. Basically, the OAS is used to reconcile value with market price. On the left-hand side of the previous equation is the market's statement: the price of an MBS. The average present value over all the paths on the right-hand side of the equation is the model's output, which we refer to as its *value*. Calculating the OAS is an iterative process. The value (i.e., the right-hand side of the equation) is calculated and compared to the security's market price. If the value is higher than the market price, the spread is increased; if it is lower, the spread is decreased. The value is then recalculated and compared again to the market price. The process is repeated until the value equals the market price; under this condition, the spread is the security's OAS.

The next question is how the OAS should be interpreted, and how it can be used by investors. What a portfolio manager seeks to do is to buy securities where value is greater than price. By using a valuation model such as the Monte Carlo model, and the OAS observed for comparable bonds, an investor could estimate the value of a security, which at this point would be sufficient in determining whether to buy a security. Put differently, the OAS of a similar security could be used to generate the bond's theoretical value; the investor can judge richness or cheapness by comparing the theoretical value to the bond's market price. Alternatively, the investor can compare the OAS generated at the market price to that available for either similar securities or an investment benchmark (such as a cost of funds). This allows the investor to judge whether the bond offers value relative to other securities, as well as whether the bond's purchase would help meet investment objectives.

In describing the model above, it is important to understand that the OAS is measuring the average spread over the Treasury forward rate curve, not the Treasury yield curve. It is an average spread since the OAS is found by averaging over the interest rate paths for the possible Treasury spot rate curves. (Of course, if the LIBOR curve is used, the OAS is the spread over that curve.)

This spread measure is superior to the nominal spread which gives no recognition to the prepayment risk. The OAS is "option adjusted" because the cash flows on the interest rate paths take account of the option of the borrowers to prepay.

Option Cost

The implied cost of the option embedded in an MBS can be obtained by calculating the difference between the option-adjusted spread at the assumed volatility of interest rates and the zero-volatility spread. That is,

Option cost = Zero-volatility spread – Option-adjusted spread

The option cost measures the prepayment (or option) risk embedded in the MBS. Note that the cost of the option is a byproduct of the option-adjusted spread analysis, not valued explicitly with an option pricing model. It is sometimes used as a proxy for the annual cost of hedging the bond's optionality. The correct interpretation is the cost in option-adjusted spread of volatility. Note that this cost is reduced as volatility declines; in this context, the relationship in the above equation indicates that OAS increases as volatility declines, all other things equal.

Selecting the Number of Interest Rate Paths

An interesting question raised in the prior discussion relates to the question of the number of scenario paths, N, needed to value a mortgage related security. A typical analysis might be for 256 to 1,024 interest rate paths. The scenarios generated using the Monte Carlo model look very realistic, and furthermore reproduce today's Treasury curve (or whatever the benchmark securities or curve used in the valuation analysis). By employing this technique, one is effectively saying that Treasuries are fairly priced today and that the objective is to determine the returns of the security being evaluated relative to those of the benchmark.

The number of interest rate paths determines how "good" the estimate is, not relative to the truth but relative to the model used. The more paths, the more average spread tends to settle down. It is a statistical sampling problem.

Most models employ some form of *variance reduction* to cut down on the number of sample paths necessary to get a good statistical sample.[1] A variance reduction technique allows one to obtain price estimates within a tick (i.e., 1/32nd of a point). By this we mean that if the model

---

[1] The *mean standard errror* (MSE) is a commonly used measure of how good the estimate is from a Monte Carlo simulation model and is defined as

$$\text{MSE} = \sqrt{\frac{\text{Variance of the trial values}}{\text{Number of trials}}}$$

A confidence interval for the estimate of the value sought can be construct using the MSE. The smaller the MSE, the greater the precision of the estimated value. As can be seen from the definition of the MSE, one approach to reducing the MSE to a satisfactory level is to increase the number of trials. However, this approach can be costly. An alternative approach is the variance reduction approach and involves reducing the variance of the trial values. In the Monte Carlo simulation literature, several variance reduction methods have been suggested. For a discussion of two variance reduction methods used in pricing derivative instruments, the antithetic variates method and the control variates method, see John M. Charnes, "Sharper Estimates of Derivative Values," *Financial Engineering News* No. 26(June–July 2002), pp. 6–7. For a discussion of other variance reduction methods, see Chapter 11 in Averill M. Law and W. David Kelton, *Simulation Modeling and Analysis*, 3rd ed. (New York: McGraw-Hill, 2000).

is used to generate more scenarios, price estimates from the model will not change by more than a tick. So, for example, if 1,024 paths are used to obtain the estimated price for a tranche, there is little additional information to be had from the model by generating more than that number of paths. (For some very sensitive CMO tranches, more paths may be needed to estimate prices within one tick.)

Several vendor firms have developed computational procedures that reduce the number of paths required but still provide the accuracy of a full Monte Carlo analysis. The procedure is to use statistical techniques to reduce the number of interest rate paths to similar sets of paths. These paths are called *representative paths*. For example, suppose that 2,000 sample paths are generated. Using a statistical technique known as principal component analysis, these 2,000 sample paths can be collapsed to, say, 16 representative paths. The security is then valued on each of these 16 representative paths. The theoretical value of the security is then the weighted average of the 16 representative paths. The weight for a path is the percentage of that representative path relative to the total sample paths.

Mathematically this is expressed as follows:

N = number of sample interest rate paths
J = number of representative paths
W_j = number of sample interest rate paths represented by representative path j divided by the total number of sample interest rate paths
$RPath(j)$ = representative path j

Then the theoretical value is

$$\text{Theoretical value} = W_1\, PV[RPath(1)] + W_2\, PV[RPath(2)] + \ldots + W_J\, PV[RPath(J)]$$

Pitfalls with the OAS Measure

As a measure of relative value, OAS is clearly superior to the static cash flow yield measures discussed in the first part of this chapter. Despite this, an investor must be aware of the pitfalls of this measure.[2] As the OAS is a product of a Monte Carlo simulation, the modeling risk associated with the simulation will also be present in the OAS. In addition, the Monte Carlo method requires that the interest rate paths be adjusted

---

[2] These pitfalls have been described and documented in David F. Babbel and Stavros A. Zenios, "Pitfalls in the Analysis of Option-Adjusted Spreads," *Financial Analysts Journal* 48 (July–August 1992), pp. 65–69.

so that the securities or rates comprising the benchmark curve are valued properly. If the on-the-run Treasury curve is used, for example, the modeled value of each Treasury is equal to its market price or, equivalently, its OAS is zero. The process of adjusting the interest rate paths to achieve that result is itself subject to modeling error. Another pitfall with the OAS methodology OAS is that it assumes a constant OAS for each interest rate path and over time for a given interest rate path. If there is a term structure to the OAS, this is not captured by having a single OAS number.

Arguably the greatest weakness of the Monte Carlo simulation, as well as the OAS values it produces, is its dependence on a prepayment model. Modeling prepayments is a highly complex endeavor in itself; in addition, the behavior of both borrowers and lenders changes over time, which in turn changes how borrowers prepay their loans both with and without refinancing incentives. As we discuss in Chapter 12, utilizing OAS as a valuation tool requires the user to be aware of the potential biases of the prepayment model, as well as the sensitivity of the securities being analyzed to different prepayments in a variety of scenarios.

TOTAL RETURN ANALYSIS

Monte Carlo simulations and option-adjusted spreads are greatly superior to the earlier methods of projecting return. As with the other measures discussed previously in this chapter, a major drawback is that they also implicitly assume that the securities being analyzed are held to maturity. While some conservative investors operate in this fashion, many investors will invest in securities to be held over finite horizons. In order for them to analyze bonds in a fashion consistent with their investment management style, they must incorporate different analytical techniques. A commonly used technique, called *total return analysis*, allows the investor to evaluate returns over different horizons and interest rate scenarios. It has the additional advantage of allowing the investor to specify reinvestment returns, which is quite helpful in analyzing securities such as inverse floaters and inverse IOs.

The total return from an MBS is defined by the following parameters:

- The cost of the security at the time of purchase.
- The security's projected cash flows, which include scheduled and unscheduled principal payments, interest, and reinvestment income (interest-on-interest and interest-on-principal).
- The security's projected value at the horizon date.

The total percentage return (i.e., the returns over the time horizon) can be calculated as follows:

$$Periodic\ total\ return\ =\ \frac{Total\ horizon\ proceeds}{Total\ cost} - 1$$

The return can be annualized, in this case, by multiplying them by 2; the generalized calculation is

$$Annualized\ total\ return\ =\ [Periodic\ total\ return]^{\frac{12}{Number\ of\ months\ in\ period}}$$

assuming that the period in question is less than 12 months.

Exhibit 10.2 shows the total return calculation for a Fannie Mae 6.0% pass-through over a six-month horizon. The total cost of the security is the dollar price plus accrued interest; the proceeds are the interest paid to the investor on the declining monthly balance, the principal paid back to the investor (valued at par), and reinvestment income (at the specified reinvestment rate).

The analyses performed by total return models are typically much more sophisticated than the calculations shown in the exhibit. The models typically allow returns to be generated in multiple interest rate scenarios, assuming parallel and nonparallel interest rate shifts. They will also typically generate scenario returns under variable assumptions, that is, if implied volatilities were to change.

In addition, the models normally allow for much greater flexibility in generating the inputs than implied by the exhibit. As an example, the security's horizon price is simply an input into the calculation, as is the projected prepayment speed over the horizon. Total return models perform similar calculations, but utilize valuation and prepayment models to generate the horizon prices and prepayment assumptions in both the base case and chosen scenarios. A number of different metrics can be used to calculate the horizon price, and can be divided into either "constant" inputs (i.e., OAS, nominal spread, price, etc.) or "user-generated" measures. As an example, variable spreads could be used to generate returns under different rate scenarios. Historical data could be used to calculate spreads for a security at different interest rate levels; these spreads could be used to generate horizon prices and returns for various rate scenarios.

For MBS, a number of other factors are important to the return calculations. As mentioned, reinvestment assumptions can have a major impact on returns for certain types of securities. In addition, the path-

EXHIBIT 10.2   Example of Total Return Calculation for 30-year Fannie 6.0s Held Over Six-Month Horizon

Assumptions	
Current balance invested at settlement	10,000,000
Initial price	100 10/32
Horizon price	100 20/32
Reinvestment rate (%)	5.00%
Prepayment speed	20% CPR
Settlement date at purchase	10/12/06
Settlement date at horizon	4/12/07
Original cost	
Face value × Price	10,031,250
Accrued interest	18,333
(1) Total cost	10,049,583
Interim cash flows	
Principal received (par value)	1,104,904
Interest received from security	285,879
Reinvestment income	12,239
(2) Total interim cash flows	1,403,022
Value at horizon	
Remaining principal	8,895,096
Dollar value of remaining principal	8,950,690
Accrued interest	16,308
(3) Total value at horizon	8,966,998
(4) Interim cash flows + Horizon value (lines 2 and 3)	10,370,020
(5) Periodic return (line 4/line 1)	3.189%
Annualized total return (line 5 × 2)	6.377%

dependency of mortgages and MBS cash flows suggests that changes in the timing of rate shifts will impact total returns under varying rate scenarios. Most models allow the user to specify whether the rate shift should occur immediately, at the horizon, or gradually over the horizon. The latter is typically more realistic than an instantaneous shift; however, it is more difficult to specify the terms of the shifts, so that the analysis can be replicated over time for other securities. Finally, total return models also typically calculate other return metrics, such as cash P&L, return on equity (ROE), and financing-adjusted returns.

While the additional flexibility of total return analysis is a key attribute of the methodology, it is also a disadvantage because these models are highly dependent on inputs such as the horizon price. The need to project prices at the horizon (in addition to prepayment speeds) adds an additional element of uncertainty to the analysis. Another drawback is that the models typically do not incorporate dynamic rates scenarios in the analysis. As we will subsequently discuss, many types of structured securities have attributes that can only be assessed under variable interest rate conditions, where rates undergo multiple changes or "whipsaw" scenarios.

CHAPTER 11

Measuring MBS Interest Rate Risk

With the exception of cash equivalents, all fixed income investors are exposed to *interest rate risk*. Interest rate risk is defined as the risk of principal losses due to changes in the level of interest rates. The risks associated with MBS are more difficult to measure than other securities, however. This is because of the incremental risks associated with predicting and measuring prepayment speeds in different interest rate regimes. The two measures of interest rate risk most commonly used by managers are *duration* and *convexity*. Duration is a first approximation as to how the value of an individual security or the value of a portfolio will change as interest rates change. Convexity attempts to measure the change in the value of a security or portfolio that is not explained by duration; it is a second approximation of the relationship between a bond's price and the level of interest rates.

This chapter discusses some of the ways the interest rate risks associated with MBS are measured. The above-mentioned difficulties in measuring risk manifest themselves in a variety of techniques used to calculate duration, as well as additional measures used to gauge the different risks that impact MBS pricing. The chapter also addresses the exposure of MBS to changes in the configuration of the yield curve, as well as other factors that impact the value of a security or portfolio

DURATION

The risk measure most commonly utilized by fixed income traders and investors is duration. In its basic form, duration calculated in any fashion estimates the percentage change in the price of a fixed income security, given a 100 basis point change in the yield curve. Basic duration measures make the following assumptions:

- The spread of the security relative to its pricing benchmarks remains unchanged.
- The yield curve shifts in a parallel fashion.
- The spread of current coupon mortgages to Treasuries remains unchanged.
- The level of volatility remains constant.

(In some instances, duration is defined by a change in the security's yield. However, the constant-spread assumption means that these definitions are identical.)

Exhibit 11.1 shows an interpretation of duration in an economic context. Duration measures the rate of change in a bond's price, given a change in yield. As such, it is a first-order rate of change (akin to speed when measuring movement), and can therefore be conceptualized as the first derivative of the bond's price/yield function, if such a function existed in reality. As illustrated in Exhibit 11.1, it can be graphically represented as the slope of the tangent line at a single point in a line representing the bond's price/

EXHIBIT 11.1 Illustration of Duration as Risk Measure

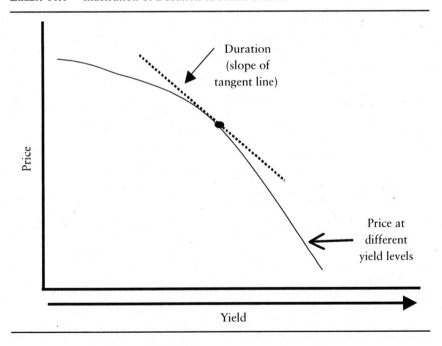

yield function. (If the bond's profile were linear, duration would be the line's slope; in actuality, the price/yield function for virtually all bonds, even those with no embedded options has some degree of curvature.)

As noted above, duration is defined as the percentage change in a security's price, given a change in yield. However, the dollar price change will not be the same for two bonds with the same duration, if their prices are different. For example, consider two bonds, W and X. Suppose that both bonds have a duration of 5, but that W is trading at par while X is trading at 90. A 100 basis point change in yield for both bonds will change the price by approximately 5%. This means a price change of 5 points (5% times $100) for W and a price change of 4.5 points (5% times $90) for X. The dollar price change of a bond can be measured by multiplying duration by the full dollar price and the rate change in basis points (in decimal form). The price sensitivity of a bond is often called its *dollar duration*, and is calculated as follows:

$$\text{Dollar duration} = \text{Duration} \times \left(\frac{\text{Dollar price}}{100}\right)$$

Analytical systems will often calculate dollar duration directly, using various terms for the measure. A metric called the *DV01* is a short-hand term for the *dollar value of a basis point*. This is different from dollar duration in that it indicates the dollar value of one basis point, rather than 100 basis points; as such, it is typically a very small number. Another term often used for dollar duration is *DP/DY*. (The term comes from calculus, defined as delta P given a delta Y.) Because this represents the price change for a 100 basis point change in yield, it is more directly comparable to duration than the DV01 term.

Calculating Duration

There are two general approaches to calculating duration. One popular approach is to calculate duration from the security's cash flows. This metric is called *modified duration*. It adjusts a metric referred to as Macaulay duration, from a measure formulated in 1938 by Frederick Macaulay.[1] This duration is specified as follows:

$$\text{Macaulay duration} = \left[\frac{1\,\text{PVCF}_1 + 2\,\text{PVCF}_2 + 3\,\text{PVCF}_3 + \ldots + n\,\text{PVCF}_n}{k \times \text{Price}}\right]$$

---

[1] Frederick Macaulay, *Some Theoretical Problems Suggested by the Movement of Interest Rates, Bond Yields, and Stock Prices in the U.S. Since 1856* (New York: National Bureau of Economic Research, 1938.)

where

k = number of periods, or payments, per year (e.g., $k = 2$ for semiannual pay bonds and $k = 12$ for monthly pay bonds)

n = number of periods until maturity (i.e., number of years to maturity times k)

$PVCF_t$ = present value of the cash flow in period t discounted at the yield to maturity

The "modification" in modified duration is made as follows:

$$\text{Modified duration} = \frac{\text{Macaulay duration}}{(1 + \text{Yield}/k)}$$

To accommodate the unique nature of MBS, the cash flows used to calculate modified duration are generated using a static prepayment speed or vector. (This measure is sometimes referenced as a *cash flow yield*.) Typically, yield matrices (a method of viewing MBS attributes discussed in Chapter 12) show a bond's modified duration, as well as the yield and weighted average life, for a number of prepayment speeds.

As defined above, the change in the price of a bond when yields change is solely due to discounting the bond's cash flows at the new yield. The measure thus implicitly assumes that the bond's cash flows are constant. This makes sense for option-free bonds such as noncallable Treasury securities, as the payments made by the U.S. Department of the Treasury to holders of its obligations do not change when the yield curve changes. However, the same cannot be said for MBS. For these securities, a change in yield will alter the expected cash flows because it will change expected prepayments speeds. This makes modified duration a flawed measure for estimating the interest rate risk of an MBS.

Effective Duration

The best method to measure a bond's price sensitivity is to change interest rates by a small amount and estimate how its price will change. This measure is generally called *effective duration*. The projected price changes can be calculated by a variety of methods. When an option-adjusted spread model is used to estimate the price changes, the metric is known as *option-adjusted duration* or OAD. Note that for a noncallable bond such as a U.S. Treasury, the estimates for modified and effective duration are equivalent. Effective duration is greatly superior for measuring the riskiness of MBS and securities with embedded options, however, since it accounts for changes in the cash flows of the bond in question due to rate changes.

Effective duration is calculated as follows:

$$\text{Effective duration} = \left[\frac{V_- - V_+}{\Delta y \times 2}\right] \times 100$$

where

Δy = change in the yield of the security (in basis points)
V_- = the estimated value of the security if the yield is decreased by Δy
V_+ = the estimated value of the security if the yield is increased by Δy.[2]

The change in yield referred to above is the same change for all points in the yield curve. Put differently, the methodology is based on parallel shifts in the yield curve. (Metrics for determining a bond's price volatility when the yield curve undergoes nonparallel shifts will be addressed later in this chapter.) The 2 appears in the denominator in order to compute the average percentage price change resulting from an increase and decrease in the yield change.

To illustrate the above formula, assume a bond priced at par where its price is projected to rise to 100-24 if rates decline by 25 basis points, and the price declines to 99-00 if rates increase by the same amount. The effective duration is calculated as follows:

$$\text{Effective duration} = \left[\frac{100.75 - 99}{25 \times 2}\right] \times 100 = 3.5$$

Option-Adjusted Duration

As mentioned above, option-adjusted duration (OAD) is a subset of effective duration, although the terms are sometimes used interchangeably. A critical issue that arises in calculating effective duration is how to generate projected prices in the different rate scenarios. Option-adjusted spread models are the most commonly used methodology for generating the estimated values of V_- and V_+. The process for calculating OAD is as follows:

Step 1: Calculate the bond's OAS at its current market price, as described in Chapter 10.

---

[2] Since V_- and V_+ are present values, the calculation of effective duration (as well as convexity later in this chapter) takes accrued interest into account.

Step 2: Shift the entire set of interest rate paths (i.e., the "rate tree") up and down by the same number of basis points (i.e., Δy the in the effective duration calculation).

Step 3: Generate cash flows for the interest rate paths in each tree.

Step 4: Calculate V_- and V_+ by discounting the cash flows to the new trees, using the OAS calculated in step 1.

Step 5: Calculate the effective duration, as described above.

A key choice to be made with the models relates to the size of the rate shift. A shift that is too large may not provide much useful information; a shift that is too small will not generate a significant change in the prepayment model, and thus will not materially change the bond's cash flows. Most models default to a 25 basis point shift of the yield curve in each direction. (Note that this does not change the quotation definition of duration as the percentage change given a 100 basis point change in rates. This refers strictly to the best method for calculating effective duration.)

Empirical Duration

Durations can also be calculated from market data. The most widely used of these measures, calculated using historical price and yield data, is *empirical duration*. Empirical duration is the sensitivity of a MBS to changes in Treasury or swap yields estimated empirically from historical prices and yields. Once the benchmark yield (e.g., the 10-year Treasury) is chosen and a series of daily prices and yields are assembled, regression analysis is used to estimate the relationship between the price of the MBS and the yield of the benchmark. The regression coefficients are calculated using the following form:

$$\Delta \text{ MBS price} = a + b(\text{Change in benchmark yield})$$

The empirical duration is then calculated as follows:

$$\text{Empirical duration} = \frac{b(\text{Change in MBS price/Change in benchmark yield})}{\text{MBS price}}$$

For 30-year MBS pass-throughs, empirical durations using 10-year Treasuries and swaps are most commonly used, although calculations versus other sectors of the curve are also useful.

There are advantages and disadvantages to the empirical duration methodology. The advantages are:

- The duration estimate does not rely on any theoretical formulas or analytical assumptions.
- The estimation of the required parameters is fairly easy to compute using regression analysis.
- The only inputs that are needed are a reliable price series and Treasury yield series.

However, there are significant disadvantages to the empirical duration metric that limits its usefulness. Empirical duration is, by definition, a backward-looking measure. The metric shows how mortgages have behaved vis-à-vis the benchmark in the past, but is not as reliable as a forward-looking measure. This is particularly the case during periods when the price history may lag current conditions such as during a period of sudden interest rate volatility. In addition, the question arises with respect to how long a data series should be used. A longer time series (utilizing, for example, data from the last 120 trading sessions) typically gives the most robust and stable output. However, because the technique equally weights relatively old and recent observations, the resulting sensitivity could be very different than may be expected under more current conditions. A short data series, on the other hand (using, for example, 20 days of data) will account for current market conditions and behavior, but will provide volatile and relatively unreliable durations.

The most serious shortcoming of the empirical duration measure is its lack of applicability across all products. Since the availability of a reliable price series is an essential element of the methodology, it is not typically useful for calculating durations of structured products, where robust and reliable time series of prices do not exist. (While it is possible to track the pricing of 10-year PACs, for example, the illiquidity of the sector relative to pass-throughs, as well as differences across various securities, makes such a data series of questionable value.) The ability to make reliable comparisons of risk across products is therefore limited.

Hedge Ratios and Treasury Equivalents

A simple and convenient tool used by traders and investors to quote durations is through a *hedge ratio*. The hedge ratio is simply the ratio of the duration of the MBS in question to that of a convenient benchmark. Hedge ratios are normally quoted versus Treasury securities (typically using 5- and 10-year Treasury notes). They allow the trader to quickly calculate how they will hedge the purchase or sale of a security. For example, if Fannie 6.0s have a hedge ratio of 0.5 versus 10-year Treasuries, a purchase of $100 million Fannie 6.0s would be hedged with a sale of $50 million 10-year Treasuries.

Another simple quotation device used is *Treasury equivalents*. It uses the hedge ratio of an MBS to quickly calculate how many Treasuries must be bought or sold to quickly neutralize (or "flatten") the position after a trade. For example, 10-year equivalents would be calculated, using the hedge ratio of the MBS versus 10-year Treasuries, as follows:

$$10 - \text{Year equivalents} = \text{Hedge ratio} \times \text{MBS position}$$

In the above example, since the hedge ratio of Fannie 6.0s to the 10-year Treasury is 0.5, every $1 million purchase of Fannie 6.0s must be hedged with a $500,000 sale of 10-year Treasuries, and vice versa.

These measures are convenient devices for quickly executing trades, and quoting the amount of securities necessary to hedge those trades. The measures, however, are only as accurate as the duration being used to generate the quoted value.

CONVEXITY

As discussed, duration is a first approximation of the expected price change for a small change in yield. As the yield changes grow large, the estimation error grows larger; this is particularly true for MBS, where the prepayment option introduces significant curvature into the bond's price/yield function. *Convexity* is a second approximation of the expected price change. It represents how much the bond's duration is ·expected to change, given changes in yields. An illustration of convexity is shown in Exhibit 11.2. The exhibit highlights the change in the slope of the tangent lines at different points in the bond's price/yield relationship.

Using the earlier example from physical science, since duration can be viewed as the equivalent of speed, i.e., the rate of change (in feet per second, for example), convexity is the equivalent of acceleration; it measures the rate of change of the rate of change (in feet per second per second).

Convexity is measured in a fashion similar to the effective duration calculation. (There is no meaningful convexity calculation that can be generated from a bond's modified duration.) Using the term V_0 to indicate the security's current value, convexity is calculated as follows:

$$\text{Convexity} = \frac{(V_- + V_+) - 2V_0}{V_0 \times \left(\frac{\Delta y}{1,000}\right)^2}$$

where Δy is, as before, the change in yield in basis points. To illustrate the calculation, we return to the earlier example of a bond with a base-

EXHIBIT 11.2   Illustration of Convexity as Risk Measure

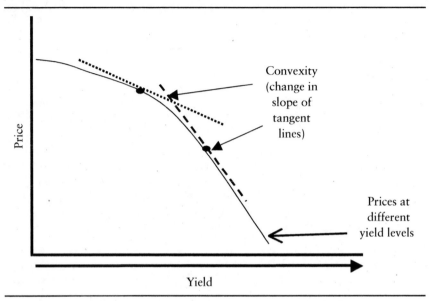

case price of par, and prices when rates fell and rose by 25 basis points of 100-24 and 99, respectively. The convexity of a bond with this profile is calculated as follows:

$$\text{Convexity} = \frac{(100.75 - 99) - (2 \times 100)}{100 \times \left(\dfrac{25}{1{,}000}\right)^2} = \frac{1.75 - 200}{0.0625} = -4$$

It is possible to approximate the percentage price change due to convexity as follows:

$$\text{Convexity price adjustment} = \text{Convexity} \times (\Delta y)^2 \times 100$$

where Δy is the change in yield in percentage terms (i.e., 100 basis points is quoted as 0.01). In the previous example, the convexity adjustment for a 100-basis-point change in the bond's yield can be estimated as follows:

$$\text{Convexity price adjustment} = -4 \times (0.01)^2 \times 100 = -0.04\%$$

The approximate price change attributable to both duration and the convexity adjustment can be found by simply adding the two estimates. In the above example, the price change approximated by duration of 3.5% and the convexity adjustment of –0.04% are added to give the total estimated price change, for a 100 basis point move in yields, of 3.46%.

Note that when a bond's convexity is negative, the bond's gain in a rally scenario is less than its loss when rates rise. (The opposite, of course, is true for bonds with positive convexity.) This can be demonstrated through an exaggerated example. Imagine a security with a duration of 4 and a convexity of –30. The convexity adjustment for a 200 basis point change in rates would be estimated as follows:

$$\text{Convexity price adjustment} = -30 \times (0.02)^2 \times 100 = -1.2\%$$

The approximate price change for a rate increase of 200 basis points would be:

Estimated price change due to duration	= –8.0%
Convexity adjustment	= <u>–1.2%</u>
Total estimated price change	= –9.2%

For a rate decrease of 200 basis points, the estimate price change would be:

Estimated price change due to duration	= +8.0%
Convexity adjustment	= <u>–1.2%</u>
Total estimated price change	= +6.8%

The gain in the rally scenario of 6.8% is less than the loss of 9.2% if rates rise. This phenomenon is attributable to the fact that the sign of the convexity adjustment is unchanged if rates either rise or decline; the sign of the price change attributable to duration, however, is different depending on the direction of the rate change.

However, the most common use of convexity is as a comparative measure. If two bonds with similar durations and spreads have significantly different convexity measures, the bond with the "better" (i.e., less negative) convexity is considered to offer better value, all other factors constant. Using the duration and convexity numbers generated by the different models to gauge relative value will be discussed in Chapter 12.

One common mistake in the MBS market is to confuse the effects of convexity and spread widening. For example, it is common to hear a bond's so-called *price compression* (i.e., the "stickiness" in a bond's price at a certain point above par value) being attributable to its "negative convexity." Often, the bond's spread widens at a certain price level because fewer investors will purchase bonds at prices substantially over par. Spreads also widen to compensate investors for accepting increased model risk, that is, the possibility that valuation models may underestimate prepayment speeds).

This phenomenon is illustrated in Exhibit 11.3. The exhibit contrasts two situations associated with price changes of a hypothetical bond due to declining yields. In one case, the bond's price is moving up the original price/yield curve; the change in the bond's price can be approximated using duration and convexity. The other scenario occurs when the price/yield curve shifts, due to changes in the bond's spread. This type of exogenous change is the result of a shift in the price/yield curve, and cannot be estimated using duration and convexity.

YIELD CURVE RISK

As discussed previously, duration and convexity are measures of what is called *level risk* if the yield curve shifts in a parallel fashion. That is, if all Treasury rates shifted up or down by the same number of basis points, these measures do a good job of approximating the exposure of a security or portfolio to a change in the level of rates. However, yield curves cannot be expected to change in a parallel fashion. Consequently,

EXHIBIT 11.3   Illustration of Price Effects: Convexity versus Spread Widening

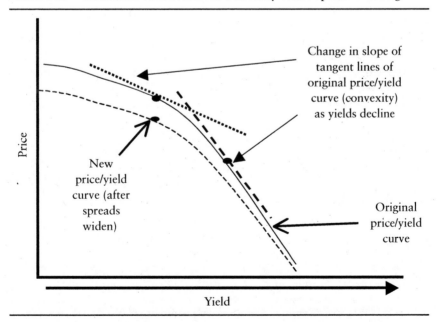

two MBS portfolios with the same duration can perform quite differently when the yield curve shifts in a nonparallel fashion.

Several approaches have been suggested for measuring the exposure to a shift in the yield curve. A popular approach for measuring yield curve risk is to change the yield for a particular maturity of the yield curve and determine the sensitivity of a CMO or portfolio to this change, holding all other yields constant. The sensitivity of the change in value to a particular change in the yield is called *rate duration*. There is a rate duration associated with every point on the yield curve. Consequently, every bond has a profile of rate durations representing each maturity on the yield curve.

The most commonly used approach, first proposed by Thomas Ho,[3] focuses on a series of key maturities on the spot rate curve. The durations for each maturity "bucket" are called *key rate durations*. The specific maturities on the spot rate curve for which key rate durations are measured can vary, but typical maturity buckets used are 6 and 12 months, and 2 through 30 years. The spot rate in each bucket is changed by a predetermined amount, holding the rest of the spot rate curve constant, and the percentage price change for the security is calculated for each bucket. (Changes in spot rates between any two key rates are calculated using interpolation.)

As we discuss in Chapter 12, key rate durations (or *partial durations*, as they are sometimes called) offer a useful way to observe how a bond or portfolio can be expected to perform under non-parallel yield curve shifts. It must be considered, however, that since key rate durations are a form of effective duration (in that they are calculated from projected price changes, given changes in yields), they will be subject to the same biases and weaknesses. For example, a key driver of these calculations is the prepayment model utilized. Depending on how the functionality of the model is specified, different models may generate a variety of inconsistent values.

OTHER RISK MEASURES

In addition to the duration and convexity measures discussed in this chapter, there are other measures that aid in assessing the relative riskiness of different securities, as well as how they will impact the duration of portfolios into which they may be included. In calculating the different measures, the parameter in question is shifted, holding the remain-

---

[3] Thomas S.Y. Ho, "Key Rate Durations: Measures of Interest Rate Risks," *Journal of Fixed Income* 2 (September 1992), pp. 29–44.

ing factors constant. This allows for the measurement of risks external to effective duration and convexity.

Commonly used measures include the following prepayment duration, volatility duration, and spread duration.

Prepayment Duration

Prepayment duration is a metric that measures how much the bond's price can be expected to change given a change in the multiple of the prepayment model. An example would be to generate values at 80% and 120% of the prepayment model. This measure helps in assessing the exposure of a bond to changes in overall prepayment speeds. Its weakness, however, is that by taking a multiple of the model, it does not account for changes in the prepayment model's functionality. As an example, the market may expect slower turnover during periods of housing market weakness, even as the refinancing propensity may be heightened. A simple multiple of the prepayment model cannot accurately account for this difference.

Prepayment duration is typically quoted as the inverse of the price change resulting from an increase in the prepayment model; a value of 1.0, for example, indicates that the bond's price will decline by 1%.

Volatility Duration

Volatility duration is a measure that estimates how much the bond's price can be expected to change given a change in the level of volatility. The issue of scale arises with volatility duration, as with returns generated using different volatility assumptions (discussed in Chapter 12) in that there are a number of ways to quote volatility. For example, a 10% change in percentage or Black volatility can mean either a 10% change in the level of volatility, or a change of 1,000 basis points in volatility. It is clearly important to specify the changes correctly and consistently.

Spread Duration

Spread duration measures how sensitive a security's expected price is to changes in the bond's spread, typically its OAS. Spread duration is different from effective duration in that the incremental change in the bond's yield associated with the spread change does not impact the prepayment model. Thus, the impact of changes in spread can be isolated from the overall change in the bond's yield. This is useful for assessing the riskiness of bonds that are highly sensitive to small changes in projected prepayment speeds.

ILLUSTRATION OF RISK MEASURES

Exhibit 11.4 shows the different risk measures discussed in this chapter for a variety of agency pass-through coupons and CMOs. The exhibit shows the following measures:

- Price and nominal spread (at the Bloomberg medians).
- Option-adjusted spreads (including zero-volatility OAS and option cost).
- Option-adjusted duration and convexity.
- Additional price sensitivity measures (spread, prepayment, and volatility durations).

From this exhibit, a few consistent patterns can be noted. For example, the OADs of MBS are consistently lower than their modified durations. This represents the effects of changing prepayment speeds on MBS prices, also manifested in the negative convexity exhibited by most MBS. The sign of the prepayment duration varies across different bonds, indicating that the effects of faster prepayment speeds on different securities are not consistent. This contrasts with the consistency seen for the volatility durations of the different bonds, indicating that increased levels of volatility are almost always associated with lower prices for MBS.

SUMMARY

There is no single perfect measure, or set of measures, for evaluating the price risks associated with MBS. Some measures, such as modified duration, clearly are inferior means of measuring the risks associated with MBS. However, measures such as option-adjusted duration and convexity have the potential for inaccuracy, due to price changes resulting from either modeling error or factors external to the models. Ultimately, a variety of measures and techniques should be used by investors to assess and understand the risks associated with the securities under consideration.

EXHIBIT 11.4 Prices, Spreads, and Risk Measures for Different Agency Pass-Throughs and CMOs*

	Bond Type	Coupon	Price	Spread/Treasuries	OAS	Zero-Vol. OAS	Option Cost	WAL	Modified Duration	Opt.-Adj. Duration	Opt.-Adj. Convexity	Spread Duration	Prepay Duration	Volatility Duration
Pass-throughs	Fannie 30-year	5.5	99 7/32	107	5	56	51	6.5	4.8	3.8	-1.67	4.4	-0.1	-0.2
	Fannie 30-year	6.0	100 29/32	111	1	64	63	4.4	3.5	2.5	-2.10	3.5	0.1	-0.2
	Fannie 30-year	6.5	102	83	-5	45	49	2.6	2.2	1.3	-1.74	2.7	0.2	-0.1
	Fannie 15-year	5.0	98 22/32	73	0	26	25	5.0	4.1	3.4	-0.97	3.8	0.0	-0.1
	Fannie 15-year	5.5	100 8/32	82	-2	36	38	4.7	3.8	2.7	-1.48	3.5	0.1	-0.1
	Fannie 15-year	6.0	101 19/32	92	4	45	41	4.3	3.5	2.2	-1.47	3.2	0.1	-0.1
PACs	Short	5.5	100 17/32	52	8	21	13	2.5	2.3	1.7	-0.88	2.2	0.0	0.0
	Short	6.0	101 12/32	76	5	37	33	2.8	2.5	1.2	-0.97	2.2	0.1	-0.1
	Intermediate	5.5	99 19/32	99	20	55	35	7.9	6.2	4.0	-2.19	5.2	0.1	-0.2
	Intermediate	6.0	101 3/32	125	24	78	54	7.7	6.0	2.9	-1.85	4.4	0.1	-0.2
	LCF	5.0	93 26/32	93	3	39	36	18.4	11.4	8.5	-0.81	10.0	0.2	-0.5
	LCF	5.5	97 20/32	110	6	55	49	18.4	11.1	7.4	-0.27	9.1	0.3	-0.5
	LCF	6.0	100 24/32	133	12	81	69	14.6	9.4	5.2	-1.53	7.0	0.2	-0.4
Sequentials	Front	5.0	99 1/32	68	17	37	20	2.6	2.3	2.0	-0.87	2.1	0.0	0.0
	Front	5.5	99 30/32	80	12	42	30	2.7	2.4	1.6	-1.25	2.0	0.0	-0.1
	Front	6.0	101 6/32	100	-2	52	55	3.8	3.3	1.9	-1.94	2.9	0.0	-0.1
	LCF	5.0	91 31/32	100	5	47	42	22.5	12.7	9.9	-0.71	10.2	-0.2	-0.6
	LCF	5.5	96 11/32	115	7	62	55	23.4	12.6	9.0	-1.13	9.8	0.1	-0.6
Supports	Front	5.5	97 24/32	177	19	241	223	2.5	2.2	5.7	-4.21	1.9	-0.8	-0.2
	Intermediate	5.5	96 21/32	154	27	137	110	8.1	5.4	5.0	-2.84	3.5	-0.6	-0.3
	Intermediate	5.0	94 3/32	124	23	83	60	11.2	7.1	6.3	-2.42	4.6	-0.9	-0.3

* The model uses the OAS model licensed by Polypaths LLC, and Countrywide Security's prepayment model. Price as of 12/15/06

CHAPTER 12

Evaluating Senior MBS and CMOs

The process of evaluating and analyzing agency and senior private label MBS is unique, particularly for structured securities. Investors typically assume that principal will be returned with 100% certainty, an implicit expression of confidence in both the agencies and senior/subordinate credit enhancement. The driver of performance of these securities is thus not *if*, but *when* principal is paid to the bondholder. While sophisticated techniques such as Monte Carlo simulation and total return analysis (described in Chapter 10) are quite useful, they are best utilized as tools comprising one component of extensive comparative analysis. Simple and straightforward tools, such as yield matrices and vector analysis, are also quite useful in understanding the fundamental attributes of different securities, as well as making comparisons between securities and across sectors. While such techniques are "quantitative" in the sense that they generate a series of numbers, it is more productive to view them as qualitative devices for evaluating tranches and contrasting different securities. A thorough analysis of senior MBS (as we will refer to both agency-backed and senior private label securities throughout this chapter) utilizes both qualitative and quantitative techniques to understand, value, and compare different securities.

In this chapter, we discuss techniques and metrics that investors and traders commonly utilize to evaluate MBS. We demonstrate how basic tools, such as yield tables and prepayment vectors, can be used in conjunction with the results obtained from higher-level analytical models to make relative value judgments. It will also discuss how the assumptions associated with metrics such as option-adjusted spreads (OAS) and total rate of return (TR) discussed in Chapter 10 should be considered when attempting to use model outputs in a framework of analysis. As opposed to an all-encompassing list of MBS analysis techniques, this chapter

241

should be construed as an introduction to how investors can evaluate MBS and senior structured tranches using techniques and models of varying degrees of sophistication.

YIELD AND SPREAD MATRICES

The most basic analysis used in evaluating structured MBS is the yield matrix or yield table. While limited in its scope and flexibility, it is quite useful in allowing traders and investors to observe the basic attributes of the security in question, as well as measure and quote its spread over market benchmarks. In the context of MBS analysis, a yield matrix is a format that allows the user to observe changes in average lives, durations, and yields under different prepayment scenarios, offering a simple but robust means of evaluating securities.

While there are many variations on yield matrices, they all typically designed to show the attributes and parameters of MBS under different prepayment assumptions. The tables are commonly constructed to show a range of prepayment assumptions on the horizontal axis. Prepayment speeds can be quoted using a variety of conventions (i.e., as CPRs, PSAs, or PPCs) as well as user-defined prepayment "vectors." (In this context, a prepayment vector is a series of monthly CPRs that encompass a single prepayment scenario that unfolds over time. We discuss vectors in more depth later in this chapter.) The vertical axis can show a number of different parameters, including prices (giving a yield-to-price table or, in some cases, spread-to-price tables), yields (creating a price-to-yield matrix), and index levels. The table also typically shows the bond's average life, modified duration, and principal payment "window" under the different prepayment scenarios. An example of a yield-to-price table for a sequential CMO, run at prices around par value, is shown in Exhibit 12.1.

For the user's convenience, yield matrices also typically show the bond's basic parameters. For example, Bloomberg tables show the following data on structured bonds:

- Deal and tranche name
- CUSIP number
- The bond's coupon rate and maturity date
- The tranche type
- Information on the deal's collateral (including issuer, coupon, WAC, WAM, and WALA)
- The bond's effective PAC band (in the case of a PAC)
- Recent historical prepayment speeds

EXHIBIT 12.1 Price-Yield Table for a Hypothetical Sequential Agency CMO: 5.5% Coupon Backed by Conventional 5.5s, 6.0% WAC, 2 Months WALA

| | | PSA | | | | | | | |
		115	125	145	175	225	450	850	1250
	99 28/32	5.54	5.54	5.54	5.53	5.53	5.51	5.49	5.47
	99 28/32	5.51	5.50	5.50	5.49	5.48	5.44	5.39	5.34
	100	5.47	5.47	5.46	5.45	5.43	5.37	5.28	5.22
	100 4/32	5.44	5.43	5.42	5.40	5.38	5.29	5.18	5.09
	100 8/32	5.40	5.40	5.38	5.36	5.33	5.22	5.08	4.96
	Ave. life	4.3	4.1	3.7	3.3	2.8	1.8	1.3	1.0
	Mod. dur.	3.6	3.5	3.2	2.9	2.5	1.7	1.2	1.0
	Sprd/Tsys	70	69	67	65	62	47	28	17
Principal	First pay	Mar-07	Mar-07	Mar-07	Mar-07	Mar-07	Mar-07	Mar-07	Mar-07
Window	Last pay	Jul-15	Feb-15	Apr-14	May-13	Apr-12	Apr-10	Mar-09	Oct-08

In the agency CMO market, yield tables are often constructed using so-called Bloomberg median speeds.[1] Since most market participants utilize these speeds, the market treats them as a consensus estimate for prepayment speeds both in the current rate regime as well as parallel-shift rate scenarios. (In fact, a Bloomberg user's default settings can be set to call up the median speeds.) However, Bloomberg does not publish median prepayment speeds for private label deals, as collateral in this sector of the market tends to be much more heterogeneous than in the agency sector. This forces investors to supply their own prepayment assumptions for a bond, based on the rate environment and collateral characteristics.

However, the use of Bloomberg medians as prepayment consensus speeds, as is typically done in the agency CMO market, arguably obscures the prepayment performance of a bond based on its actual collateral attributes. Interestingly, this runs contrary to the trend of using loan- and borrower-level attributes to better estimate prepayment performance. This is why intelligent use of yield tables requires more than rote usage of consensus speeds and market spreads. A well-constructed yield table gives the user a good snapshot of a bond's profile at that point in time, and facilitates the analysis of the bond's attributes. In this context, we will compare different bonds that have similar average lives in the base case in order to illustrate how a yield table can and should be utilized.

Aside from the yields themselves, the most important and commonly used attributes in a yield matrix are the average lives and duration of the bond at different prepayment speeds. These metrics give the investor a sense of the bond's "profile," which in turn will influence its performance under different interest rate and prepayment scenarios. A bond's profile serves as an indicator of both its riskiness and the costs associated with hedging it. Greater degrees of average life and duration variability are typically associated with wider spreads, as investors collectively demand greater returns to compensate for the incremental increases in risk.

The timing of a bond's principal payments (i.e., its "window") is also an important attribute. Quoted as either elapsed time or actual dates, a bond's principal window indicates when the bond's principal cash flows begin and end under different prepayment scenarios. The window can have a significant impact on a bond's performance; it also influences the bond's accounting treatment. Some implications of the principal window include:

---

[1] These are the median of the prepayment projections reported to Bloomberg by a number of Wall Street dealers on a periodic basis.

■ Bonds with tight principal windows and delayed principal payments, or a principal "lockout," are easier and more convenient to hold for the investor's accountants. This is especially true for investors that have accounting systems created to manage Treasury securities and corporate bonds, which have one bullet principal payment at maturity.

■ Bonds with tight principal windows will typically outperform wide-window bonds in regimes when the yield curve is steep, because the shortening of the bond's life and duration as the bond ages puts upward pressure on its price, all other factors the same. This so-called "rolldown" impacts the returns generated through total return analysis. We discuss this phenomenon later in this chapter.

■ Bonds with a principal lockout will often perform better under scenarios where interest rates experience a sharp short-term decline. Since they do not receive unscheduled prepayments immediately, their cash returns are not affected by the resulting spike in prepayment speeds. By contrast, a bond that receives principal payments immediately will have its yield and returns impacted by early fast prepayment speeds, particularly if the bond is trading at a sizeable premium or discount.

■ The principal window is a good indicator of how a bond's structure might behave. For example, the presence of so-called "cash flow breaks" in some PAC2s and support bonds (caused by the barbelling of cash flows discussed in Chapter 6) is also typically shown in yield tables, and is often indicated (as it is in Bloomberg) by a tilde (~) in the cash flow window field.

To illustrate how yield matrices can be used, we compare yield tables for different types of CMO tranches backed by the same collateral, using Bloomberg median speeds. Exhibit 12.2 shows a yield table for a hypothetical support CMO with an average life at pricing that is comparable to the sequential shown in Exhibit 12.1. Both bonds were structured using the same assumptions for the collateral (i.e., 2-WALA conventional 5.5s with a 6.0% WAC). As the collateral assumption is the same for both bonds, the tables show the same PSA assumptions in instantaneous parallel shifts of the yield curve. Most notably, the median prepayment speed in the scenario when rates are assumed to increase 300 basis points is 115% PSA for both bonds. In comparing the two bonds, the following similarities and differences are noteworthy:

■ In the base-case assumption of 175% PSA, the two bonds have similar average lives, modified durations, and yields.

■ The sequential bond's average life only extends one year from the base case in the +300 basis point scenario (which equates to extending by 30%). By contrast, the support bond's average life almost quadruples,

extending from 3.0 years in the base case to 11.5 years in the +300
basis point scenario.

■ In rates-down scenarios, both bonds lose yield, as they are shown at
prices above their parity price.[2] In the scenario where rates decline
300 basis points (which generates an assumed median prepayment
speed of 1,250% PSA), the sequential loses 23 basis points of yield;
the support bond loses 54 basis points of yield, as its cash flows
(reflected by its average life and duration) shorten more than that of
the sequential.

For ease of comparison, Exhibit 12.2 shows the support bond at the
same price (and approximately the same yield and spread) as the
sequential in Exhibit 12.1. In reality, the greater volatility of the support
bond's profile and return means that it should trade at a significant concession to the sequential bond. The tricky part of analyzing MBS (where
more sophisticated analysis is required) is in deciding *how much* of a
concession is fair, especially in more complex cases where the major
components of value are not held constant.

The yield matrix for a PAC bond is fairly straightforward, in that its
cash flows (i.e., its yield, average life, modified duration, and principal
windows) are constant within the effective PAC band. A yield matrix for
a representative intermediate PAC, run at a variety of prepayment speeds,
is shown in Exhibit 12.3. Traders and investors typically compare PACs
with similar coupons and collateral attributes based on a number of factors shown in the yield table, including the effective band, principal window, average life, and the dollar price at a given spread.

Exhibit 12.4 shows the yield table of a PAC2, structured with a
135% to 175% PSA band. The profile of the bond, on its face, is somewhere in between that of the sequential and support bonds shown in the
earlier exhibits; for example, the PAC2's average life extends roughly
four years in the +300 scenario (which equates to roughly 120% over
the base case), as compared to the 30% extension of the sequential.
However, the average life of the PAC2 at 100% PSA is 13.1 years, significantly longer than the 4.7 years of the sequential structure. Since the
bond is a PAC2, by definition it is subordinate in principal priority to
other bonds in the structure (i.e, the PAC1s); scrutiny of its performance
at speeds other than the Bloomberg medians is important for evaluating
this type of structure.

---

[2] Parity is the level where the bond's yield equals its coupon. For a bond that pays
semiannually with no payment delay, the parity price is the bond's par value (i.e.,
100% of face value). For fixed rate MBS, parity prices are typically below par, due
largely to the effects of the payment delay on the bond's yield.

EXHIBIT 12.2 Price-Yield Table for a Hypothetical Agency Support CMO: 5.5% Coupon Backed by Conventional 5.5s, 6.0% WAC, 2 Months WALA

| | | | | | PSA | | | | |
		115	125	145	175	225	450	850	1250
	99 24/32	5.55	5.55	5.54	5.53	5.52	5.48	5.43	5.39
	99 28/32	5.54	5.53	5.52	5.48	5.45	5.36	5.24	5.15
	100	5.52	5.51	5.49	5.44	5.38	5.24	5.05	4.90
	100 4/32	5.51	5.49	5.46	5.39	5.32	5.12	4.86	4.65
	100 8/32	5.49	5.48	5.43	5.34	5.25	5.00	4.68	4.41
	Ave. life	11.5	9.3	5.7	3.0	2.0	1.1	0.7	0.5
	Mod. dur.	7.9	6.6	4.5	2.7	1.9	1.0	0.7	0.5
	Sprd/Tsys	74	74	73	64	51	20	-6	-24
Principal	First pay	Mar-07	Mar-07	Mar-07	Mar-07	Mar-07	Mar-07	Mar-07	Mar-07
Window	Last pay	Feb-25	Sep-23	Jul-20	Feb-13	Jul-10	Nov-08	Mar-08	Dec-07

EXHIBIT 12.3 Price-Yield Table for a Hypothetical Agency PAC: 5.5% Coupon Backed by Conventional 5.5s, 6.0% WAC, 2 Months WALA

					PSA			
	85	100	175	250	300	500	800	1200
99 24/32	5.547	5.545	5.545	5.545	5.543	5.534	5.522	5.508
99 28/32	5.522	5.518	5.518	5.518	5.515	5.492	5.461	5.429
100	5.498	5.491	5.491	5.491	5.486	5.449	5.401	5.349
100 4/32	5.473	5.465	5.465	5.465	5.457	5.407	5.340	5.270
100 8/32	5.449	5.438	5.438	5.438	5.428	5.365	5.280	5.190
Ave. life	6.2	5.5	5.5	5.5	5.1	3.3	2.3	1.7
Mod. dur.	5.1	4.7	4.7	4.7	4.3	2.9	2.1	1.6
Principal First pay	Oct-12	Mar-12	Mar-12	Mar-12	Nov-11	Mar-10	Apr-09	Sep-08
Window Last pay	Nov-13	Mar-13	Mar-13	Mar-13	Jul-12	Aug-10	Jun-09	Nov-08

EXHIBIT 12.4 Price-Yield Table for a Hypothetical Agency PAC2 CMO: 5.5% Coupon backed By Conventional 5.5s, 6.0% WAC, 2 Months WALA

		PSA								
		100	115	125	145	175	225	450	850	1250
	99 24/32	5.55	5.55	5.54	5.54	5.54	5.54	5.52	5.50	5.48
	99 28/32	5.54	5.53	5.51	5.49	5.49	5.49	5.46	5.41	5.37
	100	5.53	5.50	5.48	5.45	5.45	5.45	5.40	5.32	5.26
	100 4/32	5.51	5.48	5.45	5.41	5.41	5.41	5.34	5.23	5.14
	100 8/32	5.50	5.46	5.41	5.37	5.37	5.37	5.28	5.14	5.03
	Ave. life	13.1	7.5	4.8	3.5	3.5	3.5	2.2	1.5	1.2
	Mod. dur.	9.1	5.7	3.9	3.0	3.0	3.0	2.0	1.4	1.1
	Sprd/Tsys	73.8	73.0	69.6	63.6	63.6	63.6	50.6	32.3	20.3
Principal	First pay	Apr-07	Mar-07	Mar-07	Mar-07	Mar-07	Mar-07	Mar-07	Mar-07	Mar-07
Window	Last pay	Oct-22	Mar-20	Dec-17	Jul-14	Jul-14	Jul-14	Nov-09	10/1/200	Jun-08

This is not to say that 100% PSA is necessarily correct or reasonable as a measure of prepayment speeds in high-interest rate regimes. However, it has traditionally been considered a benchmark of prepayment speeds for out-of-the-money MBS, at least before increased housing turnover and cash-out refinancings pushed base-case prepayment speeds higher, as discussed in Chapter 4. It therefore serves as a reasonable prepayment speed for evaluating a bond's performance in regimes of very slow prepayment speeds, particularly for tranches subject to complex cash flow allocation rules.

Prepayment Vectors and Dynamic Prepayment Scenarios

Based solely on its profile shown in the yield table, a case can be made that the relative riskiness of the PAC2 is not much greater than that of the sequential. However, such an assessment depends in part on which prepayment speeds are shown in the matrix, as discussed previously. Moreover, this conclusion can be drawn only when the attributes of the bond (and its profile under a variety of assumptions) are understood. In this vein, yield tables can both obfuscate and illuminate the true attributes of a bond, depending on how they are used.

In order to further illuminate the structural attributes and expected performance of a bond, prepayment vectors are often utilized within the yield table. As described previously, a prepayment vector incorporates variable prepayment speeds over time. An example might be to run a bond at 200% PSA for 12 months, then at 1,200% PSA for 12 months, and then revert to 100% PSA for the remaining life of the deal. This type of analysis is useful in a number of ways. It is helpful to observe bond yields and average lives under different prepayment assumptions than the standard formats and models routinely generated by most systems. Variable or "dynamic" prepayment speeds, which would presumably reflect multiple interest rate regimes, are also a more accurate representation of real-world conditions, as opposed to the more static assumptions underlying the median speeds. In addition, the ability to run dynamic scenarios also helps to expose attributes of a bond that are not apparent under more standard prepayment assumptions. Vectors that utilize dynamic prepayment assumptions are particularly useful in evaluating structured bonds, such as PAC2s, that are subordinate in priority to other tranches in a structure. The nature of the cash flow rules, and the fact that the proportions within the structure change with every monthly cash flow, make dynamic prepayment vectors quite useful. While the vectors used can become very elaborate, simple scenarios can also provide highly useful information.

An example of a scenario for utilizing vectors might be to view the yields and average lives of a bond under a faster prepayment "ramping" assumption. As discussed in Chapter 3, the PSA model assumes that loans season (or approach a predetermined prepayment plateau) over the course of 30 months.[3] An investor who believes that 30 months is too long of a seasoning ramp might construct vectors where the prepayment speeds ramp faster to the same terminal speed, that is, the CPRs increase more each month than assumed in the PSA convention. For example, 100% of an adjusted model might have a ramp that begins at 0.4% CPR in month 1 and increases 0.4% per month for 15 months, terminating at 6% CPR. Vectors are also utilized frequently for loan types where the prepayment behavior of the loans typically exhibits a large change over the life of the loan. For example, prepayment speeds for hybrid ARMs typically spike when the loans approach their reset dates. As described in Chapter 4, risk-averse borrowers typically refinance into either a new hybrid ARM or a fixed rate loan at that point, depending on the yield curve and rates available for different products. No prepayment model that exists at this writing accounts for this well-understood behavior.

The vectors typically used to evaluate CMOs and structured products are often constructed to "stress" the bond and the deal's structure. This is highly useful in examining a bond's profile under different dynamic scenarios, as well as assessing what types of scenarios would cause the structure to break down. Such scenarios do not necessarily have to be reasonable in economic terms; rather, they are often constructed purely for evaluative purposes. For example, consider the PAC2 bond shown in Exhibit 12.4. As discussed in Chapter 6, the bond is structured to take the support cash flows of a deal and, by assigning them a schedule, make them stable within a range of prepayments. Because the bonds are structured from support cash flows, however, the ability to support the structure of the PAC2s is compromised if prepayment speeds spike, even for a very short period. Exhibit 12.5 shows a yield table for the PAC2 tranche if prepayment speeds are run extremely fast (i.e., at 10,000% PSA) for the first two months after the deal is issued. Note that the profile of the bond changes considerably from that shown in Exhibit 12.4, even though the projected surge in prepayments is only assumed to last for two months. While this assumption may seem unreasonably onerous, keep in mind that 10,000% PSA in the first month after issuance is 20% CPR (10,000% × 0.2%). While this assumption is extremely fast, it is certainly possible; more importantly, the scenario shown in the exhibit is useful for evaluating the bond in question in terms of how it is structured, and what scenarios might cause its profile to change dramatically.

---

[3] 100% PSA assumes 0.2% CPR in month 1, increasing 0.2% CPR until reaching 6.0% CPR in month 30.

EXHIBIT 12.5 Price-Yield Table for a Hypothetical Agency PAC2 CMO: First Two Months Run at 10,000% PSA, 5.5% Coupon Backed by Conventional 5.5s, 6.0% WAC, 2 Months WALA

| | PSA (Beginning in Month 3) | | | | | | | | |
	115	125	145	175	225	450	850	1250
99 24/32	5.56	5.56	5.56	5.55	5.53	5.49	5.45	5.42
99 28/32	5.55	5.55	5.54	5.52	5.47	5.39	5.29	5.22
100	5.54	5.54	5.53	5.49	5.42	5.28	5.13	5.02
100 4/32	5.53	5.53	5.52	5.47	5.37	5.18	4.97	4.82
100 8/32	5.52	5.52	5.51	5.44	5.32	5.08	4.81	4.61
Ave. life	22.4	21.3	16.4	6.8	2.6	1.3	0.8	0.6
Mod. dur.	12.5	12.2	9.9	4.8	2.4	1.2	0.8	0.6
Principal First pay	Mar-07	Mar-07	Mar-07	Mar-07	Mar-07	Mar-07	Mar-07	Mar-07
Window Last pay	Jul-33	Nov-32	Apr-31	Jan-28	Apr-11	Nov-08	Mar-08	Dec-07

EXHIBIT 12.6 Average Lives and Modified Durations for a Hypothetical Agency: PAC2 CMO, Run at Variable Initial Speed, then 10.5% CPR for Life

		Initial CPR	10.5	15	20	25	30	35	40	45
		Thereafter	10.5	10.5	10.5	10.5	10.5	10.5	10.5	10.5
2 months at	Ave. life		3.6	3.8	3.9	4.1	4.4	4.8	5.4	6.2
initial speed	Mod. dur.		3.1	3.2	3.3	3.4	3.6	3.8	4.1	4.5
3 Months at	Ave. life		3.6	3.8	4.1	4.5	5.2	6.2	7.7	10.1
initial speed	Mod. dur.		3.1	3.2	3.4	3.6	4.0	4.4	5.1	6.1
4 Months at	Ave. life		3.6	3.9	4.3	5.1	6.3	8.3	10.0	6.2
initial speed	Mod. dur.		3.1	3.3	3.5	3.9	4.5	5.4	6.0	3.8

Another approach would involve using different CPRs in order to gauge the sensitivity of a bond's profile to prepayment spikes. Exhibit 12.6 shows the average lives and durations of the PAC2 used in the prior example under different stress scenarios. The terminal speed utilized across all scenarios is 10.5% CPR (which corresponds to 175% PSA at month 30). In this case, a variety of CPRs are assumed for first few months of the bond after settlement. Note that as the early speeds increase, the average life and duration of the bond also increases; in addition, the bonds also extend when the "spike" speeds are assumed for a longer period.

Both these results are counterintuitive because faster prepayment speeds typically result in shorter average lives. What is happening is that the spike in speeds resulting from a "whipsaw" rate scenario pays off the deal's support bonds very quickly. In the scenario of 40% CPR for four months, the support tranches are fully paid off my month 21. At that point, the PAC2 becomes the support for the high-priority PACs, that is, the PAC1s, in the structure. By month 68, the collateral no longer generates sufficient principal to meet the schedule of the PAC1s. At that point, all principal payments are directed to the PACs; as a result, the average life and duration of the PAC2 extends. This phenomenon is illustrated in panels A and B of Exhibit 12.7. The exhibits show the remaining tranche balances for the PAC1s, PAC2, and support bond over the life of the simple deal examined in this and the previous section. In panel A of Exhibit 12.7, the collateral is run at a constant 10.5% CPR for the life of the bond, and the PAC2 is almost entirely paid off after six years. Panel B of Exhibit 12.7 shows the same deal when the collateral is run at 40% CPR for four months, and 10.5% CPR thereaf-

EXHIBIT 12.7   Outstanding Balances for $400 Million PAC

Panel A: Support Deal at Constant 10.5% CPR

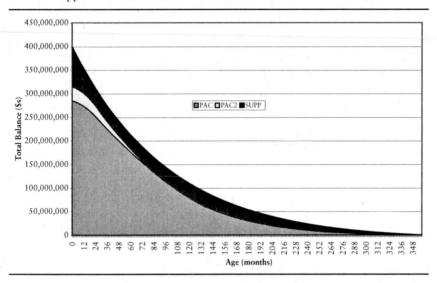

Panel B: Support Deal Run at 40% CPR for Four Months, 10.5% CPR Thereafter

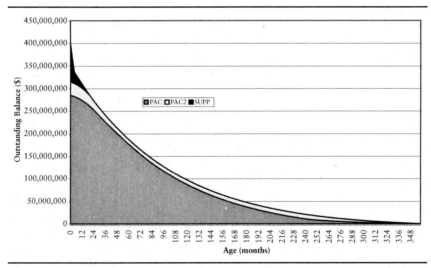

ter (i.e., the third scenario in Exhibit A.6). Note that the support bond is paid off early in the life of the deal. By contrast, the PAC2's balance remains unchanged until after month 240, and is not completely paid off until the maturity of the entire deal.

This discussion highlights the fact that some CMO tranches can be less stable than implied by yield table analysis run at constant prepayment speeds. This is because a yield table is similar in scope to a corporate balance sheet; it is a snapshot of the security's profile at a given point in time. Dynamic scenarios are a fairly easy way to uncover a bond's potential instability, particularly in more complex structures.

While PAC1s are typically quite stable, investors can stress-test them in a fashion similar to that used to evaluate PAC2s. For example, a vector might be created with a very fast speed in the first month (fast enough to prepay all the supports, typically in excess of 90% CPR), and then 6.0% CPR for life. While this does not represent a realistic scenario, it can expose structural weakness in a bond due to a priority shift written into the structure's cash flow rules, which is not typically evident from a static yield table. It also serves as a useful tool, in conjunction with a standard table, to compare ostensibly similar PACs from different deals.

Another type of dynamic prepayment analysis used to evaluate PACs addresses the issue of "PAC band drift." This technique attempts to analyze how much the effective band of a PAC changes if prepayment speeds are outside the range defined by the band for a period of time. In undertaking this analysis, a number of factors should be kept in mind. The definition of the "effective band" is the range of prepayments in which the bond's schedule can be met. This means that the effective band on a PAC may shrink, even if the schedule falls short at a particular speed by a few cents. In addition, the intrinsic nature of the PAC structure discussed in Chapter 6 means that variable prepayment speeds will impact the effective bands of PACs with various average lives differently. The effective band of long PACs, for example, are typically more sensitive to fast speeds, and more inclined to shrink, than those of the short and intermediate PACs within the structure. (To review, the slow prepayment scenarios drive the PAC schedule early in the deal; at a certain point in time, however, the upper band takes over and dictates the schedule. Therefore, bonds created before the so-called crossover point will not be affected by fast speeds to the same extent as PAC tranches later in the structure.)

For example, the 5.5-year PAC shown in Exhibit 12.3 has a structuring band of 100% to 250% PSA. At issuance, however, the effective band of this bond was roughly 100% to 290% PSA, reflecting the effects of time on a PAC band discussed in the earlier chapter. However, prolonged faster speeds will eventually erode the bands of all the PACs in a deal; the fast speeds eventually pay off all of the support tranches, leaving the PACs to behave like sequential bonds.

EXHIBIT 12.8   Effective Band for a Hypothetical PAC Run at Fast Prepayment: Speeds for Different Periods of Time Immediately after Issuance

Months	Band	Early Prepayment Speed (% PSA)							
		300	400	500	600	700	800	900	1000
6	Lower	102	103	104	105	106	108	109	110
	Upper	266	265	263	262	260	258	256	255
12	Lower	106	110	114	118	123	127	133	139
	Upper	265	260	255	249	243	237	231	224
18	Lower	114	122	132	143	155	170	n/a	n/a
	Upper	263	251	239	226	213	198	n/a	n/a
24	Lower	124	140	157	n/a	n/a	n/a	n/a	n/a
	Upper	260	237	213	n/a	n/a	n/a	n/a	n/a

Exhibit 12.8 shows the effective band of the 5.5-year PAC when run at fast speeds for a number of different initial periods. The length of time that the bond prepays faster than the upper band is clearly a key driver, and is at least as important as the level of early prepayments.

Using Yield Matrices to Evaluate Floaters and Inverse Floaters

Evaluating floaters and inverse floaters is done in a similar fashion, although the parameters are typically somewhat different. Tables for CMO floaters typically show the bond's margin and cap (typically the hard cap for corridor-cap floaters), along with the other bond attributes and deal parameters.

Rather than using yield as the primary output, as is typically the case in fixed rate bonds, a yield table on a CMO floater typically shows discount margin (DM) at different prepayment speeds. By definition, the DM is the mortgage yield less the index level. In theory, it gives the investor the spread over a benchmark that can be returned to the investor, and is typically interpreted as spread over a funding target.

This is somewhat misleading, however. The bond's yield is not adjusted to reflect the day-count convention of the index. Thus, DMs for CMO floaters are calculated based on a 30/360 day-count convention, while the LIBOR index is based on an actual/360 day count. If the yield were adjusted to reflect the day-count difference, the floater's DM would typically be 3 to 5 basis points lower. Investors that buy floating rate securities to gain spread over a funding target typically make such an adjustment.[4]

Inverse floaters can, and often are, evaluated based on a traditional yield table (i.e., showing yields at different prices). This assumes that the index off which the coupon is set is held constant. Another way of evaluating an inverse is to run a matrix that shows the bond's yield at different index levels, given a price. This type of "index matrix," shown in Exhibit 12.9, is arguably a more useful technique, as it shows how sensitive the bond's yield is to changes in the index. (While the coupon's change is a function of the inverse leverage or multiple, the yield is also impacted by factors unique to the cash flow as well as the dollar price.) It also gives the investor a sense of how the bond's yield can be expected to behave in different yield curve scenarios. A parallel shift in the yield curve means that yields should change roughly as shown in the diagonal, as indicated. (For example, a 115% PSA corresponds to a +300 basis points scenario, as does an 8.25% LIBOR assumption; a −300 basis points scenario corresponds to a 1,250% PSA and a 2.25% LIBOR in this example.) However, at a 115% PSA assumption and a 4.25% LIBOR (corresponding to

EXHIBIT 12.9 Yield-to-Index Table for a Hypothetical Agency Inverse Floater: 5.5% Coupon Backed by Conventional 5.5s, 6.0% WAC, 2 Months WALA, Priced at 92-16, 5.25% LIBOR

		PSA						
		115	125	145	175	450	850	1250
LIBOR	2.25	18.06	18.10	18.18	18.30	19.38	20.52	21.41
	3.25	14.00	14.04	14.13	14.26	15.39	16.56	17.47
	4.25	10.00	10.05	10.14	10.29	11.45	12.65	13.58
	5.25	6.07	6.12	6.22	6.37	7.57	8.79	9.74
	6.25	2.21	2.26	2.36	2.51	3.74	4.99	5.96
	7.25	0.87	0.92	1.03	1.18	2.41	3.67	4.64
	8.25	0.87	0.92	1.03	1.18	2.41	3.67	4.64
	Ave. life	9.4	8.9	8.0	7.0	3.4	2.3	1.8
	Dur.	7.2	6.9	6.4	5.7	3.0	2.0	1.6
Principal	First pay	Jul-15	Feb-15	Apr-14	May-13	Apr-10	Mar-09	Oct-08
Window	Last pay	Jul-17	Dec-16	Jan-16	Nov-14	Nov-10	Jul-09	Jan-09

---

[4] LIBOR-based floaters created off some types of deals, such as subprime ABS floaters, are structured to pay on an actual/360 basis.

a major bearish steepener), the bond's yield is 10.00%. Assuming a significant flattener with 7.25% LIBOR and a 1,250% PSA assumption, by contrast, the bond has a yield of 4.64%. We will discuss other aspects of inverse floater valuation later in this chapter.

MONTE CARLO AND OAS ANALYSIS

As explained in Chapter 10, option-adjusted spread (OAS) is a metric that attempts to show how much incremental spread is being earned over a benchmark forward curve, taking account of the cost of options embedded in the security. The methodology involved in generating Monte Carlo simulations and calculating option-adjusted spreads and durations was outlined in Chapters 10 and 11. Our discussion here is focused more on using OAS as a method of gauging relative value, with the proviso that OAS can be utilized by investors in a variety of ways. While it is tempting to view the bond with the greatest OAS as the "best" bond, this is often not the case; as with other metrics, OAS and its related methodologies are tools to be used in evaluating bonds. The output generated by a model must be considered in light of both the model's predilections and the limitations of the methodology itself. In this section, we highlight some ways that the methodology can be used, both on its own merit and as an input to other forms of analysis.

As discussed in Chapter 10, the calculation of OAS using Monte Carlo simulations is a highly complex process. The generation of the underlying yield curve, the first step in the process of generating the analysis, is a complex undertaking in its own right; the additional complexity of integrating the model's other components and inputs, such as volatility and prepayment functionality, suggests that the results obtained can be highly model-specific.

In this and the following section, we illustrate some analytical techniques by comparing the results obtained for three bonds. The bonds in question are all hypothetical bonds with a base-case average life of 4.0 years, structured from 2-WALA conventional 5.5s with a 6.0% gross WAC. The three bonds utilized were (1) a 4.0-year sequential; (2) a 4.0-year PAC with a 100% to 250% PSA band and a 2-year principal payment window; and (3) a 4.0-year PAC2 with a 135% to 175% PSA band. All prices and spreads are hypothetical, constructed to illustrate analytical techniques rather than to conform to market levels at any point in time. We deliberately used bonds with the same base-case average life and collateral, in order to be able to conduct an apples-to-apples comparison and thus minimize some of the complexities involved in the analysis. Exhibit 12.10 contains a matrix that shows the profile of the three bonds used for the rest of this chapter, along with the prices and spreads used in the analysis.

Exhibit 12.11 contains a table showing the output of a standard OAS model for the three bonds. Included in the table are the most commonly used metrics, including:

- LIBOR OAS
- Zero-volatility (Z-Vol) OAS
- Option Cost
- Option-adjusted duration (OAD)
- Option-adjust convexity (OAC)

The table also contains the output of the prepayment model, including 1-year, 3-year, and long-term (or life) CPRs. Since the three bonds were structured using the same collateral assumption, the projected speeds for the three bonds are the same.

EXHIBIT 12.10   Profile of the 4.0-year Sequential, PAC, and PAC2 Used in OAS and Total Return Analysis

		PSA						
		100	115	150	175	250	400	600
Sequential (+85/ Curve, 99-16)	Yield	5.60	5.60	5.61	5.61	5.62	5.64	5.66
	Average life	5.8	5.3	4.4	4.0	3.1	2.3	1.8
	Mod. duration	4.6	4.3	3.7	3.4	2.8	2.1	1.7
	Principal window (months)	144	131	109	97	74	51	38
PAC (+65/ Curve, 100-6)	Yield	5.41	5.41	5.41	5.41	5.41	5.39	5.35
	Average life	4.0	4.0	4.0	4.0	4.0	3.5	2.6
	Mod. duration	3.5	3.5	3.5	3.5	3.5	3.1	2.4
	Principal window (months)	25	25	25	25	25	12	7
PAC2 (+100/ Curve, 99-00)	Yield	5.64	5.67	5.76	5.76	5.86	5.99	6.12
	Average life	13.6	8.6	4.0	4.0	2.5	1.7	1.3
	Mod. duration	9.3	6.3	3.4	3.4	2.3	1.6	1.2
	Principal window (months)	200	171	116	116	41	26	19

EXHIBIT 12.11 OAS Model Output for Three Hypothetical Securities

Bond	Price	Spread/ Treasury	Average Life	Modified Duration	OAS	Zero-Vol. OAS	Option Cost	OA Duration	OA Convexity	Model Prepayment Speeds (CPR%)		
										12-month	36-month	Long-term
Sequential	99 16/32	85	4.0	3.4	10.8	43.9	33.0	2.5	-1.57	6.1	9.1	11.6
PAC	100 6/32	65	4.0	3.5	11.9	26.2	14.3	2.6	-1.74	6.1	9.1	11.6
PAC2	99	100	4.0	3.4	0.2	65.3	65.1	2.2	-0.99	6.1	9.1	11.6

A cursory viewing of Exhibit 12.11 shows that the PAC has the highest OAS of the three bonds; by contrast, the zero-volatility OAS (Z-Vol. OAS) is highest for the PAC2, reflecting its high-static spread. The PAC2 also has the highest option cost. (As described in Chapter 10, option cost is the difference between the OAS and Z-Vol. OAS, and can be interpreted as the cost of hedging the interest rate volatility implied by the model.) Interestingly, the PAC has the lowest option cost, but the most negative convexity of the three bonds. While often used as equivalent measures, the two metrics measure different attributes of the bond. The option cost measures how much market volatility costs the bond in option-adjusted spread; the convexity measures the nonlinearity of the bond's price profile.

Depending on the interpretation, Exhibit 12.11 suggests that the 4.0-year PAC may either be the "best" bond (as it has the highest OAS and lowest option cost) or the "worst" bond (since it has the lowest Z-Vol. OAS and the most negative convexity of the three securities in question). The temptation to use one metric or another as a sort of relative-value "magic bullet" is normally counterproductive. Rather than giving a simple summation of relative value, this type of analysis is most useful as a basis for further inquiry into the attributes of the different securities, and what conditions might cause one bond to offer better returns than another.

Given the complexities of the OAS methodology, the output generated by OAS models can vary greatly due to both biases within the model and changes in the level of inputs. One of the most important drivers of OAS functionality is the prepayment model. As shown in Exhibit 12.10, prepayment model generates prepayment vectors for each interest rate path, which are in turn used to generate the cash flow vectors central to the analysis. Therefore, the output of the prepayment model has a profound impact on the spreads and metrics ultimately displayed by the model; in turn, the functionality and biases implicitly contained in the prepayment model are one of the most important drivers of the OAS model's output.

Changes in the market levels used as inputs, as well as variations in how the inputs are handled, can also result in marked changes to the output of the model. For example, an important input is the level of implied volatility. Higher implied volatility (or "vols") typically reduced option-adjusted spreads; however, the response to higher vols is often quite dependent on the nature of the bonds being analyzed.

Therefore, using OAS effectively requires the user to be cognizant of both the potential biases of the model being utilized, as well as how the bonds being analyzed might be impacted by changes in the market environment. One way of accounting for these factors is to rerun the analysis while changing the model's parameters. To illustrate this, we recalculated the OAS of the three bonds in Exhibit 12.11 by running multiples of the prepayment model (shown in panel A of Exhibit 12.12, using 80% and 120% of the model) and the level of volatility (running at 90% and 110% of the market levels, as shown in panel B of Exhibit 12.12). With respect to the prepayment model, the spread of the PAC2 is clearly the most sensitive of the three bonds to changes in the prepayment functionality. In part, this is due to its lower dollar price; more importantly, changing the prepayment model increases (at a lower model multiple) or decreases (at a higher multiple) the probability that the collateral will prepay at speeds below the band, which would make it a much longer cash flow. The PAC2 is also the most sensitive to changes in volatility, although all three bonds are less responsive to this change than to changes in the prepayment model.

This output is useful in a number of ways. If, for example, the prepayment model is considered to be "fast" or "slow" relative to either historical experience or the market consensus, the output of the model must be interpreted in this context. If a relatively "fast" model generated a high OAS for a PAC2, the outsized spread might be largely attributable to the biases of the model, rather than the attractiveness of the bond. The same output from a "slow" model, by contrast, might well indicate a very cheap bond. In addition, the prepayment environment is not static; as discussed in Chapter 4, prepayment speeds reflect factors such as the state of the housing market, the shape of the yield curve, and the availability of alternative products. Therefore, even if the user is comfortable with the output of a model, changes in the prepayment

EXHIBIT 12.12 OAS Output for Three Hypothetical Securities

Panel A. Using Multiples of Prepayment Model

	OAS		OAS Change from Base Case	
	80%	120%	80%	120%
Sequential	7.5	13.4	−3.3	2.6
PAC	13.8	8.2	1.9	−3.7
PAC2	−33.7	23.6	−33.9	23.4

Panel B. Using Multiples of Implied Volatilities

	OAS		OAS Change from Base Case	
	90%	110%	90%	110%
Sequential	15.5	6.0	15.5	6.0
PAC	14.8	8.7	14.8	8.7
PAC2	7.3	−6.8	7.3	−6.8

environment may impact the relative attractiveness of a bond. The PAC2 in the example would be much less attractive if base-case prepayment speeds were to slow due to profound housing market weakness and resulting slower turnover.

In this light, the simple changes imposed on the prepayment model in panel B of Exhibit 12.12 are themselves somewhat biased. While using a simple multiple of the prepayment model is a fairly robust test in most cases, prepayment functionality is multidimensional. Model attributes such as base-case prepayment speeds, the ramping behavior, and the response to refinancing incentives all are important. Running the prepayment model at different percentages of the base model does not fully change the model's functionality. While this is an easy test that gives useful results for most bonds, certain cash flows (such as support POs and inverse IOs) require more robust stressing of the prepayment model in order to fully grasp the bond's prepayment sensitivities.

These considerations are also important in evaluating potential returns on securities that do not have fixed payments. This includes the hybrid ARM product, which comprises a significant share of the mortgage universe. As discussed in Chapter 4, the prepayment behavior of a hybrid ARM varies based on how soon the bond resets, and whether it has already experienced its first reset and is now experiencing periodic rate adjustments. The value of a hybrid ARM security is highly dependent on expected prepayment speeds. A major factor relates to what proportion of the bond will be outstanding when the underlying loans reset. This is because the bond's floating rate tail has great value, especially if the yield curve is flat, as the security's coupon rate will reset to very high levels; this makes it a high-yielding security with a very short duration. Therefore, OAS analysis of hybrid ARMs is highly dependent on the veracity of both the pre- and postreset prepayment model projections; a robust analysis of the hybrid ARM product involves running spreads and valuations at various multiples of the prepayment model both before and after the reset date.

Therefore, the output of OAS models should not be viewed as isolated indicators of relative value. OAS is much more useful when viewed as one tool in an arsenal of different techniques. Rather than signaling value in isolation, the results should be interpreted in the context of what the investor needs to believe in order to like one bond over another.

TOTAL RETURN ANALYSIS

As discussed in Chapter 10, the concept of total return (TR) methodology is a robust measure of expected returns over a defined horizon. This analysis is commonly used by investors that manage assets versus market benchmarks or indexes, as well as by investors looking to evaluate and compare projected performance under different interest rate scenarios. In the following section, we demonstrate some ways that TR analysis can be used, using the same three bonds evaluated in Exhibits 12.11 and 12.12.

Total return is arguably a more realistic and robust measure of performance than yield for a number of reasons. Most importantly, it relaxes some of the unrealistic assumptions underlying yield measures; it allows for the assumption of different reinvestment returns, as well as the prospect that the bond will be held to a predefined horizon, rather than to maturity. It also allows returns to be generated under a variety of different interest rate and prepayment scenarios. However, this increased flexibility means that some assumptions must be explicitly made prior to generating the analysis. These assumptions include:

- The method used to determine the terminal price of each security at the horizon. Often, an assumption of constant OAS is made, meaning that the bond's price is regenerated at a point forward in time, using the current level of OAS as the pricing benchmark. Other spreads, such as static spreads over swaps, can also be used, along with user-defined prices generated outside the TR model. Alternatively, the analyst can assume that spreads will change as time elapses; therefore, variable option-adjusted or static spreads can be used to calculate the terminal price.
- The time horizon to be evaluated (which often depends on the investor's typical holding period).
- When curve shifts would take place (i.e., instantaneous, at the horizon date, or gradually).[5]
- The nature of the yield curve shifts. (As we will subsequently discuss, a thorough analysis involves both parallel shifts as well as changes in the configuration of the yield curve.)
- The reinvestment rate to be assumed. A commonly used method should use a so-called *run off strategy*, which means that all interest and principal proceeds are held in the form of cash. Under this assumption, a spread around LIBOR or some cash benchmark is typically assumed. Alternatively, the investor may assume that proceeds will be reinvested in similar securities, which means that the reinvestment rate should be the same as that of the bond being analyzed.

---

[5] While the impact of different rate shift timing is *de minimus* for most fixed income securities, the exposure to changing prepayment speeds makes MBS path-dependent, as noted in Chapter 10. Therefore, the returns will vary under the same rate-change scenario if the timing of the shift is changed.

Total return analysis also has some biases that need to be taken into account. As noted above, the terminal price of the bond is often generated using a spread at the horizon date. In addition, the average lives and durations of bonds with tight principal windows shorten more than those with wide windows. (At its extremes, the average life of a bond with a bullet maturity will shorten pro rata with the passage of time; a pass-through that amortizes over a 30-year schedule might only shorten 0.1 to 0.2 years in average life for every year that passes.) Depending on the shape of the yield curve, a tight-window bond's horizon price will rise as time elapses more than that of a wide-window bond. The value of the so-called rolldown effect is greater when the yield curve for its class of securities is steeper, vis-à-vis when the product's yield curve is flat. (This "curve" is a function of both the benchmark yield curve and spreads for each point on the yield curve.) This means that the results of total return analysis will be impacted by the cash flow window; the magnitude of the effect is a function of the shape of the product yield curve, as well as whether market spreads will widen as the bond ages and its price rises.

Exhibit 12.13 shows projected 12-month total returns for the three agency CMOs in various parallel-shift scenarios, using instantaneous changes to the spot curve, constant-OAS horizon pricing, and a LIBOR-flat reinvestment assumption. For the sake of comparison, we also show

EXHIBIT 12.13   12-Month Total Returns for 4.0-Year Agency CMOs and Bullet Agency Debenture In Parallel-Shift Scenarios

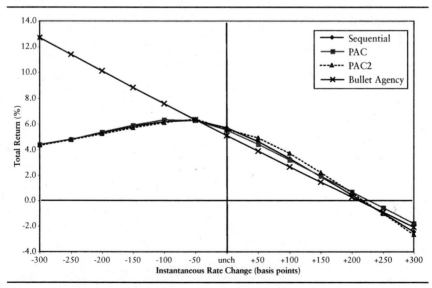

the returns for a par-priced, noncallable agency debenture, with a four-year maturity. While the returns of the debenture are virtually linear with respect to rate changes, all of the tranches exhibit returns that tail off in rally scenarios beyond a 50-basis-point shift, reflecting the impact of faster prepayment speeds on returns.

Exhibit 12.14 shows the parallel-shift return data in Exhibit 12.13 as incremental returns versus the noncallable debenture. This framework is very useful in defining the scenarios where thes bonds can be expected to outperform or underperform each other. The returns of the three securities in rally (i.e., rate decline) scenarios are very similar. The PAC2 can be expected to outperform the other two MBS in cases of moderate rate increases; the PAC will outperform both bonds when rates rise more than 200 basis points.

As noted, the return analyses shown in Exhibits 12.13 and 12.14 are based on parallel shifts in the yield curve. However, nonparallel yield curve shifts can result in very different results, depending upon the structure and type of the bond in question. Panels A and B of Exhibit 12.15 show incremental returns for the three tranches versus the non-callable agency debenture in nonparallel shift scenarios. Panel A of Exhibit 12.15 shows projected 12-month returns when the short end of the curve (i.e., 2-year and shorter rates) are changed, while the long end of the curve (10-year and longer rates) are held constant. Panel B of Exhibit 12.15 shows

EXHIBIT 12.14   Difference in 12-Month Total Returns Between 4.0-Year Agency CMOs and Bullet Agency Debenture in Parallel-Shift Scenarios

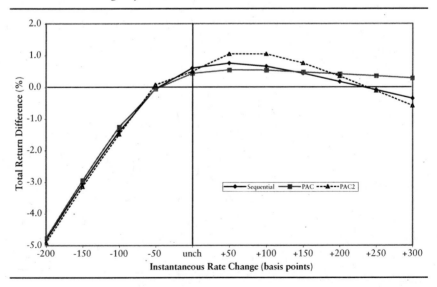

EXHIBIT 12.15   Difference in 12-Month Total Returns Between 4.0-Year Agency CMOs and Bullet Agency Debenture in Yield Curve Change Scenarios

Panel A. Change in 2-Year Yield, 10-Year Yield Unchanged

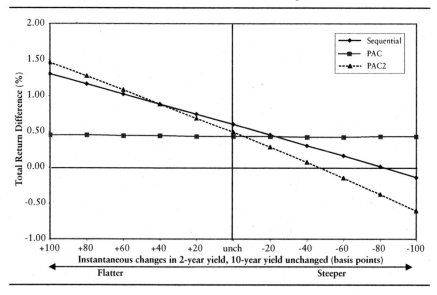

Panel B. Change in 10-Year Yield, 2-Year Yield Unchanged

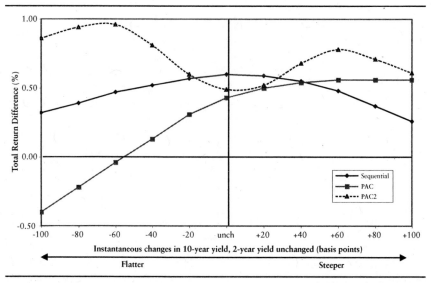

the opposite scenario, where the short end is held constant while the long end is changed. (In both cases, the "belly" of the yield curve can be envisioned to pivot off the sector held constant.) Both exhibits are scaled to show yield curve "flattening" as the areas on the left of the horizontal axis, while yield curve "steepening" is illustrated at levels on the right side of the axis.

The striking aspect of these two exhibits is how much different the return profiles are for the three bonds, despite their identical base-case average lives and similar modified and option-adjusted durations. In Panel A of Exhibit 12.15, the incremental returns of the PAC over the noncallable debenture are virtually insensitive to changes in the short end of the curve, while the sequential and PAC2 bonds both outperform the debenture in a flattening scenario (which in this case can be considered a "bear flattener" scenario) but lag the debenture as short rates decline and the curve steepens (i.e., a *bull steepener*).

In the case where the 10-year yield is changed, as shown in Panel B of Exhibit 12.15, the results are quite different. The PAC's incremental returns lag those of the sequential when the curve flattens (a *bull flattener* scenarios), but outpace them when the curve steepens (a *bear steepener* case). Interestingly, the PAC2 exhibits the best performance in cases of significant swings in either direction.

The differing incremental performance of the three bonds in the nonparallel curve shift scenarios reflects aspects of their structures related to those highlighted in the earlier discussion of yield curves and prepayment vectors. For example, bonds with schedules (such as PACs) will typically underperform sequentials (as well as unstructured securities such as pass-throughs) when the long end of the yield curve rallies. This is because of the impact of changing prepayment projections on the schedule. Lower long rates and a flatter yield curve cause the prepayment model to project faster future prepayment speeds. In turn, this causes the balances of the support bonds to pay down faster, resulting in less support for the PACs. The constant-OAS horizon pricing assumption therefore imputes wider static spreads and weaker price performance of the PACs in these scenarios, negatively impacting their total returns vis-à-vis bonds without schedules.

This effect is best illustrated by using key rate or partial durations. As discussed in Chapter 11, key rate durations attempt to measure the sensitivity of a bond's price when discrete segments of the yield curve are changed. Exhibit 12.16 shows the partial durations of the three bonds used in the analysis. Note that the PAC has a very uneven duration profile. It has relatively high positive exposure in the three- and five-year sectors; its durations in the longer rate buckets, however, are very negative, revealing the bond's vulnerability in the bull flattener sce-

EXHIBIT 12.16 Key Rate Durations for 4.0-Year Agency CMOs

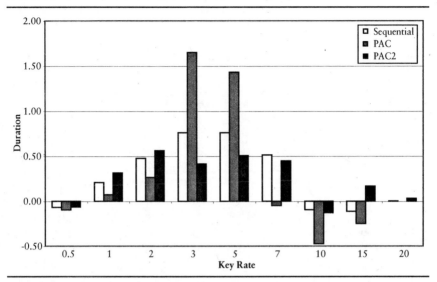

nario. Its returns are not impacted by the bear flattener, however, as it has very little duration exposure to short rates. While the other two CMOs also have negative long durations, their magnitude is quite small in comparison to the PAC; this is consistent with their relative performance versus the PAC in curve-flattening scenarios.

While TR analysis is very useful, it has implicit weaknesses that should be taken into account. In the analysis shown in Exhibits 12.13, 12.4, and 12.15, we did not adjust for the different option-adjusted durations of the four securities utilized. A true duration-neutral analysis means that, to equalize the durations, some of the bonds in the structure will need to be evaluated as part of a portfolio that consists of CMOs and cash. (Lengthening a bond's duration can be accomplished by using a short position in cash, essentially leveraging the portfolio.) However, the CMO-and-cash portfolios are effectively portfolio barbells, with low-duration cash combined with securities exhibiting positive durations. Barbelled portfolios exhibit their own performance attributes with respect to changes in the yield curve configuration; typically, barbells will outperform as the yield curve flattens and lag when it steepens. Therefore, investors undertaking TR analysis need to take account of this potential bias; one potential solution would be to limit comparisons to securities with similar durations, in order to eliminate or minimize the biases imposed with barbelled portfolios.

Another important issue is a weakness discussed previously with respect to yield tables. The analysis is designed to project returns in either static or rate-change scenarios that move in one direction. However, the discussion on yield tables and vector analysis demonstrated that some bonds are more sensitive than others to yield curve shocks and dynamic changes in interest rates. Most TR models do not allow such scenarios to be taken into account. In addition, it is difficult to identify factors driving returns for these bonds in different scenarios; the interaction between the cash flows within a deal is often unpredictable, and the returns can be quite model-specific.

This is highlighted by the incremental performance of the PAC2 shown in Panel B of Exhibit 12.15. The incremental performance vis-à-vis the two other tranches in the bull flattener case is likely due to the PAC2's positive performance at faster prepayment speeds, as indicated previously. In the bear steepener case, the bond's schedule prevents the bond from extending as much, at least in scenarios of modest long-rate changes. However, these results would be different in a dynamic scenario where long rates first fell and then rose; as discussed previously, the PAC2's support would immediately erode, and its performance (particularly in bearish long rate scenarios) would likely suffer.

COMPARING THE ANALYSIS OF AGENCY AND PRIVATE LABEL TRANCHES

In Chapter 8, we contrasted structuring techniques utilized in agency and private label CMO deals. As a corollary of the discussion of valuation techniques for various MBS, the relative ease of valuing bonds in the different sectors should be addressed. While the same techniques are typically used to evaluate agency and non-agency bonds, differences between the products often make valuing private label bonds more difficult and subjective. In some cases, these differences stem from the structures themselves; however, other differences also contribute to the wider dispersion of dealer quotes for senior private label securities vis-à-vis those created from agency deals.

■ Agency CMO structures have a greater degree of standardization than do private label deals. Agency PACs, for example, are structured using PAC bands to generate the schedule; while somewhat restrictive, this technique allows for a fair degree of transparency with respect to the attributes of the PACs being created. Moreover, the bands utilized to structure PACs are fairly consistent across deals. (Typically, current-coupon PACs are structured with lower bands in the area of 100% PSA, and upper bands ranging from 250–300% PSA.) The super-stable structures discussed previously in this chapter have schedules that are generated manually, through an iterative trial-and-error process. While allowing for greater structuring flexibility, this technique creates more heterogeneous structures; this makes private label bonds more difficult to analyze than agency PACS, even though they are fundamentally similar securities.

■ There is much less consensus on prepayment speeds for the loans backing private label deals than for the pools that collateralize agency CMOs. As noted previously in this chapter, Bloomberg publishes a series of median prepayment speeds for fixed rate agency collateral that are calculated from model projections reported by multiple Wall Street dealers. These "Bloomberg medians," calculated for both base-case and parallel-shift rate scenarios, are treated as consensus prepayment projections by traders and investors. The existence of *de facto* consensus prepayment speeds generally makes valuing agency tranches easier, thus enhancing the liquidity of the agency CMO sector. By contrast, Bloomberg does not publish median speeds for jumbo-balance and other non-agency loan cohorts. The dearth of published consensus prepayment projections, along with the heterogeneity of their collateral pools, makes the analysis of non-agency tranches both laborious and highly model-dependent. In turn, this increased uncertainty makes price and spread quotes less consistent across dealers.

■ There are fewer investors active in the private label sector than in agency-backed products. Despite the fact that the incremental credit risk of triple-A rated private label security over agency tranches is quite small, some investors limit their MBS purchases to agency-backed bonds as a form of risk management. This is particularly true for those investors without particular expertise in the MBS sector who wish to limit their perceived credit exposure and seek the presumed safety associated with the agency guaranty. The smaller constituency of the private label sector results in reduced liquidity for non-agency bonds. This manifests itself in reduced liquidity, wider bid/ask spreads, and greater uncertainty in price discovery.

■ Finally, it often takes longer to run private label bonds in analytical systems. For example, many non-agency deals have collateral files with hundreds of different loan strata. This can dramatically increase the computation time required to calculate metrics such as OAS and effective duration, and thus reducing the time available to contemplate valuation. Operational issues can also limit the ability to perform the type of "model stressing" advocated earlier in this chapter, particularly if the bond in question is being evaluated under multiple market scenarios. This difficulty is magnified if the trader is attempting to value or trade a portfolio of bonds.

However, valuation differences across sectors become less evident when evaluating support and "whippy" paper, as well as MBS derivatives such as IOs and inverse floaters. Irrespective of sector, these bonds are intrinsically difficult to price. In addition, valuations tend to be highly model-specific, based on differences in how the yield curve, volatility, and prepayments are modeled.

Therefore, it is reasonable to conclude that the more generic agency CMO tranches are easier to value than comparable bonds structured in the private label sector. Much of the cross-sector differences fade, however, when attempting to evaluate more complex securities, as they are difficult to evaluate regardless of sector and collateral type. One consistent challenge to private label trading, however, is the issue of model performance described above. This has created demand for models that run faster without sacrificing accuracy, such as the option-theoretic approach discussed in the appendix.

EVALUATING INVERSE FLOATERS

Evaluating complex securities such as inverse floaters and inverse IOs presents special challenges to investors. As discussed in Chapter 7, these bonds are created from either a collateral pool or, more commonly, from a collateral or "parent" tranche. In addition, their coupons are both variable and, especially for "payer" inverses, leveraged with respect to changes in the reference rate or index. Before addressing some valuation techniques, it will be helpful to establish a framework for understanding and conceptualizing the bonds in an economic context.

Since both the inverse floater and floating rate tranche are created from a fixed rate parent tranche, the following relationship is true:

> Long a fixed rate parent tranche
> = Long a capped floater + Long an inverse floater

(As discussed in Chapter 7, the floater must be capped, since the parent tranche has a fixed coupon rate.)

Recasting this relationship in terms of an inverse floater gives us

> Long an inverse floater = Long a fixed rate parent tranche
>   – Long a capped floater

Or, equivalently,

Long an inverse floater = Long a fixed rate parent tranche
+ Short a capped floater

Thus, the owner of an inverse floater has effectively purchased a fixed rate tranche and shorted a capped floater. However, shorting a floater is equivalent to borrowing funds, where the interest cost of the funds is a floating rate and the floating rate is the reference rate plus the spread. Consequently, the owner of an inverse floater has effectively purchased a fixed rate asset with borrowed funds, and thus owns a leveraged position in the parent tranche. This is consistent with the discussion in Chapter 7 of the leverage embedded in an inverse floater.

In this framework, the nature of inverse floaters is fairly straightforward. However, valuing and evaluating inverse floaters can be quite difficult, given the complexity of their cash flows and returns. As with other types of tranches, there are a number of techniques that can be utilized in evaluating and comparing different inverse floaters. However, there is no one guide to value, and the difficulty of valuing the bonds is magnified by both their complexity and the amplified impact of small modeling errors on the values generated.

As with other senior tranches, Monte Carlo simulations can be used to directly generate either OAS-based prices or an OAS at a given price, which can be compared to other comparable securities. For inverse floaters and bonds where the coupon is contingent on a reference rate, however, using this approach requires a special understanding of how the Monte Carlo process generates interest cash flows, based on the parent bond's coupon and the reference rate.

The model begins by simulating the path of short-term interest rates, as before. Then, from the path of short-term rates, two other paths are created. The first is the path of short rates used for both the generation of prepayment rates and discount rates for the cash flow vectors; the second is a path for the inverse floater's reference rate. In constructing the simulated path for the reference rate, it is necessary to make an assumption about the relationship between the short-term rate and the reference rate. Thus, if the reference rate is one-month LIBOR, the model must make an assumption about the relationship between one-month LIBOR and the one-month risk-free rate. If one-month LIBOR is assumed to be X basis points over the one-month risk-free rate, then on the simulated path for the reference rate, the rates are assumed to be X basis points above the simulated short-term path of rates. Therefore, for a given month on a given interest rate path, there is a value for both the reference rate and the refinancing rate.

Given a prepayment model, the coupon reset formula for the inverse floater, and the structure of the deal, cash flows can be determined for each month on each interest rate path. A critical assumption in this methodology is the relationship between the reference rate and the short-term rate. (Of course, the calculation is much simpler for LIBOR OAS values, as the short-term rate and the reference rate are similar, if not identical.)

Given a required OAS, the value of an inverse floater is computed by calculating the value of each interest rate path and then averaging the values. Alternatively, the OAS can be computed given the market price of the inverse floater. In practice, it is difficult to use this methodology without a good idea of what the required OAS should be to generate a theoretical price (or, at a given price, what an acceptable OAS might be) for a bond in question. This method is most useful for those participants that are actively trading the sector during times when comparable bonds are trading. This allows the analyst to use the output of the models to value a variety of structures and leverages.

An alternative means of valuing the bonds is by computing its so-called "creation value." Many CMO tranches can be viewed in the context of where they can be created, and traders typically shape their valuations based on their knowledge of where the various tranches can be created (assuming, of course, that they are createable). Judging creation value on one bond, however, presupposes that the trader has a good idea of where the remaining tranches would trade at that point in time, along with the pricing of the appropriate collateral. Given that knowledge, along with values for the yield curve, the structuring model would generate a value and spread for the tranche in question. Under certain conditions, the generation of creation value is particularly helpful for inverse floaters and other tranches that are difficult to value in isolation. As we will discuss, however, this should not necessarily be viewed as a hard value, but rather as a guide in generating and judging valuations.

Chapter 7 showed how tranches can be split into floater/inverse floater combinations, depending on the attributes of the parent tranche and the floater to be created. We can express the relationships among the collateral tranche, the floater, and the corresponding inverse floater as follows:

$$\text{Parent tranche} = \text{Floater} + \text{Inverse floater}$$

That is, the sum of the value of the floater and the value of the inverse floater must be equal to the value of the collateral tranche from which they are created. This relationship holds for both the face value and the dollar value of the bonds; if this relationship is materially violated, arbitrage profits are possible. The relationship can therefore also be expressed as follows:

MV of inverse floater = MV of parent tranche – MV of floater

where MV is the market value of each tranche in question. This expression states that the value of an inverse floater can be found by valuing both the collateral tranche and the floater, and then calculating the difference between the two values. In this case, the value of an inverse floater is not found directly, but instead inferred from the value of the collateral tranche and the floater. The market value of the parent tranche and the floater can be determined through a variety of techniques, including the type of Monte Carlo simulations discussed previously.

The same relationship also holds if dollar prices are used. In this case, however, the leverage of the inverse must be taken into account. For example, an inverse with 4× leverage means that there are four times as many floaters as inverse floaters in the structure. If the parent tranche's face value is \$100 million, there are \$80 million in floaters and \$20 million in inverse floaters. Thus the following relationship holds:

$$100 \times \text{Parent tranche price} = (20 \times \text{Inverse price}) + (80 \times \text{Floater price})$$

This can also be expressed as

$$[20 \times (1 + 4) \times (\text{Parent tranche price})]$$
$$= (20 \times \text{Inverse price}) + [20 \times (4 \times \text{Floater price})]$$

Dividing both sides by 20 results in

$$[(1 + 4) \times (\text{Parent trance price})] = \text{Inverse price} + (4 \times \text{Floater price})$$

This can be generalized for any leverage L as

$$[(1 + L) \times (\text{Parent tranche price})] = \text{Inverse price} + (L \times \text{Floater price})$$

Solving for the inverse floater price results in

$$\text{Inverse price} = [(1 + L) \times (\text{Parent tranche price})] - (L \times \text{Floater price})$$

There are a number of important implications associated with this price relationship. First, it is typically not difficult to price the floater, especially if it is comparable to other tranches being created in the market. The greater difficulty is usually associated with the determination of the parent tranche's price. However, the pricing of the parent tranche has a major impact on the pricing of the inverse, due to the impact of the leverage. Put differently, the above equation indicates that every point that the parent tranche is mispriced results in a $1+ L$ mispricing of the inverse floater. In the previous example, a one-point mispricing of the parent tranche would result in the inverse price being off by five points.

The second implication is that, in this context, the price of the inverse is not related to the level of the reference rate. Rather, the reference rate is reflected in the value of the floater, specifically in the value of the cap associated with the floater. Were rates to rise to a level near that of the floater's effective cap, the market value of the floater would fall; if the price of the parent tranche remained stable, the inverse's price would therefore increase. Finally, the impact of factors such as the shape of the yield curve and the levels of implied volatilities impact the pricing of the inverse through their effect on the value of the parent tranche and the floater.

As noted, creation value can be a useful guide to the value of an inverse under certain conditions. It is particularly useful in gauging the value of bonds comparable to those being produced in the new-issue market. However, it is not feasible to assess creation value for bonds that cannot, at that point in time, be created. If the production coupon for 30-year pools is 5.5%, for example, it would be impossible to judge the creation value of a bond backed by Gold 7.0s, as none of the components could be priced effectively. This is especially true in the context of the pricing errors that would occur as a result of the inverse's leverage on its price. Finally, structures are often quite complex. Using the standard analytical systems (such as Bloomberg), it is often difficult to deduce exactly how some structures work; in addition, more than one complex bond will need to be valued. For example, the presence of two-tiered index bonds (TTIBs) in a structure requires the analyst to understand how the cash flows are allocated to both the TTIB and the inverse floater; in addition, the TTIB would need to be valued, along with the floater and the parent tranche, in order to value the inverse. In most cases, this is too complex an undertaking, and too prone to error, to be useful.

SUMMARY

A logical conclusion from the discussions in this chapter should be that no one technique or methodology can give a complete understanding of how different MBS, particularly structured securities, can be expected to perform under real-world conditions. Tools such as yield tables, option-adjusted spreads, and total return analysis should be viewed as complimentary methodologies. Rather than viewing one metric as giving "better" results, a variety of methods, models, and techniques should be utilized in analyzing bonds and undertaking relative-value comparisons.

An Option-Theoretic Approach to Valuing MBS*

Throughout this book, the importance of understanding the underpinnings of prepayment behavior has been emphasized as well as their effects on mortgage-backed security (MBS) valuations. Prepayment speeds are the dominant consideration in MBS analysis. The evolving nature of borrower behavior was first described in Chapter 4. In Chapters 10 through 12, how prepayment projections are taken into account in valuation, relative value, and risk models was examined. Most prepayment models in current use are econometric models that have been calibrated to historical prepayment data. Although the right to refinance a mortgage is widely recognized as a call option granted by the lender to the homeowner, *option-theoretic* models are not currently used in prepayment modeling despite their use for valuing corporate bonds and agency debentures with embedded option. There are two reasons often cited for not employing option-theoretic models to value an MBS: (1) most borrowers do not exercise the option optimally and (2) empirically it has been found that option-based models are not able to explain observed prices of MBS.

In this appendix, we describe a relatively new approach for valuing MBS developed by Kalotay, Yang, and Fabozzi (KYF hereafter)[1] and

---

[1] For a complete description of the model, see Andrew Kalotay, Deane Yang, and Frank J. Fabozzi, "An Option-Theoretic Prepayment Model for Mortgages and Mortgage-Backed Securities," *International Journal of Theoretical and Applied Finance* 7, no. 8 (December 2004), pp. 949–978. See also Andrew Kalotay, Deane Yang, and Frank J. Fabozzi, "An Option-Theoretic Approach to MBS Valuation," Chapter 33 in Frank J. Fabozzi (ed.), *The Handbook of Mortgage-Backed Securities: 6th Edition* (Burr Ridge, IL: McGraw-Hill, 2006). For an option-based model for mortgage refinancing, see Andrew Kalotay, Deane Yang, and Frank J. Fabozzi, "Optimal Mortgage Refinancing: Application of Bond Valuation Tools to Household Risk Management," Andrew Kalotay Associates (October 2006).

---

* This appendix is coauthored by Frank Fabozzi, Andrew Kalotay, and Deane Yang.

show how it can be used to value pools of mortgages and MBS issued by Ginnie Mae, Fannie Mae, and Freddie Mac (i.e., high-grade pools, where neither the credit risk of the homeowner nor that of the issuer is a significant factor). The approach distinguishes between prepayments that do not depend on interest rates and refinancings that do. Turnover and curtailment comprise what in the model is referred to as "baseline prepayments." These prepayments are modeled using a vector of prepayment speeds, while refinancings are modeled using a pure option-based approach. In the model, the full spectrum of refinancing behavior is described using a notion of "refinancing efficiency." Borrowers are classified as follows:

- *Financial engineers:* borrowers who refinance at just the right time
- *Leapers:* borrowers who refinance too early
- *Laggards:* borrowers who wait too long to refinance

The initial mortgage pool is partitioned into "efficiency buckets," with the size of each bucket calibrated to market prices. The composition of a seasoned pool is then determined by the excess refinancings over baseline prepayments. Leapers are eliminated first, then financial engineers, and finally laggards. The composition of the mortgage pool gradually shifts towards laggards over time, automatically accounting for the "prepayment burnout" behavior observed in the market.

OPTION-THEORETIC MODELS FOR VALUING MBS

Historically, several option-theoretic approaches to valuing MBS have been proposed. These models were first introduced in the academic literature in the early 1980s but did not appear to have been used by participants in the mortgage market then or now.[2] These models assumed optimal refinancing decisions by homeowners and exogenous reasons for other prepayments and later extended by incorporating transaction cost or other market frictions to explain why nonoptimal refinancing decisions were observed in the market. The chief pitfall of these models was they assumed the refinancing behavior of all homeowners was iden-

---

[2] See, Kenneth B. Dunn and John J. McConnell, "A Comparison of Alternative Models for Pricing GNMA Mortgage-Backed Securities," *Journal of Finance* 36 (1981), pp. 471–483; Kenneth B. Dunn and John J. McConnell, "Valuation of Mortgage-Backed Securities," *Journal of Finance* 36 (1981) pp. 599–617; and Richard Stanton, "Rational Prepayment and the Valuation of Mortgage-Backed Securities," *Review of Financial Studies* 8 (1995), pp. 677–708.

tical and optimal under specified economic conditions, implying that all refinancings occur simultaneously in a given mortgage pool.

Wall Street firms sought to develop models that overcame the drawbacks of the option-theoretic models in the academic literature. In 1987, two researchers then at Merrill Lynch, Andrew Davidson and Michael Hershovitz, developed a model that they coined the "threshold refinancing pricing model."[3] While in their model, they also attributed nonoptimal refinancing as being due to transaction costs, but assumed that a mortgage pool is heterogeneous with different homeowners facing different transaction costs. Similar heterogeneous pool models have also been proposed and analyzed by other practitioners and in the academic literature. While the Davidson-Hershovitz model was implemented at Merrill Lynch, it never gained wide acceptance in the mortgage market and was eventually abandoned. One key problem in earlier option-theoretic models was the unrealistically high transaction costs required to fit market prices for MBS.

AN OPTION-BASED PREPAYMENT MODEL FOR MORTGAGES

The KYF model is similar in some regards to earlier option-theoretic models, but differs in crucial aspects. It is similar because the model of refinancing behavior is based on an optimal option exercise strategy. They also model heterogeneity by decomposing the mortgage pool into buckets and assuming that each bucket represents different refinancing behavior. The crucial features distinguishing the model from the others are the following:

- Mortgage cash flows and the cash flows of MBS are discounted using different yield curves, a procedure not followed in previous option-theoretic models.
- Prepayments are classified as one of two different types and then each is modeled differently. The first type, turnover, is assumed to be independent of interest rates, and the second, refinancings, is assumed to depend on interest rates.
- Refinancing behavior is not modeled in terms of transaction costs but in terms of an "imputed coupon," which is defined later.

This immediately affords a simple and natural way to model the credit profile and the credit impairment of the homeowner (as an OAS).

---

[3] Andrew Davidson and Michael Hershovitz, "The Refinancing Threshold Pricing Model: An Economic Approach to Valuing MBS," Merrill Lynch Mortgage-Backed Research, November 1987.

The model handles real transaction costs in a straightforward manner.[4] In addition, the model provides a simple means of parameterizing the full range of possible suboptimal refinancing tendencies ("leapers" to "laggards").

Existing prepayments models are based upon overly complex descriptions of prepayments. They all have many input parameters to set or calibrate and run into the danger of overfitting. The KYF model, in contrast, is a parsimonious prepayment model that uses the simplest possible mechanisms to account for all crucial factors that drive the price of an MBS. The KYS model employs only a few input parameters set at reasonable and realistic values, is able to reproduce the market prices of new mortgage pools and pass-through securities, and how they change as market conditions change. The prepayment process of the mortgagor is modeled in considerable detail, the basic idea being that once a simple and realistic formulation of the prepayment process is obtained, it will be clear how "turning the knobs" affects cash flows and value.

The KYF model makes a distinction between interest rate-driven refinancings and all other prepayments. It assumes that the sole purpose of refinancings is to reduce interest expense. Using the term more broadly than is customary, they refer to all other prepayments as turnover. While the distinction between refinancing and turnover is admittedly somewhat blurry—home sales may in fact depend on interest rates—for modeling purposes they consider the approach adequate.

Model of Turnover

While reasons such as defaults, disasters leading to a destruction of the property, and property appreciation may explain turnover, the primary cause of turnover is sale of the property. (As discussed in Chapter 4, a proxy for turnover is annualized existing home sales as a percentage of the total number of homes.) A prepayment attributable to the mortgagor seeking to take advantage (monetizing) the appreciation in the value of the mortgage property is referred to as a "cashout" refinancing, and its impact on prepayment speeds is often generally ascribed to "turnover."

In the KYS model, turnover is described in terms of a vector of monthly prepayment speeds over the legal life of the mortgages (e.g., a vector of prepayment rates quoted in terms of the PSA benchmark). Data from periods of high interest rates—and therefore low rates of eco-

---

[4] Therefore, the "lifetime refinancing cost" as studied in the academic literature is considered.

nomical refinancing—turnover is somewhere between 75% PSA and a 100% PSA. KYS show how their model can determine the market-implied turnover rate. Their results are in good agreement with expert opinion and historical experience, i.e. that find that 50% PSA is too low, and 150% PSA is too high. In their illustrations, a turnover rate of 75% PSA is used and is referred to as the "baseline rate." Assuming that the interest rate for new mortgages incorporates the market's expectation of turnover, they estimate the baseline rate.

Model of Refinancing Behavior

From the perspective of the mortgagor, the risks entailed in the refinancing decision are obvious: *ex post*, refinancing is seen as premature if rates continue to decline, while waiting is perceived to be a mistake if rates rise. There are rigorous option-based valuation tools available to assist borrowers with the timing decision. Many corporate and municipal bond issuers routinely employ the "efficiency" approach described below in their refunding decisions.[5] Why the concept of refinancing efficiency has been absent from the MBS literature is an enigma.

The basic idea is to treat the mortgagor's right to refinance as a formal call option, exercisable at any time at par.[6] Given the prevailing mortgage rates and a market-based interest rate volatility, the mortgagor can determine the value of the refinancing option and compare it to the attainable savings (expressed in present value terms). The ratio of savings to option value is the so-called *refinancing efficiency*. Although refinancing efficiency cannot exceed 100%, it will reach 100% if rates are sufficiently low. At 100% efficiency the expected cost of waiting for interest rates to decline further exceeds the cost of the new mortgage. Financially sophisticated borrowers will refinance when refinancing efficiency reaches 100%.

An optionless yield curve is needed to compute the savings and option value. While optionless borrowing rates are readily available for institutional borrowers, commonly quoted residential mortgage rates are technically immediately callable and this point is addressed next.

---

[5] See William M. Boyce and Andrew J. Kalotay, "Optimum Bond Calling and Refunding," *Interfaces* (November 1979), pp. 36–49; and C. Douglas Howard and Andrew J. Kalotay, "Embedded Call Options and Refunding Efficiency," in *Advances in Futures and Options Research* 3 (Elsevier, 1988). For a review of the underlying theory, see Andrew J. Kalotay, George O. Williams, and Frank J. Fabozzi, "A Model for Valuing Bonds and Embedded Options," *Financial Analysts Journal* 49 (May–June 1993), pp. 35–46.

[6] As discussed in Chapter 1, some loans are structured with prepayment penalties.

Few homeowners possess the financial sophistication described so far. In the KYF model, those that do have that capability are referred to as *financial engineers*. Most homeowners refinance too early (at an refinancing efficiency less than 100% of the option value) or too late (they continue waiting after refinancing efficiency has reached 100%). Early refinancers are referred to as *leapers* in the model, while those who act late are referred to as *laggards*. Together, financial engineers, leapers, and laggards span the entire spectrum of refinancing behavior. KYF establish that a rational leaper cannot refinance much sooner than a financial engineer; doing so would actually result in a loss, rather than in savings. For this reason, they focus on laggards, rather than on leapers.

KYF provide a formal definition for leapers and laggards. Their parameterization is a natural extension of the definition of the financial engineer, characterizing refinancing behavior by assigning the mortgagor an *imputed coupon*. The mortgagor will refinance whenever a financial engineer would refinance a maturity-matched mortgage with the imputed coupon. For example, consider two 7% mortgagors who refinance suboptimally—one does so when a financial engineer refinances a 6% mortgage and the other when a financial engineer refinances a 7.5% mortgage. Because the former's imputed coupon is 6% and actual is 7%, we refer to the borrower as a 1% laggard (who refinances late). Similarly, the one with an imputed coupon of 7.5% is a 0.5% leaper (or equivalently a –0.5% laggard), who refinances early.

The following related assumptions are made in the model:

1. The turnover rate is uniform across all types of mortgagors, be they leapers, laggards, or financial engineers.
2. Migration over time across behavioral types is not allowed: once a laggard, always a laggard.
3. The refinancing decision of a financial engineer does not depend on the expected turnover of the pool. In other words, the cash flow savings and the option value are calculated assuming the full remaining term of the mortgage.

Burnout

Prepayment burnout, or simply *burnout*, refers to the observed slowdown of interest rate driven prepayments following periods of intensive refinancings. It is attributed to the changing distribution of the pool: The most aggressive mortgagors (leapers) are the first to refinance, leaving behind the slower reacting laggards.

Conventional MBS analysis handles burnout by changing the parameters of the prepayment function. One possible refinement is to partition the pool by prepayment speeds, so that the earliest prepayments will be attributed to the fastest sector.[7]

From the pool factor—the ratio of the mortgage pool's remaining principal balance outstanding to the mortgage pool's original principal balance outstanding—the extent of prepayments can be inferred. Contractual (i.e., regularly scheduled) amortization determines at any given time the maximum possible value of the pool factor, assuming no prepayments at all (i.e., 0% PSA). Any difference between this maximum value and the actual value is due to prepayments. Although conventional prepayment models do not explicitly distinguish between turnover and refinancing *ex post*, low pool factors for high-coupon mortgage pools are understood to be primarily due to refinancings.

In the KYF model, burnout requires no special treatment. The assumed turnover determines a baseline value for the pool factor. Any difference between the baseline pool factor and the actual pool factor is attributed to refinancings. Because the model specifies the order in which mortgagors refinance (leapers first, followed by financial engineers, and then by laggards), the pool factor unambiguously determines who has left and who still remains in the mortgage pool. In statistical terms, the pool factor determines the *conditional distribution* of leapers and laggards, given an initial distribution.

Therefore, burnout is a natural consequence of the model. Given two otherwise identical mortgage pools, the one with the smaller pool factor will automatically prepay more slowly.

VALUATION OF MORTGAGES

To understand the KYF option-based mortgage valuation model, we begin with a discussion of the term structure of optionless mortgage rates. While these rates are readily observable in virtually all other sectors of the credit markets, in the realm of residential mortgages they are virtually nonexistent. One of our principle objectives is to determine, in terms of basis points, the market cost of the prepayment option. By carefully distinguishing between turnover and refinancings, KYF establish that turnover actually reduces the cost of the option.

The Term Structure of Mortgage Rates
Arbitrage-free valuation of a fixed income instrument requires as an input an optionless yield curve. This curve can be converted into spot

---

[7] Alexander Levin, "Active-Passive Decomposition in Burnout Modeling," *Journal of Fixed Income* 10 (March 2001), pp. 27–40.

and discount rates by bootstrapping, or into a lattice to value an instrument with an embedded option.[8]

Because conventional residential mortgages are immediately prepayable, an optionless yield curve cannot be observed directly. In addition, standard mortgages rates are for amortizing structures rather than bullets. KYF analyze mortgages assuming that an optionless yield curve is actually observable. Later on the KYF framework explains how this yield curve can be inferred from prevailing mortgage rates.

KYF first discuss the effect of servicing cost. The cash flows received by an investor is net servicing cost: The higher this cost is the lower, the value of the mortgage. Given the annual servicing cost, the fair value of an optionless mortgage with a specified interest rate and maturity can be determined. Or one can determine the interest rate on a new optionless mortgage that sells at par. Exhibit A.1 shows their assumed optionless bullet mortgage rates. This mortgage curve is 80 basis points above the fixed side of a maturity-matched LIBOR swap curve. Note that the yield curve is steeply upward sloping and that the 30-year "bullet" (i.e. non-amortizing) rate is 5.60%.

Exhibit A.2 shows the fair interest rate of optionless amortizing mortgages of various maturities. For example, in the absence of servicing cost, the fair rate on a 30-year level-pay mortgage is 5.15%, 45 basis points below the 30-year bullet rate. The reason for the difference is the upward sloping yield curve—the average life of a 30-year mortgage is only 18.75 years. In general, the shorter the final maturity the

EXHIBIT A.1   Optionless "Bullet" Mortgage Yield Curve

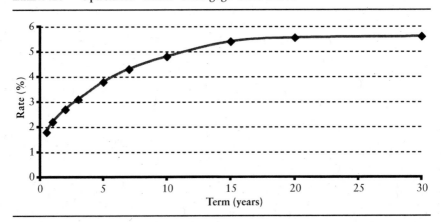

---

[8] See Kalotay, Williams, and Fabozzi, "A Model for Valuing Bonds and Embedded Options."

EXHIBIT A.2   Fair Coupon on Nonprepayable Mortgages

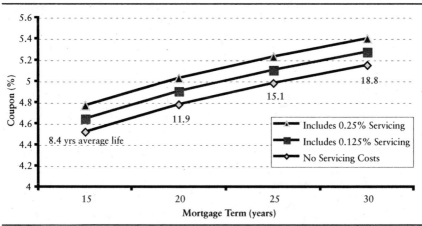

EXHIBIT A.3   Fair Coupon of 30-Year Prepayable but Nonrefinanceable Mortgage (Including 0.125% Refinancing Cost)

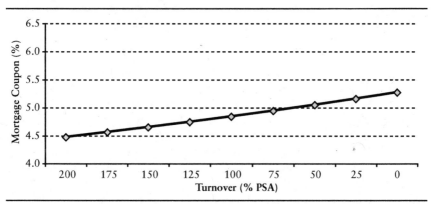

lower is the rate. Also shown in Exhibit A.2 are fair mortgage rates incorporating service costs. The servicing cost is essentially additive. For example, if the annual servicing cost is 0.25%, the fair mortgage rate increases from 5.15% to 5.40%.

Consider a large pool of new 30-year mortgages and assume that its annual turnover can be accurately predicted. KYF parametrize turnover as a multiple of the PSA speed; in particular 0% depicts no prepayments at all. The annual servicing cost is assumed to be 0.125%. Exhibit A.3 shows how turnover affects the rate of a new 30-year nonrefinanceable mortgage. As in Exhibit A.2, because of the upward-sloping yield curve the higher the turnover (i.e. the shorter the average life) the lower will be the mortgage interest rate.

Expert estimates of the annual servicing cost vary between 0.0625% and 0.25%. In the examples presented by KYF and that are reproduced below, it is assumed that the cost is 0.125%, resulting in a rate of roughly 5.28% for a new 30-year mortgage

How Turnover Affects Mortgage Rates

KYK calculate the fair interest rate of optionless mortgages. Consider hypothetical mortgages that *can be prepaid but cannot be refinanced.* This notion is the exact analogue of the familiar "callable but not refundable" feature of corporate bonds. But while for bonds this notion is relatively unimportant, for mortgages it is extremely significant because turnover is an important, if not the principal source, of prepayment activity.

The Refinancing Decision

KYF then analyze the effect of the refinancing option. First they develop a model of how mortgagors can approach the refinancing decision using the notion of refunding efficiency. For illustration purposes, they consider mortgages with 25 years remaining to maturity. Because they report all values as a percentage of the outstanding face amount, the dollar size of the mortgage is irrelevant. For illustration purposes they assume that refinancing expenses amount to 1%.

For valuation purposes the mortgagor and the investor should use the same yield curve (and associated lattice), because both are looking at essentially the same cash flows.

The textbook approach[9] to determine savings assumes that the new mortgage is optionless and matches the amortization schedule of the outstanding one, for the remaining 25 years. In practice the terms tend to be mismatched and the new mortgage is immediately repayable. (KYF examine this issue but we will not cover it here.) Consider a 6% mortgage with 25 years to maturity; its remaining average life is about 15.5 years. The rate of a matching refinancing mortgage turns out to be 5.41%. The savings are equal to the difference between the present values of the existing mortgage and the new one. A computation shows that the amount saved (net refinancing cost) would be 5.05% of outstanding principal. On the other hand, at 16% volatility the option value (accounting for potential future refinancing costs) is 5.675% of

---

[9] See John D. Finnerty and Douglas R. Emery, *Debt Management* (Boston, MA: Harvard Business School Press, 2001).

the outstanding principal amount. The resulting refinancing efficiency is their ratio, 89.2%. For a 6.25% mortgage the savings is 8.602% to 1.010% and the refunding efficiency is 99.5%. Exhibit A.4 displays how the refinancing efficiency responds to changes in of the mortgage yield curve. For example, the yield curve would have to decline 23 basis points, corresponding to a 5.18% refinancing rate, in order that the efficiency of the 6% mortgage reach 100%.

It can be concluded that a financial engineer would refinance a 6% mortgage with 25 years to maturity if he or she could obtain a matching 5.18% mortgage (an annual saving of 82 basis points before transaction cost), while the target rate for a 6.25% mortgage is about 5.40% (a saving of 85 basis points).

Note that efficiency depends not only on the refinancing rate but also on the shape of the yield curve and the interest rate volatility, here assumed to be 16%. At a higher volatility the option value would increase and, therefore, the 100% efficiency level would require a lower rate. (Standard econometric models do not consider the effect of interest rate volatility on prepayment speed.)

As mentioned already, in practice the new mortgage does not match the maturity structure of the outstanding one and it is also repayable. How does the refinancing efficiency approach cope with these considerations? The basic idea is that as long as the refinancing mortgage is fairly priced, its precise structure is irrelevant; its maturity and coupon structure can be arbitrary. For example, it is possible to determine the savings from refunding a 25-year, fixed rate mortgage with a 30-year, adjustable rate mortgage. Returning to the example of the 6% mortgage with 25

EXHIBIT A.4   Refinancing Efficiency for 25-Year Mortgages

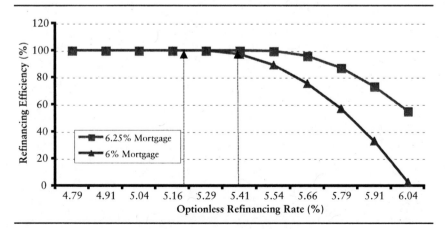

years left to maturity, we saw that it should be refinanced if it is possible to obtain a matching 5.18%, 25-year mortgage. But the mortgagor could also opt for a 30-year, nonrefinanceable mortgage with a slightly higher rate (say 5.22%) or even a 30-year, refinanceable rate (say 5.62%, more about this later). The practical problem is that a mismatch introduces interest rate risk, and therefore the savings are not guaranteed. For example, if interest rates rise, refinancing a fixed rate mortgage with one that floats (i.e., a short-reset ARM) can result in a loss rather than a savings. Note that this problem does not arise when the mortgages are matched, because the periodic cash flow savings are known.

The refinanceabilty of the new mortgage poses a similar problem. Because a refinanceable mortgage bears a coupon higher than an otherwise identical optionless mortgage, the nominal cash flow savings are lower. On the other hand, there is the potential of additional savings should rates continue to decline further. The critical question is whether or not the refinancing feature is fairly priced by the market.

Adjusting both savings and option value for possible mispricing of the new mortgage is straightforward. If such mispricing favors the borrower, the adjusted refinancing efficiency will be higher, and this should advance the timing of refinancing.

The Market Cost of the Refinancing Option

KYF extend the valuation method described above to determine how many basis points the market charges for the refinancing option on a new 30-year mortgage. Exhibit A.3 serves as a reference: it shows the nonrefinanceable rate at an assumed turnover.

Exhibit A.5 displays the basic results reported by KYF. The critical assumptions are that the interest rate volatility is 16%, the refinancing cost is 1%, and the refinancing decisions are optimal (i.e., every mortgagor is a financial engineer). Each of these assumptions can be easily changed. For now, the implications of the KYF findings are reported.

Exhibit A.6 shows the cost of the refinancing option as a function of turnover, obtained by subtracting the optionless rates from the refinanceable rates. Observe that the lower the turnover the more the market charges for the refinancing option: for example, at a turnover of 0% PSA, the cost would be 86 basis points, while at 150 PSA it is only 20 basis points. As indicated earlier, KYF assume that the expected turnover rate for a new mortgage pool is 75% of PSA; at that rate the current estimated cost of the refinancing option would be roughly 40 basis points. This result seems reasonable and it provides additional justification for using the 75% PSA assumption for turnover in this context.

EXHIBIT A.5 Fair Coupon for 30-Year Mortgages (Including 0.125% Servicing Cost)

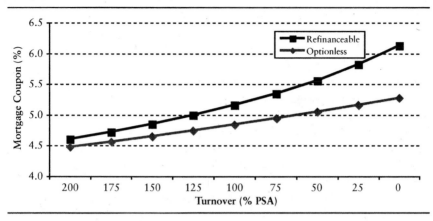

EXHIBIT A.6 Cost of Refinancing Option

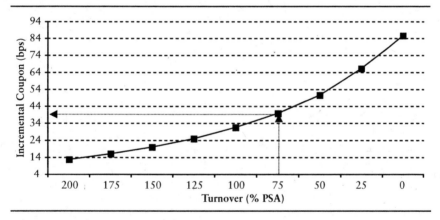

The above results are based on the assumption that every mortgagor is a financial engineer. This assumption to a specified leader/laggard behavior can be easily modified, or it can be more generally assumed that the initial pool can be represented by some distribution of leaders and laggards. KYF state that the cost of the refinancing option of new mortgages depends primarily on turnover, and only weakly on leaper/laggard distribution. At the same time, they observe that as the pool ages it becomes skewed toward laggards, and therefore the leaper/laggard distribution is critical in valuing seasoned pools.

In summary, KYF show that a financial engineer would refinance a long-term mortgage with a like nonrefinanceable mortgage if he or she could save about 85 basis points. But the market offers only refinanceable mortgages at roughly 40 basis points higher. Therefore a financial engineer will refinance a long-term mortgage when the market rate is about 45 basis points (85 to 40) below the rate of the outstanding mortgage.

Seasoned Mortgages and Tranches

For seasoned mortgages, KYF assume that the mortgagor is a financial engineer and, in order to demonstrate certain points, that the servicing cost is zero. Exhibit A.7 shows the values of pools of conventional (i.e., uninsured) 30-year mortgages over a wide range of coupons. In anticipation of valuing mortgage derivatives products (collateralized mortgage obligations and mortgage strips), the exhibit also displays the interest and principal components. Note that the value initially increases, reaching a peak of roughly 101 at a 6% coupon. As the coupon further increases, the value declines to slightly above 100. There are reasons for this phenomenon.

Consider the right side of Exhibit A.7. Because a financial engineer will refinance a mortgage whose coupon is very high without delay, the value of such mortgage is expected to be very close to 100. The slight premium observed in the exhibit is due to the additional interest received by the investor during the period from when the homeowner notifies the mortgage servicer of his or her intent to refinance to the actual refinancing date.

It is less intuitive, however, how the value of a mortgage can exceed 101 if the refinancing option is optimally exercised. The 1% refinancing

EXHIBIT A.7 Value of Principal and Interest Components of Conventional Mortgage Pools

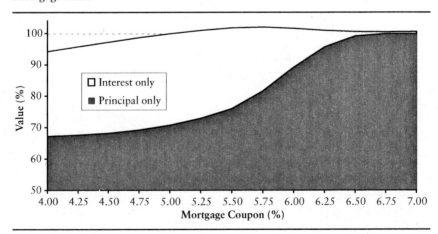

cost is clearly insufficient to explain this phenomenon. The fundamental reason is that the mortgagor's refinancing decision disregards turnover. *In essence, the mortgagor refinances only when it would make sense to do so with a maturity-matched mortgage.* In the refinancing decision, the mortgagee does not take into account the possibility of having to prepay the mortgage for reasons unrelated to interest rates. Because when he or she refinances a mortgagor does not plan on moving in the foreseeable future, such a "myopic" decision policy seems realistic. The effect of turnover on the value of the mortgage is extenuated when the yield curve is steeply` upward sloping, as is the case here. While financial engineer mortgagors are patiently waiting for interest rates to decline to a level where refinancing is optimal, some of them end up prepaying for unrelated reasons.

A CLOSER LOOK AT LEAPERS AND LAGGARDS

The Range of Leaper/Laggard Spreads

While the ultimate goal of the KYF model is to value MBS, it is worthwhile to continue to focus on the underlying unsecuritized mortgage pool. The differences between the MBS and the pool are twofold. First, only a specified portion of the mortgage interest is passed through to the MBS holder, and second, because of credit enhancement and liquidity considerations, the MBS cash flows are preferable to the mortgage cash flows—and hence discounted at a lower rate. KYF reexamine these issues in the valuation of MBS.

As discussed above, implementation of the KYF model requires a user-specified turnover rate and leaper/laggard distribution. They provided anecdotal evidence to the reasonableness of using 75% PSA for the turnover rate. Assuming this and that the mortgagor is a financial engineer, they calculated the fair interest rate of a new refinanceable mortgage.

They then relax the assumption that every mortgagor is a financial engineer, and consider how a heterogeneous pool affects value based on the rigorous definition for leapers and laggards provided earlier: using financial engineers as a point of reference they specify behavior by a spread relative to the financial engineer. Next, they establish the relevant range of these spreads.

KYF use the following argument to establish that leaper spreads should be less than 0.5%. Consider a 0.5% leaper with a 6% mortgage (i.e. a 6% mortgagor whose imputed coupon is 6.5%). As explained earlier, a financial engineer will refinance a 6.5% mortgage when market rates (of refinanceable mortgages) are in the 6.0% range. Accordingly, a 0.5% leaper would refinance his or her 6% mortgage immediately at the time he or she receives the mortgage, a behavior which is clearly non-sensical. Prepayment of a 6% mortgage when rates are at 6% can be attributed only to turnover, not to refinancing. Therefore, they cap leaper spreads at 0.25%.

Laggard spreads on the other hand can be much wider, but unless the mortgagor is credit-impaired they should not exceed 1.5%. A 1.5% laggard would not refinance his or her 6% mortgage until market rates have fallen below 4%. Given the readily available information about current mortgage rates (the so-called *media effect*), anyone who does not refinance a 6% mortgage when rates are at 4% is unlikely to ever refinance.

While the behavior of mortgagors can vary widely, it is reasonable to assume that when a new mortgage pool is assembled, it is dominated by mortgagors in the +25 to –25 basis point range. But, as discussed earlier, the distribution tends to become more and more laggardly as the pool ages.

The Effect of Leapers and Laggards on Value

Leaving all other assumptions (turnover equal to 75% PSA, refinancing cost equal to 1%, servicing cost equal to 0.125%, etc.) unchanged, Exhibit A.8 shows the fair coupon and the cost of the refinancing option for new 30-year mortgages over the relevant range of leapers and laggards. The cost of the option is obtained by subtracting the 4.95% optionless rate corresponding to 75% PSA (shown in Exhibit A.3). Evi-

EXHIBIT A.8 Fair Coupon (with 0.125% Servicing Fee) for 30-Year Refinanceable Mortgage across Behavior Spectrum

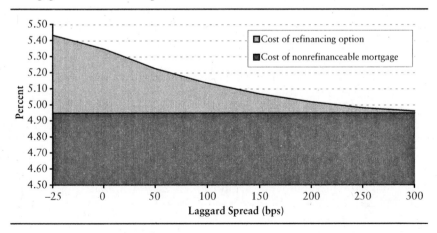

EXHIBIT A.9   Mortgage Value Depends on Refinancing Behavior

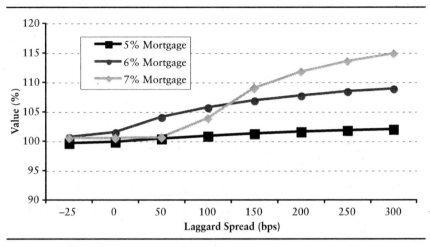

dently with the exception of extreme laggards, behavior has little impact on the cost. This confirms that the market rate of new mortgages can be explained by the assumption that financial engineers dominate the initial pool.

Exhibit A.9 displays how refinancing behavior affects the value of 30-year, 5%, 6%, and 7% unsecuritized mortgage pools and in the process also demonstrates how the KYF approach captures the burnout phenomenon. For leapers or financial engineers, the value of a premium 7% mortgage is barely over par, but laggardly behavior greatly increases the value because the mortgages will remain outstanding longer. As the amount outstanding (i.e., the factor) declines, the mix automatically shifts towards laggards, increasing the dollar price of the amount that remains outstanding.

Laggard Spread Distribution

How refinancing behavior, as depicted by laggard spread, affects the value of an unsecured mortgage pool was shown earlier. For a given a distribution of laggard spreads, the value of the pool and that of the corresponding MBS can be determined. Next we outline the KYF approach for creating a laggard distribution.

KYF recommend inferring the distribution from the market prices of actively traded securities. In their illustration, they confine themselves to a very simple family of distributions, namely the negative exponential distribution anchored at 0 basis points laggard spread.

EXHIBIT A.10   Naive Laggard Distribution

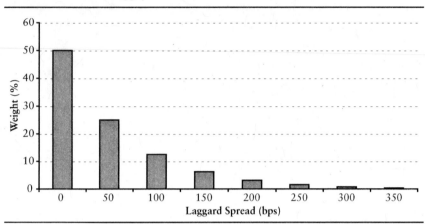

In implementing the model, they represent the distributions by placing appropriate weights in evenly spaced buckets along the laggard axis. Exhibit A.10 demonstrates the process. Starting with the financial engineers at the origin, the buckets are spaced at 50 basis point intervals. The weight is assumed to decline from bucket to bucket by a factor of 0.5. Accordingly the weight assigned to financial engineers is 0.50 and the weight of 50 basis point laggards is 0.25, and so on. This distribution is used as a point of reference and referred to it as the *naïve distribution*.

The naïve distribution can be modified by either adjusting the spacing of the buckets (say to 40 basis points) or the rate of decline (say to 0.6). While the two representations are mathematically equivalent, in numerical implementation one of them may turn out to be preferable to the other.

KYF illustrate how the rate of decline affects the value of unsecured mortgage pools, keeping the spacing of the buckets at 50 basis points. They consider pools of 30-year mortgages over a wide range of coupons, assuming that refinancing behavior follows the naïve distribution. Exhibit A.11 shows the values of new pools (factor equal to 1.0), and of seasoned pools following major refinancing activity (factor equal to 0.5). Evidently, the values are barely distinguishable for moderate coupons. In contrast, for high-coupon mortgages, the value of a seasoned pool is much higher; in fact, as the coupon increases, the value of a new pool actually declines, exhibiting negative duration. In the case of a seasoned pool with a small factor, the same phenomenon would occur only at a much higher coupon level.

EXHIBIT A.11   How Factor Affects Value of Pool of 30-Year Mortgages Naïve
Laggard Distribution

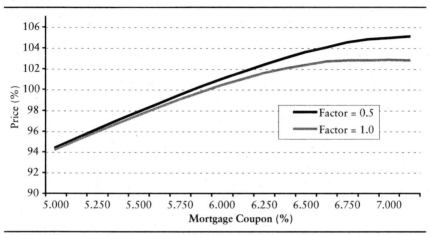

VALUATION OF MBS

The description thus far has focused on the KYF approach to valuation
of unsecured mortgage pools. Here we describe their model for valuing
MBS. All other factors being the same, there are two major reasons why
an MBS is preferable to an uninsured mortgage pool. First, because it is
credit enhancement (either through the GSEs or the subordination
mechanism), an MBS is more creditworthy. Second, because an MBS is a
security, it is more liquid than the underlying mortgage pool. For these
reasons the cash flows of an MBS are discounted at a lower rate than
those of an unsecured mortgage pool.

Valuation Framework

KYF represent the yield curves for an MBS and for a mortgage pool by
respective OAS's relative to a benchmark swap curve. As long as the
OASs are fixed, the yield curves will be perfectly correlated. For the reasons just cited, the OAS of an MBS should be lower than that of its
underlying mortgage pool. In the KYF examples that follow, it is
assumed that the OAS of every MBS is the same and demonstrate that
robust and sensible results are obtained even under this simplistic
assumption. Of course, one could fine-tune the analysis by using MBS-
specific OASs.

EXHIBIT A.12   Fair MBS Coupon as Laggard Spacing Changes (adjacent weights decline by 50%)

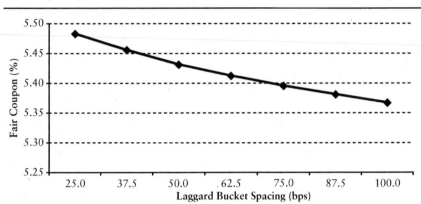

Based on its duration, and because the credit of a residential mortgage is comparable to a corporate bond with a single-A rating, KYF estimated that at the time they prepared their illustration the OAS of an unsecured mortgage pool should be roughly 70 to 90 basis points to the swap curve. In the valuation of MBS, the fundamental role of the mortgage OAS is to project refinancing activity; the value of the mortgage pool is only of secondary interest. The higher this OAS, the slower will be the rate of refinancing, and the greater will be the value of an MBS with an above-market coupon.

As discussed, the OAS of an MBS should be much tighter than that of a mortgage pool. A reasonable comparable is the OAS of an debenture of similar duration by the GSE that issued the MBS. The OAS of intermediate agency debentures at the time that they prepared their illustration was roughly 25 to 35 basis points to the swap curve. This OAS has no effect on the cash flows; its sole function is discounting. The higher it is, the lower will be the value of the MBS.

Exhibit A.12 shows the values of new MBS. The coupon of the MBS is assumed to be 50 basis points below the weighted average coupon (WAC) of its mortgage pool. The mortgage OAS in their illustration was assumed to be 80 basis points, the MBS OAS was therefore 30 basis points, and the naïve distribution used to describe refinancing behavior (buckets placed 50 basis points apart, weights of adjacent buckets decline by a factor of 2).

Implied Prepayment Distribution

KYS apply the model to real market prices. Exhibit A.13 shows the terms of 14 Fannie Mae MBS along with their prices as of September

EXHIBIT A.13   Fannie Mae Prices of September 30, 2003

MBS	WAC (%)	Original Amortization (mos.)	Age (mos.)	WAM (mos.)	Factor	Price (%)
FNMA 5.0 TBA	5.52	360	4	355	0.99	100.000
FNMA 5.0 2002	5.64	360	12	345	0.93	100.000
FNMA 5.5 TBA	5.94	360	6	352	0.92	101.984
FNMA 5.5 2002	6.03	360	11	347	0.78	101.984
FNMA 5.5 2001	6.13	360	23	332	0.61	102.047
FNMA 6.0 TBA	6.52	360	14	344	0.84	103.188
FNMA 6.0 2001	6.59	360	25	330	0.40	103.188
FNMA 6.0 1999	6.64	360	56	293	0.30	103.313
FNMA 6.0 1998	6.65	360	61	287	0.26	103.406
FNMA 6.5 2001	7.02	360	26	329	0.27	104.219
FNMA 6.5 1998	7.07	360	63	284	0.17	104.281
FNMA 7.0 1999	7.55	360	51	298	0.16	105.563
FNMA 7.0 1998	7.49	360	67	282	0.14	105.688
FNMA 7.5 2000	8.13	360	38	313	0.09	106.563

30, 2003.[10] Note the wide range of MBS coupons and pool factors. The U.S. dollar swap curve on the same day is shown below:

Term	1 mo.	3 mo.	6 mo.	1 yr.	2 yr.	3 yr.	5 yr.	10 yr.	30 yr.
Yield (%)	1.160	1.160	1.180	1.290	1.886	2.498	3.374	4.495	5.303

The table below displays the modeling assumptions:

Turnover rate	75% PSA
Refinancing cost	1% of mortgage
Mortgage OAS	80 bps
MBS OAS	30 bps
Short-term interest rate volatility	16% (0% mean reversion)

Based on the above, they find that the laggard distribution that provides the best fit to the given prices. In this application, they created 10 equally spaced buckets and assumed that the weights of adjacent buckets decline by a factor of 2. They then varied the spacing of the buckets to determine the best fit. As displayed in Exhibit A.14, the spacing that

---

[10] The data were provided by Countrywide Securities.

EXHIBIT A.14   Determining Implied Prepayment Distribution (FNMA MBS prices of 9/30/03)

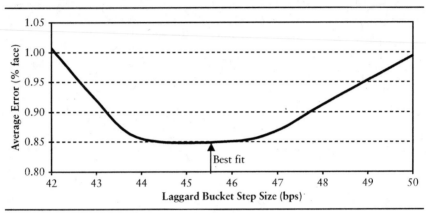

EXHIBIT A.15   FNMA MBS Prices of 9/30/03

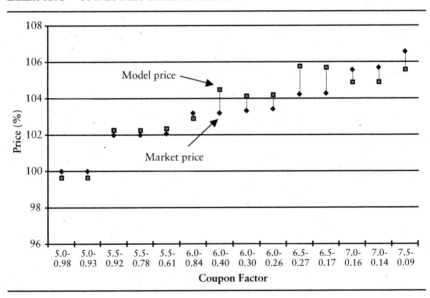

optimizes the fit occurs at 46 basis points, and it results in an average error of 0.85%. Exhibit A.15 shows the corresponding fitted values along with the actual prices of the MBS.

SUMMARY

The approach to MBS valuation described in this chapter separates "baseline prepayments"—turnover and curtailment, which are largely non-interest rate sensitive—from refinancings, which are interest rate driven. The former can be reasonably specified with a vector of prepayment speeds. The latter is represented by a distribution of mortgagor refinancing behavior—those that exercise the refinancing option too early, too late, or optimally. The model requires no historical data whatsoever. This distribution is initially calibrated to explain prices of liquid MBS. Once calibrated, the model takes current market inputs and uses option-based analysis to produce fair values that match market prices very well.

e indicates entries in exhibits.
n indicates entries in the footnotes.

Busted PAC, 121

Call risk, 16
Capital markets, importance, 37–38
Cash flow. *See* Barbelled cash flows; Senior non-NAS cash flows
  barbell process, 123
  breaks, 245
  impact, 280
  profile, smoothing, 129
  projection. *See* Interest rate path
  remainder, payment, 121, 128
  stressing, requirement, 263
  structuring, 41–43
    logic, 100–101
  yield, 228
Cash-out activity, proportion, 89
Cash-out loan, 88
Cash-out percentage, real estate aggregate value quarterly change (contrast), 89e
Cash-out refinancing, 6, 72, 76, 250
  proportion, 88–90
Cash P&L, 223
Cash window, 27
Catalyst, 175–176
CDR. *See* Conditional default rate
CDX. *See* Cumulative default rate
Charge-off rate (COR), 65, 66
Cleanup calls, inclusion. *See* Private label deals
Closed universe, 107–108
CLTV. *See* Combined LTV
CMO-and-cash portfolios, 269
CMOs. *See* Collateralized mortgage obligations
CMT. *See* Constant Maturity Treasury
Collateral, 272
  average life, 114e
    structuring, 119e
  balances, 171e
  pool, stripping, 142e, 143e
  principal, allotment, 147
Collateralized mortgage obligations (CMOs), 23n
  creation, 110
  deals, 34–35

reverse engineering. *See* Senior CMOs
  structures, 212–213
  viewpoint, 107
  evaluation. *See* Senior CMOs
  prices/spreads/risk measures, 239e
  sequential pay structure, 133e
  structure, PAC/support bond (inclusion), 119e, 124e
  structuring, fundamentals, 104–105
  trades, involvement, 113
  tranches, 209
Collateral-specific factors, 196
Combined LTV (CLTV), 6
Committee on Uniform Securities Identification Procedures (CUSIP) name, 242
Companion bonds, 117
Complete prepayment, 48
Conditional default rate (CDR), 47, 65. *See also* Monthly CDRs
  assumption, 61
Conditional prepayment rate (CPR), 48, 185
  assumption. *See* Constant CPR assumption
  relationship. *See* Single monthly mortality
  usage, 49–50
Consensus prepayment speeds, 271
Constant CPR assumption, 62
Constant Maturity Treasury (CMT), 7–8
Constant OAS, assumption, 264
Constant-OAS horizon pricing, 265
Consumer lending rates (generation), MBS markets (role), 37–41
Consumer mortgage market, overview, 3
Conventional loans, 10, 49
  products, 87
Convexity, 225, 232–235. *See also* Negative convexity
  adjustment, 234
  definition, 232
  price adjustment, 233–234
  relationship. *See* Option-adjusted duration
  risk measure, illustration, 233e
  spread widening, contrast, 235e